To Al,

Friend, Colleague,
Renaissance man,

Bill

Work and Academic Politics

William Form

Work and Academic Politics

A Journeyman's Story

Transaction Publishers
New Brunswick (U.S.A.) and London (U.K.)

Library of Congress Catalog Number: 2001041597
ISBN: 0-7658-008-2
Printed in the United States of America

Library of Congress Cataloging-in-Publication Data

Form, William Humbert, 1917-
    Work and academic politics : a journeyman's story / William Form.
        p. cm.
    Includes bibliographical references and index.
    ISBN 0-7658-0080-2
    1. Form, William Humbert, 1917- 2. Sociologists—United States—Biography. 3. Sociology—History—20th century. 4. Universities and colleges—United States—Departments. 5. Universities and colleges—United States—Faculty. 6. Universities and colleges—United States—Sociological aspects. 7. Italian Americans—Biography. I. Title.

HM479.F67 A3 2001
301'.092—dc21   2001041597

To My Guild Masters

Arthur Stinchcombe

Gerhard Lenski

Joan Huber

Irving Horowitz

Richard Hamilton

Wright Mills

Peter Rossi

Edward Laumann

Peter Blau

Amos Hawley

James Coleman

Hubert Blalock

Alex Inkeles

Seymour Lipset

Contents

Preface

I had never expected to write an autobiography, but after completing some pieces on my family and my schooling, I had the makings of a book. This is how it came about.

When I finished my term as editor of ASR in 1989, I was beyond Ohio State's compulsory retirement age and looking forward to a return to research on work and politics. The last piece I wrote before becoming editor dealt with U.S. labor politics in the New Deal (Form 1990b). The first afterwards was a chapter solicited by Maureen Hallinan, an organizational approach to institutional analysis (Form 1990a). Then my colleague Craig Jenkins and I decided to bring together the best New Deal studies but for reasons explained later, the project had to be abandoned.

Instead, I completed a long-delayed monograph on U.S. labor politics (Form 1995b) and was about to turn to a project on institutional analysis when John Pease, a former student and long-time friend at the University of Maryland, urged me to record my recollections of C. Wright Mills' four-year stint at Maryland before he went to Columbia. Mine was the only dissertation Mills ever directed. I described how I got to Maryland, contacts with faculty, and my place in the department before and after Mills appeared. Editor Jonathan Imber published it in *The American Sociologist* (Form 1995a). When I told him I had deleted much material about myself, he urged me to submit another article, "The Accidental Journey," on my years at Maryland (Form 1997a).

About this time, long discussion with Bill D'Antonio on the persistence of white ethnicity in America made me examine my own notions. Bill insisted that it was still important, which I doubted. My father, converted to Protestantism soon after arriving from Italy, had soon been Americanized. He changed the children's name from Formicola to Form when we were in college. My ethnic background rarely came up in academia. Yet race, ethnicity, and multiculturalism had become important in U.S. sociology in the 1970s. While I never doubted the stubborn persistence of race cleavages, ethnicity was another matter.

i

In response, I began to write about my experiences with ethnicity in Rochester, New York, where I grew up. "From Uli to Bill" attempts to show how Rochester's school system handled a massive influx of immigrants' children in the late nineteenth and early twentieth centuries, and how it shaped my own academic journey. The school system simply ignored the ethnic backgrounds of second generation Italian, Jewish, and Polish children, exposing them to the same education given earlier to British, German, and Irish immigrants' children. The system quickly turned second generation children into Americans who spoke only English to one another, later moved from ethnic areas, and often married spouses of other backgrounds. Claims of strong ethnic survival and multiculturalism seemed exaggerated. I sent the essay, "The Accidental Journey," to family and a few colleagues. Together, "From Uli to Bill" and the "Accidental Journey" described my experiences from grammar through graduate school.

As was my practice, I showed things I wrote to my friend and colleague, Dick Hamilton. He thought the essays were publishable and urged me to write one comparing sociology in the 1940s with the discipline today. So I sketched recollections of the seven institutions where I had taught over almost sixty years (Maryland, Hood College, American, Stephens Junior College, Kent State, Michigan State, Illinois at Urbana-Champaign, and Ohio State, quite different institutions). Writing systematically about them was difficult as it was hard to separate personal concerns from intellectual and political issues in department, university, and disciplinary association. I had neither preserved my letters, departmental records, or memorabilia nor kept a dairy. Yet to my amazement, the amount of material I could remember seemed inexhaustible.

In the midst of this, family concerns diverted my writing plans. My brother George, thirteen years my senior, died in 1995. He had had such an important impact on my life that I had dedicated *Blue Collar Stratification* (1976a) "To my brother and teacher." In my grief I wrote an essay, "For the Love of George, the Appassionato" and sent it to family and kin. The following year, my brother Arnold unexpectedly died. He was two year older than I. Again, I wrote a memorial piece; "Arnold, Il Furioso di Buon Cuor." As my sister Nancy, four years older than I, was critically ill, I wrote her profile, "Nancy, Semper Fidelis." Then family members pressured me to write a piece on my parents that I labeled "Taciturn Maria and Sober Antonio." By adding an introduction on my grandparents and a short conclusion, I had a book, *On the Shoulders of Immigrants, a Family Profile* (1999) dedicated to sister Nancy. As a family document, it was deposited in several university libraries.

Writing *On the Shoulders of Immigrants* got me to ruminate about my own life and I decided to get back to the autobiography. Writing *On the Shoulders* had yielded fresh insights on how the family, the Rochester school system, the Great Depression, and changes in U.S. universities over time had affected the course of my academic life. Over sixty years, I had witnessed transformations in society, the discipline, the university, its departments, and the American Sociological Association. I had lived through the longest economic depression that the country had ever suffered and then World War II. Instead of the anticipated depression after the war, academia experienced a quarter century of unparalleled expansion. Before the war, sociology departments of modest size were linked to social work. In the postwar period, large departments that aimed to build a scientific discipline emerged in research universities. Then the turmoil of the Vietnam War and the Civil Rights movement in the 1970s presaged decades of stasis, disagreement, and fragmentation.

These changes had to be integrated into an autobiographical account in order to show how a journeyman's experiences were shaped by the interaction of family, workplace, and politics. I trace my changing research interests: industrial sociology, urban studies, community disasters, societal stratification, comparative industrial organization, and working-class stratification. I try to illuminate how the social and political realities of departmental life affected my changing research program. Then, since I occupied various offices in the American Sociological Association over a period of about fifteen years, I describe Association politics as I saw them. I close with a comparison of departmental and disciplinary conditions at the beginning and end of my career.

Throughout this work, I use the vocabulary of the medieval guild system because academia resembles that ancient institution and because my lifelong interest in organizations and occupations makes the vocabulary appropriate. My family socialization foreshadowed or perhaps determined my interest in work, work organizations, and politics. My educational training functioned as an apprenticeship. Travelling from one university to another parallels the journeyman phase of the guild system. Universities resemble councils of guilds or disciplines and departments are like shops, both with their own social and political life. The hierarchy of professorial ranks represents the stages traversed by a journeyman. Only a few journeymen become masters. Most spend their lives as journeymen, as in my case. Finally, I think of the American Sociological Association as a guild organized on the national level.

It is not easy to avoid a self-serving tone in describing one's own life. Although I have tried to do so, I cannot vouch that my accounts of events are dispassionate. An autobiography is not a research monograph. I report experiences as I perceived them, undoubtedly neglecting facts I was unaware of and alternative interpretations of events, especially in the accounts of conflicts within departments and the American Sociological Association. If I have given offense, I beg indulgence. Other sociological autobiographies I have read have taken different approaches. Mine differs somewhat in placing more emphasis on political life in the department and guild.

In writing these memoirs, I am indebted most to Joan Huber whose support, criticisms, and advice have improved my research and writing for many years. Although busy with their own duties, my Ohio State colleagues Richard Hamilton, Craig Jenkins, and Krishan Namboodiri have read portions of the manuscript and encouraged me to finish it. I am very indebted to my oldest friend at Michigan State, Allan Beegle, who provided needed data and reviewed the chapters on the university. In the last few years, I have lunched weekly with three retired colleagues, Alfred Clarke, Simon Dinitz, and Roscoe Hinkle, who have given me many accounts of departmental and university life. None of these persons is responsible for what I have reported.

Upper Arlington, Ohio

1

Making Americans: From Uli to Bill

On a cold spring day in 1936 I sat with the Saracen's seven grandsons facing her coffin in the Italian Presbyterian Church of the Evangel in Rochester, New York. Grandmother Nunziata Polizzi Cornetti was known as the Saracen because that is what my Piedmontese grandfather called his dark and fiery Sicilian wife. I never knew my grandfather, the fair "German" who died in 1918, the year after I was born. Whenever we visited his grave at Mount Hope cemetery, grandmother would sit on the iron chair beside his stone and tell him everything that had transpired since her last visit. Then, bidding him goodbye, she would tell him that she would join him soon. But eighteen years passed before she was buried next to him on that cold spring day.

A college sophomore, I hadn't been inside the Church of the Evangel since I was in second grade. My father, Anthony Formicola, founding member and longtime elder, had led the faction that had ousted the Reverend Frasca (who claimed to be related to my mother). Perhaps feeling guilty for his part in splitting the congregation, father took his family to the "American" Lake Avenue Baptist church just four blocks from our home.

The Evangel's sanctuary was much smaller than I had remembered it and Mr. Roncone's red wall hanging behind the altar with the gold inscription *In Hoc Signo* over a golden crown was much larger. The service was conducted in Italian. Barely aware of what was going on, I felt out of place. Grandmother, a tiny old lady always in black, was a distant figure. Although I saw her daily, we had little to do with one another. She slept at our house but spent most of the day at the homes of her other children. Sometimes she would appear after supper to tell my mother the events of her day, often tales of slights, misunderstandings, even outright mistreatment, recounted with a flair for the dramatic. We children were her silent audience. While she acknowledged our presence, I don't recall that she ever called me by name. She spoke only Sicilian and my ability to speak and understand it was too primitive for conversation.

The congregation began singing an Italian hymn that mother sometimes hummed. A wave of emotion swept over me and I began to breathe heavily, trying not to cry. Cousin Mike Traino on my right frowned, jamming his elbow in my ribs. I quickly regained my composure. The Saracen's only son, Uncle Joe, sobbed audibly while his three sisters wept silently. The ten grandchildren sat impassively.

At the end of the service, the grandsons and Uncle Loreto (Aunt Giulia's husband) carried the gray coffin to the hearse at the curb. I was surprised at its lightness. At the grave, grandmother's three daughters, her son Joe, spouses, and pastor gathered around the casket, the rest of us behind them. After a few psalms and prayers, the pastor threw a handful of dirt on the coffin as it was lowered into the earth. Uncle Joe broke down, bidding his mother loud goodbyes as he was almost forcibly led away. Mother, Aunt Marietta, and Aunt Giulia sobbed quietly. We grandchildren silently followed our parents to waiting automobiles.

The four families planned to meet at Aunt Giulia's after the service. My aunts and uncle were conversing quietly in the parlor when we children arrived, chattering as usual as we crowded around the kitchen table which was spread with a simple lunch. Then the voices from the parlor grew louder. Our parents were arguing about their proper shares of the funeral and medical expenses. Such flair-ups bubbled up periodically, but usually died down quickly, as if by secret agreement.

Aunt Giulia protested that she had borne the brunt of caring for their mother in her final days, had turned her home into a funeral parlor, and suffered many inconveniences. Aunt Marietta quietly observed that, while grandmother had never lived with her, she spent most of her days at the Trainos, took meals there and was given sufficient money for all her needs. My mother, Maria, firmly stated that she had done her share; grandmother had lived with us for the past seven years. When they both became ill at the same time (mother still had a fever), grandmother had to be moved temporarily to Giulia's. Aunt Marietta and her husband Frank both worked in a tailor factory as did Uncle Joe and his wife Grace. Only Giulia was in a position to care for their mother. Mother added that it was Joe's bitter fight with their mother that had made her decide to move to our house.

Uncle Joe probably felt guilty. As the only son, he felt it was his sacred duty to care for his mother. Also, he had the largest house and the smallest family. Exploding into uncontrolled rage, he screamed that their mother had lived in his home almost 20 years before she went to live with her daughter, Maria. As oldest child, it was Maria's turn to care for mother.

Amidst the shouting, I could hear my father's insistent calls for calm. Known as the peacemaker, he typically mediated family disputes. The only one of the Saracen's three sons-in-law to call her "Mama," he would secretly slip her small sums of money. He began firmly, "Now, we all know that mother always wanted her children to love one another. She would not rest peacefully in her grave if she thought we were having these disagreements. We all loved her. It makes little sense to argue who did the most for her. Let's bury our differences, embrace one another, and peacefully work things out." My father moved to embrace Uncle Joe, who withdrew screaming, "Never! Never! Never! I'll have nothing to do with any of you until I die . . . *a la morte, a la morte*!" He stormed out of the room. After a few silent moments, we all went home. Like all family fights, this one would soon blow over.

But it lasted several years. As oldest child, my mother waited for her siblings to call on her. After all, my father's parting comment at the big fight was that our door was always open and everyone would be welcome. Turning to Uncle Joe, he had said "I will visit you soon to clear up a few things. All right?" Uncle Joe replied, "If you visit me, you do me a favor; if you don't, you do me a double favor."

Uncle Joe, second oldest child and Aunt Marietta, next in line, buried their differences first. Aunt Giulia, the youngest, was first to call on my mother, the oldest. Aunt Marietta and Aunt Giulia began to see one another, first at church, then at their homes. Aunt Marietta finally called on my mother. After several months, Marietta arranged a reconciliation between Joe and Giulia. Three years or more passed before peppery Uncle Joe unexpectedly visited my mother, brimming with energy and cracking jokes as if nothing had happened. The feud ended but family gatherings of the aunts and uncles and their children ceased, except for funerals.

During the years of the split, we cousins visited regularly. Our parents never expected us to echo their family squabbles. Relations with aunts and uncles remained cordial. We cousins saw family quarrels as routine, our parents as equally culpable, overly sensitive, too emotional, and typically Italian. Although no one said it, we were different, Americans. How did we get this way?

Assimilation in the Immigrant Generation

Although melting pot theory dominated U.S. sociology from its inception, some sociologists attacked it in the 1970s for failing to explain the generational survival of ethnicity (e.g., Glazer and Moynihan 1970; Horowitz 1977). My recollections of immigrant experiences while growing up in Rochester support the view that the assimilation of southern European immigrants was unresisted, rapid, and thorough. When children of immigrants left grammar school, their assimilation of the American-British heritage was largely complete. In my case, being born Protestant probably speeded the process but it occurred almost as rapidly among Italian Catholics (see Alba 1995).

My father, Antonio Formicola, came to the United States in 1893 at age 17. He had made big strides toward assimilation by the time I was born. Learning English in night school, he spoke it almost without accent. He became a citizen and defined himself as an American, singing patriotic songs with gusto. A Protestant convert, he was active in the organizations of the Italian Presbyterian Church of the Evangel, its theater group, Board of Elders, band, and the Odd Fellows lodge. In these activities, he met many Americans. He liked to tell a story of a stranger who could not place him ethnically.

"What are you?" the stranger asked.

"A cabinetmaker," my father replied.

"I mean, what's your nationality?"

"I'm an American, like you."

"No, I mean where were you born?

"Oh, Italy. If that's what you wanted to know, why didn't you ask in the first place?"

As a cabinetmaker with access to factory lumber and machinery, father made frames for two large engravings of George Washington and Abraham Lincoln that hung prominently on our living room walls. He named his second son "Arnold Lincoln." The family routinely attended Memorial Day parades downtown and my father hung the American flag on our front porch on all national holidays.

His political assimilation was rapid. For 13 years he and my mother were the only ones in the Ninth Ward to vote socialist. He then became interested in promoting the city manager plan as a way to overcome machine politics, going from door to door in our neighborhood to rally support for it. The sponsors of the drive, largely Republican, noted my father's oratorical skills in English and Italian and induced him to become one of them. Father joined the Columbia League (a Republican organization for Italians), was elected ward and county committeeman in the party, and remained a loyal Republican all his life. Our front room windows displayed photographs of Republican candidates for Governor and President. When Herbert Hoover's picture appeared in his race against Al Smith for President and four years later against Franklin Roosevelt, neighborhood children threw stones at the windows.

Father was a worker-foreman in the veneer department of Michelsen's bedroom furniture factory. Although Michelsen claimed German heritage, the Italians considered him American as they did almost everyone except Italians and other recent immigrants. When the Irish and German employees began to retire, Michelsen had to turn to the Italians, my father being the first that he hired. Father became his informal employment agency.

A paternalistic employer, Michelsen felt obliged to teach his Italian employees American ways in politics, manners, and other matters. At dinner father often reported Mr. Michelsen's views on the news of the day. Father would also exchange political views with Mr. Stein, a downtown Jewish clothier who hired him to make weekly collections from the Italians who bought their clothes on credit. Stein, a socialist, tried to persuade father and mother to vote for the party.

Religion and politics were father's passions. He rarely passed the opportunity to try to persuade neighbors or kin to become Protestant and vote Republican. We were the only family in the neighborhood to subscribe to the daily *Democrat and Chronicle*. Every evening father read *all* of the paper, except sports and funnies. Then he and mother discussed the news, responding to it as personal experiences that bore directly on their lives. The formidable problems of the day, they concluded, could be solved only by more education. Their children would have as much of it as they could afford.

My parents neither ignored nor deprecated their Italian heritage. On the contrary. Opposite the portraits of Washington and Lincoln in the living room, father mounted an engraving of Garibaldi, and above the dining room sideboard hung a bas relief of the Florentine religious martyr, Savonarola. On winter evenings, father would read aloud to mother from books on Italian history and novels borrowed from the public library. The family attended memorial services for Sacco and Vanzetti, wrongly executed as anarchist murderers. On September 20, the family went to church to celebrate the liberation of Rome from the

Pope and the Vatican in 1870. We children were embarrassed because father sang Garibaldi's War Hymn in a very loud voice:

> All' armi, all' armi!
> Si scopron le tombe, si leva noi morti,
> I martiri nostri son tutti risorti...

We were grateful that Mr. Scagliolo, a giant of a man with a more powerful voice, sang about the uncovering of tombs and arising of martyrs with even more vigor than father. My parents spoke a better Italian than most of our neighbors, knew more Italian history, and more closely followed news about Italy. But they had no desire to return to Italy, even for a visit. When I asked father why he felt that way, he replied, "What's the point? I left Italy because I was starving. Why go back? To see the misery? He who feeds me I call 'papa.' America has been good to me and it is my fatherland."

Yet my parents never pushed Italian ways on us. They thought that we should learn Italian but my mother's efforts to teach us the *Silibario*, a syllable book used in the early grades in Italy, were feeble. We never got much beyond pronouncing the vowels and consonants: "ba, be, bi, bo, bu."

In short, as the first generation, my parents travelled a long way toward assimilation. The church, the Republican party, the factory, the newspaper, and other agencies reached out to absorb immigrants, who went along perhaps without realizing it. The process was probably speedier with my parents than with most of our neighbors. In any event, most immigrants neither denied nor deprecated their ethnicity, identifying with both Italy and America although over time they came to think of themselves more as American without verbalizing it.

Assimilation in the Second Generation

Assimilation, well begun in the first generation, was largely completed in the second by the school system where all children in the city, including those of immigrants, were trained to become Americans. Before describing my childhood recollections of the school system in the 1920s and early 1930s, I should explain why being a Protestant speeded the process.

The Role of the Church

Rochester's Italian Protestant churches flourished roughly from 1915 to 1945, then declined. All died by 1960 (Form 2000). In their early

years, they speeded the Americanizing of the first generation by stress-
ing links to American Protestant churches and American ways. In function and structure the Italian Protestant churches mirrored their American denominations in most ways, save for the use of Italian. Even so,
they stressed the learning of English, the folkways of American voluntary associations, and the importance of education. Increasing the use
of English in services to retain second generation's loyalty eliminated
the only thing that distinguished them from the American churches.
The small Italian Protestant neighborhood churches could not survive
the second generation's residential and occupational mobility. To remain Protestant, most of the second generation married outside the Italian community. Catholics intermarried less; 46% of native born of Italian heritage in my cohort married spouses not of Italian background
(Alba 1995: p. 14).

In my case, the process proceeded even more rapidly than for most
second generation Italian Protestants because my father transferred our
membership to Lake Avenue Baptist, a downtown church four blocks
from home and a mile from the city center. Most members lived in
middle-class neighborhoods in other parts of the city. I was envious
when my Sunday School friends discussed their Christmas presents:
Lionel electric trains, Erector sets, and model cars. Although I felt deprived, my friends never made me feel poor or unwelcome. While Rochester Italians made much of American prejudice, my family experienced none of it at Lake Avenue Church. We attended Sunday School,
Christian Endeavor, choir, Boy Scouts, the orchestra, the annual picnic,
and congregational meetings.

Mrs. Charity Carmen, the church missionary whose job was to visit
members, dropped in regularly. She always asked how the children were
doing at school and invited mother to the Wednesday afternoon Sewing
Circle. Mother spoke broken English but she overcame her shyness.
She told Mrs. Carmen that all her children would go to college. My
father attended adult Sunday School after the general service while we
were in Sunday School. Father had no problems with English and clearly
knew more of the Bible than others but he never became a church officer as in the Church of the Evangel.

Mrs. Carmen arranged for a man with no son to adopt me for the
evening to attend a father and son banquet and for my brother Arnold
and me to join the YMCA. My Sunday School teacher, Claude Darling,
took his class bowling at the downtown YMCA on a Sunday afternoon.
We also went to his home for picnics and hiked in the country. He showed

all the boys how to shoot his shotgun. Most important, Mr. Darling held an annual Sunday School contest. Whoever learned the most Bible verses and had the best attendance was given a prize at year's end. In 1929 I won a silver Elgin watch, its back inscribed with my name, misspelled. My father thought that a boy my age would break a watch so he held it for me until I was old enough to care for it. On Sundays he wore it on a silver chain across his vest, an Odd Fellows pin dangling from it. When he died in 1968, 39 years later, I "inherited" my watch.

To become church members, Baptists require total immersion at the age of responsibility. My baptism as an infant in the Italian Presbyterian Church of the Evangel didn't count. By age 19, I had doubts about God's existence but Nancy and Arnold, my older siblings, had been baptized and clearly my turn had come. Before a congregational meeting, I briefly professed my faith, declaring that I had come to know Jesus, and decided to follow his teaching. The congregation voted to accept me as eligible for baptism. Mr. Blackburn, who sat in the pew next to ours, helped me don the baptismal gown. The pastor, Dr. Yeaple, guided my steps into the pool, lowering me into the warm water until it covered my head as the congregation sang "Just as I am, without one plea, But that Thy blood was shed for me." At the service the following Sunday, Dr. Yeaple extended the Hand of Fellowship, making much of his long association with our family and his joy in receiving me into the fellowship. His obvious sincerity and firm handshake made me feel fully integrated into the congregation. Ethnicity was no barrier; the church reached out to us and we were happy about it.

Schools and Manufacturing Americans

The Language "Problem"

In the late nineteenth century, the first Italian immigrants in Rochester invaded Irish neighborhoods, sending their children to nearby schools that had made no plans to accommodate them. The children spoke their parents' Italian dialects and the dominantly Irish teachers spoke no Italian. In kindergarten and first grade, the children speedily learned to speak and write standard American English. It became the sole language of the second generation and the schools no longer faced a language problem.

By the time I was born, 14 years after my parents married, Italian was no longer the family language. My parents generally conversed in it, but mother spoke to us in a mixture of Italian and English, and we children talked to each other and to our parents only in English. Our Italian vocabulary was too limited to utter coherent sentences and our efforts to converse represented a mishmash of Italian, English, and anglicized Italian words.

Of the four children only George, the oldest, could converse in Italian. He spoke only Italian when he went to kindergarten at age seven. As an adult, he spoke Italian better than most of his peers but it was not good Italian. He later studied it and spoke it grammatically. My family's language pattern was not unique. In Aunt Marietta's family, only the oldest of the four children, Angelo (later Charles), could manage Sicilian; that of his siblings (Louis, Michael, and Josephine) was primitive and anglicized. That they knew any Sicilian at all was due to grandmother's monitoring them while their parents worked in a tailor factory. Grandmother also monitored Louis, the only child of my mother's brother, Uncle Joe, and his wife, Aunt Grace, who also worked in a tailor factory. Louis could manage a primitive Sicilian. Aunt Giulia and Uncle Loreto Luchetti, a Roman, had come to the United States in their teens and spoke fairly good English to their daughters Roselynn and Loretta, neither of whom mastered their parents' good Italian.

Most neighborhood families shared my family's language practices. Regardless of how much Italian was spoken in the family, the children spoke unaccented American English to one another. I never heard second generation children conducting a conversation among themselves in Italian. Generally only the first child in immigrant families could speak the parental dialect. No grammar school teacher ever uttered an Italian word in class. Total immersion in English led children to speak unaccented American in one year. Contrary to popular opinion, only 20 percent of persons of Italian heritage in my cohort reported Italian as the language spoken at home (Alba 1995, p. 9).

Current practices of teaching immigrant children in their parents' language would have made little sense in my generation. Parents, many of them illiterate, spoke a variety of dialects that had no words for much of what their children experienced in school. Teaching them in Italian would have required most children to learn two languages: English, on which most had already made a good start and Italian, which almost no one knew.

Continuing Expansion of the School System

After the Civil War, Rochester's school system was challenged to assimilate increasing numbers of immigrants' children. A city of 90,000 in 1880 grew to 330,000 by 1930 when I entered junior high: 23 percent foreign-born, 38 percent native-born with at least one foreign-born parent, and 39 percent native-born of native parents (U.S. Bureau of the Census, 1880-1949).

In the nineteenth century, the educational system had to confront the task of assimilating the children of immigrant Germans and then the Irish. By 1900, most immigrants came from Southern and Eastern Europe, mostly Italians, Poles, and Jews from Poland and Russia. The tide ebbed rapidly when the Immigration Act of 1923 restricted migration from those countries.

Italian immigrants were mostly young adults with high birth rates. The school system's problems in dealing with the growing number of immigrants' children was exacerbated by the rising age of compulsory education. In 1900 most children began school in first grade and only a few went beyond sixth. By 1910 kindergarten was introduced and all children were expected to complete sixth, preferably eighth grade; by 1930, ninth or tenth grade. By 1940 almost all children under age 16 (tenth grade) attended school and half of those between 16 and 20 years. Median school completion rate for those over 25 was 8.8 years (U.S. Bureau of the Census, 1940). It was hoped but not generally realized that most urban youth would complete high school by age 18 or 19.

The school system expanded rapidly, especially in the 1920s and 1930s, building new grade schools to accommodate growing numbers of immigrants' children. Soon after, junior high schools were built because the age of compulsory attendance was raised. Within a few years, more high schools had to be built. From 1928 to 1942, during the longest economic depression in U.S. history, the school system expanded rapidly. Even when unemployment rates were highest, 20 percent or above, funds were found to build more schools and hire more teachers.

Early School Experiences

I began kindergarten in an old grammar school, Number Six, about six blocks from home. After a few weeks, I was transferred to Number Five, a converted nunnery four blocks from home that I attended for two years before the old wooden structure was torn down to provide the site for a new and larger school. In third grade, my school was an old brick house converted into two class rooms. Classes were held half days, two in the morning and two in the afternoon. The next year, we moved into the new John Williams School, Number Five. After the sixth grade, I was sent to the new Jefferson Junior High. I attended summer school, skipped a half grade, and transferred to West High School, one of the city's oldest. The semester after I left Jefferson, all seven junior high schools in the city were expanded into junior-senior high schools.

From kindergarten on, school brought few surprises as my older siblings, Nancy and Arnold, talked about it at home. I knew what to expect and my expectations were confirmed. Mother did not even take me to my first kindergarten class at Number Six; Nancy and Arnold simply dropped me off. Hanging our outdoor clothes in a long dark wardrobe, we entered the bright class room where we marched about, sang songs, and took naps.

I was disappointed to be transferred to Number Five. It had no mysterious wardrobe and I was no longer tracing George, Nancy, and Arnold's footsteps. However, at both Numbers Five and Six, kindergarten had three teachers, one of whom played the piano. Kindergarten was fun. My strongest recollection was the daily singing of "My Country 'Tis of Thee." We often played Soldier Boy. The children formed a circle and chose a leader carrying a bundle of American flags to march around inside while everyone sang:

"The soldier boy goes marching by, goes marching by, goes marching by,

"The soldier boy goes marching by, may I go too?

"If your heart is kind and true, you can be a soldier too."

At the word "too," the leader stopped. The child opposite the leader would then be given a flag. Placing the flag on his or her shoulder, the child followed the leader around the circle while everyone repeated the song. Again, at "too," the leader stopped to acquire another flag bearer. The number of children bearing flags grew until all the children had joined the circle and marched around the room singing as the routine ended.

One day, soon after the New Year, my cousin Josephine Traino and I were sent up a rickety flight of stairs to the first grade. As we entered the room, the teacher was showing the children flash cards inscribed with syllables and short words. She would call on a pupil to pronounce the word or syllable, then the whole class would repeat it aloud. Soon we were reading books. Then the class was moved to a larger room with two teachers. One of them formed a reading circle with half the class on a platform at one side of the room while the other half was being taught arithmetic. Each student in the reading circle was asked to read aloud a passage from the book. I read a passage about a streetcar motorman who kept ringing his bell: "ding-ding; ding-ding." I decided then and there to become a motorman when I grew up.

In second grade we had the school's only male teacher, Mr. Mancuso, dark, young, single, and of Italian background. As the other teachers always smiled at him, we children concluded that they were in love with him. Mr. Mancuso taught us to sing two-part songs. At the end of the term, he invited other classes to the auditorium (the old convent chapel) to hear our Christmas concert. My only teacher who ever uttered an Italian word in class, Mr. Mancuso told us that we could figure out the meaning of complicated words if we knew Italian, illustrating with the word "petroleum," composed of "pietra," or rock, and "olio," oil. That was the extent to which the school acknowledged our ethnic background.

At Easter one teacher had us make Easter baskets from stiff colored paper stuffed with white cotton, a yellow cotton chicken, and four colored jelly beans. One nasty day, cousin Josephine and I took our baskets home at lunchtime. Icy rain and snow pelted us and neither of us had worn gloves or rubbers. We trudged through icy slush, our feet beginning to freeze in soggy shoes, clothes and hands covered with sleet. We arrived home crying, carrying the paper baskets in our frozen hands. Setting the baskets aside, my mother put our hands under cold water then gave us thick slices of bread she had just baked, spread with olive oil and served with hot tea and warm milk. She hung our wet clothes over the kitchen stove, putting our shoes in the oven to dry.

The school system seemed indifferent to separation of church and state. Our teachers, mostly Irish Catholics, taught us to sing Protestant hymns at Christmas. Once a week the children attended the nearby Catholic church for religious instruction, a practice that the Irish bishop convinced the school system to adopt because most children rarely attended the Irish-dominated neighborhood churches (Form 1999, ch. 9). As Protestants, cousin Jo and I were the only ones to remain in class during religious instruction. Our Irish teachers who otherwise would have had a free period resented having to monitor us. I amused myself by drawing pictures of the nearby Eastman Kodak tower, motorized sleds, and horses.

Miss McCarthy, our third grade teacher, a Protestant, was impressed with the vigor with which Jo and I sang the Christmas carols she was teaching. One Sunday afternoon she and her boy friend stopped by my house to pick us up to sing carols at an old people's home. She accompanied us on the piano as we began to sing: "The snow is on the hill tops, the snow is in the glen, and Christmas has come to our glad hearts again. The storms may come a-roaring ... " I could not hear Jo, who was frozen with stage fright. After I pinched her hip, she weakly joined in. Our unmemorable performance received a loud round of applause.

Making Patriots

Rochester's schools had been designed to educate children of the original settlers, Americans of British origin. The design remained unchanged as immigrants arrived from across Europe. School authorities continued to assume that all children were to be educated as British-Americans. Teachers never referred to our ethnic backgrounds as disqualifying us from becoming Americans, for the nation's history was our history. In first grade, as we filed in the room each morning, we stood erect by our seats. Calling for silence, the teacher said, "Good morning, students." We replied in chorus, "Good morning, Miss Jones." Then everyone saluted the flag and recited the Pledge of Allegiance.

We learned about our Pilgrim and Puritan forebears in New England. That they were British and Protestant was of no consequence. They were still ours. When Lincoln declared that " ... our forefathers brought forth on this continent a new nation," he was speaking of our forebears, of our indivisible nation. When we daily sang, "My Country 'Tis of Thee," we sang of our country. We were as much a part of it as the original settlers, as the Germans who came later, and the Irish who came still later. All were Americans. As each national holiday approached, we studied its history and importance. Washington's and Lincoln's birthdays were very important but Memorial Day, which commemorated the Civil War, was more important. The most important was Armistice Day, November 11. At 11 A.M., the eleventh hour of the eleventh day, we silently stood by our seats for two minutes in memory of the fallen in the World War. Deeply moved, we recited "In Flanders fields the poppies grow ... "

To Be Clean and Healthy

The teachers well knew that immigrants' children were poor, often dirty and lacking proper deportment and manners. Their charge was to make the children of illiterate peasants into Anglo-Americans. We learned to be clean, polite, speak good English, and become Americans. The first requirement was good health. Schools were an integral part of the U.S. public health movement. After standing by our seats to pledge allegiance, each row walked to the front of the room to be inspected for lice and a clean face, neck, hands, and clothes. Those with lice were sent to the school nurse. Those with dirty hands or faces were given soap and sent to the wash room. Then the teacher reinspected them, urging them to be clean the next day. If uncleanliness persisted, the visiting nurse informed parents that their children had to appear clean in school, which generally solved the problem.

After inspection, teachers gave health lessons. They showed us how to brush our teeth, clean our fingernails, and wash our hands. We were instructed on what kind of clothes to wear, how to tie our ties, brace our stockings, and clean our shoes. We were told to use toothbrushes, with soap, salt, or soda as a dentifrice. The teacher's influence on parents was palpable. When children told parents, "The teacher says we have to have a tooth brush... two pencils...a note pad," parents felt compelled to comply.

Each semester a doctor and nurse visited the class. After each physical examination, the nurse gave the child a white, blue, or red card. White cards signified good health, blue cards, possible problems; red cards called for immediate medical attention. I got a blue card once because the doctor thought I was underweight. I took the card home and returned it, signed, to the teacher. After talking to me, the nurse decided that I was not malnourished. City nurses visited the homes of children who got red cards and arranged for the child to visit a doctor.

Dental care was part of the school health program. To clean our teeth, 20 women dental technicians set pedal-driven dental equipment and chairs in the halls each term. A dentist then inspected each child to identify those who needed care, which was most of us. A few days later, we boarded a street car to the Dental Dispensary operated by the University of Rochester's School of Dentistry. On arrival we were seated in a delightful walnut-paneled waiting room with Mother Goose frescoes painted above the panels. A large cage in the center of the room held 20 or so wildly chirping canaries. When our names were called, we climbed a long steep staircase with walls of sickly green. Taking our cards, a nurse led each child into a large high-vaulted room with 60 dental chairs in three long rows. The scene was terrifying, children screaming in fright or pain. We climbed onto the chairs, frozen in terror. Although the student dentists were patient, they used no laughing gas unless teeth had to be pulled. Since most of us made repeat trips to the dispensary, the appeal of the canaries and Mother Goose frescoes eroded rapidly. Yet, without the Dispensary, most students would not have seen the dentists whose services were available for poor children through high school.

In the 1920s, doctors recommended that children's tonsils be removed to prevent colds and sore throats. In the basement of the Dental Dispensary the University of Rochester Medical School operated a large clinic. Children of the poor (mostly those of immigrants) who were identified as needing to have their tonsils removed were sent there. I don't recall that Nancy, Arnold, or I had unusual problems with our tonsils. Yet one evening our parents took all three of us on the street car to the clinic. We entered an enormous room with perhaps 50 beds. Each of us was assigned a bed and we slept there that night. Early next morning a nurse awakened me. I climbed onto a high bed which was rolled to the operating room where I was given ether. When I awoke, I was back in my bed, one of a bedlam of crying and vomiting children. We were fed ice cream and told to rest until the bleeding stopped. After an hour or two, we met our parents who took us home for more ice cream. Within a day or two Arnold and I recovered, but Nancy had to go to a hospital to staunch the persisting bleeding.

Public health nurses wearing blue uniforms and carrying large black leather bags were a common sight in our neighborhood. They tended to the needs of poor pregnant women, directed the sick to doctors and hospitals, quarantined houses where there was a contagious disease like diphtheria. The school system taught health practices, identified children who needed medical attention, and directed them to proper health facilities. The school system along with the city's public health agencies and the University of Rochester provided health services to the children of immigrants.

Manners, Respect, and All That

Expected to be well-behaved, students were graded on cooperation and deportment. Teachers drilled students to be courteous toward them and one another. For example, "Miss Mayhew, may I please leave the room," was the required question. Permission was not granted until the student got it right. Then "Thank you" was in order and the teacher would reply "You're welcome." By the fourth grade, polite language was thoroughly inculcated into all of us. We were also taught the social circumstances that required, "excuse me," "pardon me" or, most formal, "I beg your pardon."

Discipline was generally not a problem in class or on the playground. I recall only two exceptions. The first involved a boy who persistently "sassed" the teacher. Exasperated, she finally sent him to the principal's office. After he returned, the problem persisted. The next time he was sent to the principal, she ordered him to bring his father to school. Since the father spoke no English, the teacher sent me to the principal's office to translate. She asked me to tell the father that his son disturbed the class, was disrespectful to the teacher, and persistently refused to follow her requests. But I knew too little Italian to translate. Finally, I came up with some disconnected words, "Your son...he talks, talks, talks...the teacher...angry." The father shouted, "He does?" and slapped the boy across the mouth. "Stop, stop," the principal shrieked. Turning to me, the father said "Tell her he'll be a good boy. I'll fix him when he gets home." The boy returned next day, sullen but subdued the rest of the term.

In sixth grade, Mrs. McMullen told a disruptive boy to go to the principal's office. A big tough lad, he refused to budge. When she reached for his arm to lead him to the door, he resisted. Struggling, he tore her dress, pulled off her glasses, and jerked on her necklace. Beads scattered across the floor. "Call the principal," the teacher screamed. The girl closest to the door raced down the hall. In a minute, the vice principal, a strong young man, arrived, put an arm lock on the boy, and manoeuvered him out of the room. We never saw him again.

Identifying Talent

The Eastman School of Music of the University of Rochester worked closely with the school system. My brother Arnold and cousin Louis Traino (Jo's brother) got group violin lessons for free after school at Number Five Annex, an ancient building two blocks from Number Five. Once in second grade when Jo and I were waiting at the Annex for our brothers to walk us home, we found the staircase to the steeple and saw the rope dangling from the tower that rang the school bell. I pulled on it, but it didn't ring. Then Jo and I together leaped up a foot or so and grabbed the rope with both hands. As we came down, the bell rang. Since we did not release our grip on the rope, it carried us up a foot or two and we rang it again. As we continued the vertical teeter-totter, the principal charged into the room and dragged us to his office. With a cylindrical ruler from his desk drawer, he delivered several stinging blows across our palms. Crying, we huddled in a corner of the hallway until our brothers emerged after the music lesson.

In fourth grade, the entire class took what I later learned was the Seashore Musical Ability Test. All of us were given head phones connected to a phonograph at the front of the room. A voice on the record asked us to assess whether the first note was higher or lower than the second, louder or softer, longer or shorter in duration. After a few weeks, students with the highest scores were given cards that informed parents that their child was eligible to rent any musical instrument (except a violin or piano) for $2.50 a year. In addition, free group lessons would be provided at Monroe High School on Saturday mornings. The child could also enroll in courses in music reading, harmony, and composition.

Having received one of the precious cards, I told my parents I wanted a flute. Brother George went to the Board of Education downtown to pick it up but brought home a French horn instead, his instrument. I overcame my disappointment because George immediately taught me to play it and read music. The Saturday morning lessons from red-headed Mr. Richlin, a student at the Eastman school, proved superfluous. After a few months, my grade teacher asked me to bring my horn to school. She accompanied me on the piano as we practiced a few simple songs. Before the entire student body in the assembly hall, we played "Long, Long Ago" and "The Blue Bells of Scotland."

An ensemble of the Rochester Civic Orchestra (about 30 players) gave a concert in our assembly hall. The conductor, Eugene Harrison, taught us to identify the instruments. After the performers played solos, he led the entire orchestra in several selections. Music appreciation continued in the class room.

In the 1930s, objective tests were being introduced in the schools. In fifth grade, we were given what I believe was an achievement test; in sixth grade, an intelligence test. We were not told the results but it was obvious that the teachers took them seriously. We were told to be absolutely silent while taking them and to raise our hands if we had a question. Ivan Ranaletti who sat in the twin desk next to mine tried to copy my answers. Forgetting to raise my hand to attract Miss Envelope's attention, I objected audibly, which irritated her. After the test, she reprimanded me rather than Ivan who was, I thought, the culprit. I was resentful, Ivan was angry. As we left for lunch, he challenged me to a fist fight. I had never been in one before and wanted to avoid it. I told him that my mother expected me home for lunch, but I would fight him after lunch before class.

As I apprehensively approached the school grounds after lunch, the boys had already formed a circle for the fight. Ivan was an experienced fighter. Crouching, he circled around me, pounding my face in quick bursts. I backed away, not striking a single blow, blood dripping from my nose. I began to cry and the fight was over. When I got home that afternoon, mother spotted my bloody shirt and a "shiner" on one eye. She insisted on knowing what happened. After several lame excuses, I admitted to fighting. She repeatedly asked who it was, but I remained silent. "Uli," she said angrily, using the nickname for Guglielmo, "if you don't tell me his name, I'll give you another black eye." I told her.

She took me at once to Ivan's home. When Mrs. Ranaletti appeared at the door, mother pointed to my black eye and bloody shirt. "This is what your boy did to my son!" Mrs. Ranaletti remained silent, but mother continued, "You must teach your son not to fight. That is no way for boys to behave." Mrs. Ranaletti weakly responded that she would speak to Ivan and that he would not fight me again. While he did not, he continued to push me around and I submitted to his intimidation.

Soon after, mother visited my class, the only mother in the neighborhood who annually visited her children's classes. For us, this was a supremely embarrassing experience. About ten o'clock mother would appear in her best dress, introduce herself to the teacher and ask to observe the class. The teacher would offer her a chair at the front of the room and proceed with the lesson. As I slumped in my seat trying to become invisible, she would call on me to recite. After 20 minutes of agony, mother would rise, thank the teacher, and address the class:

> Boys and girls. This is a nice school and you have a good teacher. She is kind and wants to help you. You must always pay attention to your teacher, learn, and be respectful. You are fortunate to be here. Thank you very much.

Teachers, typically pleased by mother's visit, would follow her from the room and report that I was a good boy and a good student. In this instance, however, Miss Envelope was not happy with me. After mother left, she addressed the class, smiling wryly: "It was nice of William's mother to visit us. She thinks he's such an angel, but we know that he can sometimes be unruly." I was humiliated. When I got home that afternoon, mother told me that the teacher said that I fidgeted and talked too much. I admitted that I found it very hard to sit still and did whisper sometimes. Mother reached out to administer a slap or two. Although she rarely hurt me, I avoided punishment by circling the dining room table, stopping before the china cabinet screeching, "Look out, look out, we might break the glass!" She ordered me to move away, but I refused to budge. She finally said, "I'll tend to you later."

A few weeks passed. Then one day mother and I were in the cellar where we had a gas stove and sink that we used in the canning season. As I helped her with the canning, she suggested, "Uli, let's play cowboys and Indians. You be the cowboy." Mother was rarely one to play, but I innocently consented to be tied to the post. Then she said, eyes dancing and suppressing a grin, "You were a bad boy in school and you talked back to the teacher. I do not ever want to hear that again. Do you understand?" Even though I readily agreed, she proceeded to whip me with a rope. Although she did not hurt me, this was reprehensible and I never forgave her. But I did learn to sit still and be quiet in class. I resented Miss Envelope, who seemed indifferent.

One afternoon Miss Envelope told us that the tests we took that spring had been scored. Thumbing through the notebook that contained our scores, she raised her eyes, focussed on me for a second or two, and smiled faintly. As we marched out of the room to return home, she rested her hand on my shoulder and walked a few paces with me. Leaning over the balustrade as we trooped down the stairs, she said softly, "Good night, William." "Good night, Miss Envelope," I replied, relieved that she had finally forgiven me.

In sixth grade, we got another printed test, probably for intelligence. When the results came in, Miss Envelope again thumbed through the results and gazed at me, smiling. Then she told us what to expect next semester at Junior High School. We would go into an academic, technical, commercial, or general-industrial tracks. There would be two sections for each track, eight in all. I was assigned to 7B-1, the higher section of the highest track, academic-Latin.

Junior High

The first semester at Jefferson proved tumultuous and disturbing. At Number Five all students had been of Italian background and I was among the most able. At Jefferson most of my classmates were American and equally able. Although ethnicity never became a problem, I felt socially marginal. Coming from the same school in other neighborhoods, many of my classmates were friends before they came to Jefferson. I rarely visited their homes and had little contact with them outside of class. They were self-confident, wore better clothes, and had more money. I felt poorly dressed. For lunch, I had unevenly sliced bread for sandwiches cut from mother's home made bread. Retreating to a corner of the cafeteria, I observed that most of my classmates bought a gill of milk and sat together munching neat sandwiches made with store-bought bread. Some even bought their entire lunch.

As Valentine's day approached, classmates began exchanging cards. While most boys received many cards, I received only three or four from the pretty girls seated separately on the other side of the room. We hadn't exchanged cards in grammar school and I couldn't afford to buy them. I sketched a few by hand and sent them to the girls who had sent me cards.

When the school put on the operetta, *Ali Baba*, I was assigned to the chorus. I felt that the teachers should have recognized my musical ability and given me a better role. At rehearsals, convinced that they were playing favorites, I sang when I shouldn't, moved about, and tore at my flimsy costume. Refusing to use the E-flat crook on my French horn, I transposed poorly from my F horn, disrupting rehearsals. The exasperated director finally took my horn, expelled me from band, and sent me to the principal's office for being disruptive in chorus and band. The principal, Miss Shelmadine, asked me to bring my mother to school. I wept and refused. For two days I sat in the anteroom of her office until she finally allowed me to return to class, much subdued.

Returning to the chorus, I sang listlessly and remained inconspicuous. I didn't think of asking the band director for my horn. However, as a member of the National Guard cavalry band, my brother George had a beautiful government-issued silver French horn, with valves rather than the pistons of my old horn. George lent it to me and I took it to rehearsal, going to my chair without asking permission to return. The director was dismayed but let me stay. I learned to transpose music and was no longer disruptive.

Although all of my teachers were considerate, they did not understand what was troubling me except for Mrs. Gallagher, the arithmetic teacher. A beautiful gray-eyed woman with prematurely grey hair, she sensed the problems of the three boys of Italian descent in her class. In one corner of the room sat Sam Cicorelli, the blond son of the Sicilian cobbler in my neighborhood. Mrs. Gallagher quickly recognized his talent for solving long arithmetic problems: "Begin with five, triple it, divide by three, multiply by four . . . " She praised him for arriving at the correct answer first. I usually lost track after four or five directions.

Mrs. Gallagher also brought out Amerigo, a dark shy lad who never volunteered to answer questions or go to the blackboard to do arithmetic problems. He responded brightly when she called him "Samuel" rather than "Amerigo." She waited patiently for him to answer questions. Samuel slowly became more responsive and eventually volunteered to perform at the black board. In my case arithmetic was not my strongest suit, but Mrs. Gallagher was patient. Although she called me "William," most students called me "Bill" rather than "Will," and thereafter I was "Bill."

Choir was the highlight of the week. We marched into a bright room with elevated rows of seats. Prissy Mr. Truitt directed us while Miss Apple accompanied us on piano. We sang mostly British folk songs, "The Lass With the Delicate Air," "Danny Boy," and "Coming Through the Rye." The class always ended too soon for me. Ironically, social studies, my future life work, was my worst subject.

I routinely did my homework in grammar school but didn't know that this wasn't enough in Junior High. One had to master the material to earn top grades. For the first time, I was not one of the best students. We moved from one classroom to another for different subjects. I was shy, afraid to approach my teachers. Although I was disturbed when I did not get all A's on my report card, I did nothing about it. At the end of the first semester, I was mortified to be transferred to 7A-2. It had a few more students of Italian background but the curriculum was exactly the same and the competition as stiff. Yet the atmosphere was more relaxed. I studied a little, felt more comfortable, and began to perform better.

In eighth grade, we began Latin. Vocabulary was easy but grammar was difficult and I did not do well at first. After I spent more time studying, things improved steadily. Toward the end of the semester, Ivan Ranaletti approached me in the hall as I was waiting to enter the science room. As was his wont, he gave me a shove, but this time I shoved back, grabbed him, and we started to tussle. Mr. Harmon, the science teacher, spotted and separated us. Luckily, he did not send us to the principal for violating a cardinal rule: no fighting at school.

That summer, I finally settled scores with Ivan. As the Trainos were experiencing economic hardship, they rented their home in a middle class neighborhood and moved back to their house on Lind Street, around the corner from ours. Mike and Louie had "acquired" two pairs of beautiful maroon boxing gloves. Every day Mike, Louie, Arnie, I, and a few neighborhood boys fought regular three-minute rounds, not to settle scores but to learn how to box. I overcame my fear of being hurt. In a few weeks I could not only defend myself, I could outbox everyone my size and even those a little larger. Ivan Ranaletti, who lived two blocks away, appeared one day as we were practicing. When he tarried, cousin Mike suggested that he and I put on the gloves. Ivan confidently agreed and I feigned reluctance although I was eager to fight. He came toward me in his normal crouch position. I gave him several stiff lefts to the head. As he rose from his crouch and lowered his guard, I hit him on the head with a right cross, sending him reeling. Surprised, he rushed toward me, both arms swinging wildly. I backed off, avoiding his blows, held my ground and struck his head with a series of peppery left jabs. As he retreated, I pursued him with left and right jabs, not giving him a chance to recover. Mike finally stopped the fight when I cornered Ivan against Cordaro's garage door. Ivan left quietly and never bothered me again. I regretted that it was not a bare-knuckle fight to the finish.

I was enjoying school again. Rochester's Museum of Natural History, a branch of the zoo, and the neighborhood library were situated in Edgerton Park that bordered Jefferson Junior High. I spent many hours in the museum and library. Our teachers took us on great field trips. Every week we attended a general assembly, a pleasant break from class routines. We studied parliamentary procedure every semester until it became automatic. In the first semester of ninth grade, I was elected class president and later nominated for school president, which I lost. My election speech was abstract, unfocused, and filled with big words.

Arnie and Nancy who had been attending West High School took courses that summer. After a day or two at home alone, bored (mother would not let me roam the neighborhood), I decided to attend summer school too. By taking two courses, I could skip a semester of Junior High and attend West High with Arn and Nancy that very fall. I would insist that mother buy me long pants and let me wear a belt rather than suspenders.

High School

West and East High were the city's oldest high schools. West High opened up a new world for me. We daily walked two-and-one half miles to West's beautiful building, surrounded by lawns, shrubs, and trees. The main hall was adorned with life-size statues of Athena, Augustus Caesar, and Greek Boys Wrestling. On the first day, I was enrolled in the Latin college preparatory curriculum and had to buy (not rent) five books. Every hour, the hallways became crowded as individual students moved to different rooms. Every class required home work and everyone had one or two study halls to do some of it. More had to be done at home. *All* clubs, athletics, band and orchestra were held after classes. As at Jefferson, most students bought their lunch in the cafeteria, but about a quarter of us ate our sandwiches in a corner. There I discovered other Americans who like me were poorly dressed, children of farmers who were bussed in daily.

All students at West had to meet the same graduation requirements: four years of English, three of math, two of history, two of science, and a three-year sequence in another area, for me, French. At the end of the year, we all took the required Regents Examinations; grades were posted by name on bulletin boards in the cafeteria. Every week for four years, we were required to write a theme for English class. In the first year, we all bought *Magic Casements* (Carhart and McGhee 1928), a book of poetry used all four years. Every spring, the school held a poetry contest in the assembly where students recited poems they had memorized. Prizes were given for the best renditions.

Each Friday morning, the student body met for assembly. We stood at attention as the orchestra played and the seniors marched in to sit in the front rows. Boys wore white shirts, dark trousers, and blue ties; girls, white middy blouses, blue skirts, and blue kerchiefs. The principal, Mr. Spinning, made a few announcements but most of the time was devoted to student performances: a short play, a band or orchestra selection, high school cheers and songs, or poetry renditions. Each term, the Drama Society presented a three-act play in the evening. As a member of band and orchestra, I played French horn for the assemblies and plays.

In my first semester, I enrolled in Latin, Geometry, English, French, Chemistry, History, Band and Orchestra, and one study hall. Latin, with Miss Beshquatur was dull. Geometry with Mr. Savage was interesting but tough. Chemistry met in a large lecture hall with step-rows. We looked down at Mr. Smith as he lectured and demonstrated chemistry experiments. Then we went to the adjoining laboratory to conduct our own. This was serious stuff. I decided to take Modern European rather than American History. Mr. Harris lectured and then we asked him questions. I preferred his lectures to class discussions. Mr. Harris sparked a lifelong interest in foreign affairs. I found myself turning to the foreign news in the *Democrat and Chronicle* before reading anything else, a habit I retained all my life.

In all four years of English, we had to memorize poetry. Entranced by the beauty and rhythm of the language, I always enjoyed that. I gratefully remember all the poems I had to memorize that I can recite to this day. In addition, every semester the students gathered in the auditorium to hear a faculty member in costume recite a Shakespeare soliloquy. Each semester we read a Shakespeare play, memorized at least one soliloquy and a long poem, and read at least one novel, often American.

I thrived under West High's academic demands. Our art teacher invited us to her home, showed us her studio, and served us goodies. Our band and orchestra conductor sent the best musicians to Monroe High School to join those selected from other high schools for the Inter-High band and orchestra. The orchestra gave two concerts over the NBC network. Fred Mastrodonato and I were asked to play horn in Charlotte High's orchestra for Gilbert and Sullivan's *Pirates of Penzance*. In my senior year, I was selected for honors English and French. In English we studied Chaucer and learned how to pronounce late Middle English. College courses in British prose and poetry brought few surprises. We completed the third and fourth year of French in a year and were able to converse at year's end. Our French Club gave a play in French and conducted an oral poetry contest that I won. Miss Smith took us to *Le Cercle Français*, an East Avenue club where only French was spoken. The women served us tea and cookies while we conversed in French.

West High, the search for talented students was built into the system. Whatever their backgrounds, students with merit and talent were recognized. Those who scored high on the Regents' Examinations were encouraged to apply for college scholarships. Students were also encouraged to develop their talents in extra-curricular activities. Thus, I was asked to join the inter-high school band and orchestra; others were encouraged to take part in school plays. The speech teacher, Mr. Savage, worked long and hard with Michael Parisi, who stuttered terribly, until he was able to lead the student body in school cheers. The voice teacher discovered that Tony Dibiasi had a glorious tenor. Given special lessons after school, he performed in assembly, and sang professionally in Protestant church choirs in the city.

In the middle of the Great Depression, West High gave us a classical education comparable to that given in private academies. The teachers assumed that a classical education was appropriate for all students, regardless of their backgrounds. The curriculum, designed for children of British settlers, was considered good for children of later immigrants.

Those who would not or could not handle the academic curriculum received technical training.

Tempus Mutatur et Nos Mutamur in Illis

I was 19 years old when I attended the Saracen's funeral service at the Church of the Evangel. In the 14 years since I had last been there, Lake Avenue Baptist Church and the school system had made me a middle-class American who felt out of place at Evangel. Before father died, 32 years would pass. In that interval, the ethnic situation in the city had changed drastically. My parents attended church less often after the children left town. Father's funeral, held in a funeral home, was conducted by the former pastor of the Church of the Evangel, melded meantime with an "American" church. Surprisingly, it was in English. Six years later when my mother died at age 93, her service was also held at a funeral home. It was conducted in accented English much like mother's by a lay pastor of an Italian experiential church. Thus, by the 1960s even the last rites of the Italian-born were conducted in English.

The extent of my loss of Italian as I Americanized became clear over time. Although I had studied Latin, French, and German, the first language I used in research was Spanish, in Mexico, and I learned enough to get by. When I was about to go to the International Sociological Association meetings in La Stresa, I studied Italian for a week, confident I could get along. We first visited England, France, and Germany. England was wonderful. I felt at home. There were few surprises because I had a sense of seeing what I had already known. My French was rusty, but I could make myself easily understood and felt comfortable as a tourist. In Germany, I scraped along with college German. Surprisingly, the Germans seemed more American in some ways than the British. But when Al Beegle and I arrived in Milan to board the train for La Stresa, I tried to converse with a fellow passenger in my newly acquired Italian. I didn't do well and soon gave up. Although entranced by art, architecture, and landscape on the way to Florence and Rome, I felt no sense of belonging as in England.

On my second sabbatical, I planned to study FIAT's automobile workers in Turin. This time, I prepared by studying Italian for a year at Michigan State but still could not converse fluently when I first arrived. When I visited my father's birthplace, a town in the Apennines north of Naples, I felt like a rich foreigner as I parked my new Volkswagen microbus in the town square. I took some photos but did not try to visit distant relatives. When visiting my maternal grandfather's birthplace in the foothills of the Alps northwest of Turin, I struck out again. Approaching two peasant women dragging a cart full of grapes, I asked if they knew of anyone with grandfather's name, Conet, Gonet, Cornet, or Cornetti. In a nasal Piedmontese dialect that sounded more French than Italian, they said they knew no such family. But when I left Turin, I spoke Italian fluently and no longer felt like a stranger. Rochester's educational system had done its work. When children of immigrants completed sixth grade, they spoke unaccented English, had proper manners and hygienic habits, and followed American customs. Ethnic discrimination was no issue in grammar school because all of us were of Italian background. Regardless of ethnic origin, all children were taught the same curriculum. Teachers believed that standardized tests identified talented students, whatever their backgrounds. While their faith in the tests may have been too strong, testing did reduce partiality. The teachers never doubted that they could turn the children of poor illiterate immigrants into Americans.

In junior high, I confronted a multiethnic environment where teachers could have easily been prejudiced and discriminatory. Although "Americans" were generally of higher socio economic status, they were found in all ability-graded levels, albeit in different proportions. Whatever their ethnic origin and whatever their curriculum, all students had to meet the same standards. I never witnessed a single instance of a teacher's attributing poor performance to ethnicity or social status. If anything, the opposite was true; they encouraged children of ethnics to develop their talents. To be sure, teachers ignored ethnicity in their efforts to inculcate American customs and values but neither students nor parents, eager to become American, mourned the loss.

In high school, the emphasis on merit was even greater. While the school system did not assure that poor talented students, American or ethnic, would go to college, teachers nonetheless assumed that all students in my track were capable of absorbing a classical education that would serve them well. The standardized Regents Examinations of the State Department of Education also encouraged universalism. Even without them, teachers identified the talented and directed them to special honors classes.

In view of public school success in fostering talent, why did children of immigrants feel that Americans were prejudiced and discriminatory? First, because discrimination in the community was based on class as well as ethnicity. Second, discrimination clearly occurred in the labor market. Immigrants and their children confronted barriers to employment in the city's best-paying industries: Eastman Kodak, Bausch and Lomb, the Haloid Corporation (later Xerox), Stromberg-Carlson, the Gleason Works, and the U.S. Postal System.

Job discrimination was strong during the Great Depression up to World War II. In the prosperous postwar period, it declined rapidly in employment, residence, and other arenas. Today, Rochester's new immigrants are Hispanic and African-American. The school system again faces a difficult challenge of integrating them into the mainstream. One hopes that its success with earlier children of immigrants may be repeated.

Even though second and third generation descendants of Europeans are culturally American, many still identify themselves as ethnics (Gans 1979) and others continue to label them as such. I never made a point of either hiding or emphasizing my ethnic origin, always revealing it to friends. When I did, some would say, "Bill, I didn't know you were Italian, being a Protestant and all." I told them that my parents and grandparents were born in Italy, but were buried here. The bold ones observe that Form doesn't sound like an Italian name. I explain that my father changed it when I was in college. Most can't resist asking, "What was it before it was changed?" When they enter my office and I am singing or whistling, as I often am, they comment that Italians love opera and singing. In short, they interpret my behavior in ethnic terms only when they know my heritage.

2

Pre-Apprenticeship

In high school, I never thought seriously about an occupational goal. I toyed with the idea of becoming a forester, living alone in a tower watching for fires, even writing to the Forestry School at the University of Syracuse for a catalogue. I enjoyed playing French horn in the school orchestra and considered studying at the Eastman School of Music to become a professional musician, an idea that soon died. In the midst of the Great Depression I would only join a large corps of unemployed musicians. Mother spoke vaguely of my becoming a medical missionary; the church would probably bear the expenses, but the idea was never pursued. Or I could become a pastor. Instead, I became a professor. While that was largely an accident (see chapter 3), socialization narrowed my occupational choices and the way I behaved on the job. Whether forester, musician, doctor, or pastor, I would have been oriented to work and politics. I explore below how that orientation developed in a period that I call pre-apprenticeship.

In the six institutions where I taught, my colleagues teased me about an overdeveloped work ethic. But how lucky can you get? It was probably no accident that my research in sociology focused on work and industry, the working class, and politics. In studying the automobile industry for many years, I concentrated on the historic divide between skilled and nonskilled workers and union politics. My passion for politics was both academic and personal as evident from my involvement in departmental, university, and professional affairs. I also had strong avocational interests: the French horn, house and boat building, home repairs and decorating. I also participated in political and religious organizations.

Like my siblings, by the time I went to college, I was imbued with four passions: education, work, politics, and the inextricable bond between music and religion. As a professor, I studied work and politics. Outside academia, my passions were physical work, politics, music, and religion. I was born during World War I. Its memory was fresh and vivid as I grew up, as much a part of my life as the Great Depression. World War I, the Great Depression, and World War II became a seamless reality that endured all my life.

Family Background

Father, Antonio Formicola, born in 1876, was reared in Pignataro Maggiore, an Appennine village northeast of Naples. His father was an animal broker who could barely support his family. As eldest child, Antonio was privileged to have four years of education. Then for three years he was apprenticed to a cabinetmaker who treated him as a son and taught him to play the cornet. Both played in the town band. Since Antonio could find no work after his apprenticeship, he went to the United States 1893 at age seventeen. Returning to Italy for compulsory military service, he attained the highest rank possible for conscripts, corporal major. After that, again unable to find work as a cabinetmaker, he left for the United States never to return. He became Protestant, fluent in English, married my mother, and soon became foreman in a bedroom furniture factory. Bright, gregarious, and a natural orator, he attained the highest offices in his church and lodge. At first he was a socialist then became a Republican ward and county committeeman with some local political influence. He was a sober and devoted husband and father who highly valued learning and education.

Mother, Salvatrice (later Maria), was born in 1883 in Caltanisetta, in central Sicily, the oldest of the ten children born to Luigi Antonio and Nunzia Pollizzi Cornetti. Born in 1848 near the French border in Piedmont, Luigi attended school five or six years, was apprenticed as a veterinarian, then trained as a mechanic in the Italian army. He was reared as a Waldensian (a twelfth century pre-Reformation Protestant sect), later became a Mason and antiroyalist, identities that he kept secret. While in the army, he was shipped to Caltanisetta where he met my future grandmother. After completing his military service, he worked on the Suez canal, returned to Sicily, married Nunzia, and worked in the nearby sulphur mines as an "engineer" or mechanic.

Salvatrice attended the local Protestant mission school only two years, blaming her mother for not allowing her to go on. She admired her quiet and perhaps haughty father, who preferred reading in solitude to petty socializing. During a family quarrel when he refused to have her confirmed in the Catholic Church, he revealed his religion and politics and became locally unemployable. Eventually he found work as a "engineer" on the railroad being built from Messina to Palermo. The family moved every year or two with construction of the railroad.

When an economic depression halted railroad building, Luigi could find no work and migrated to America at the age of fifty-four with Salvatrice, aged twenty. He was refused admission at Ellis Island because he had not bothered to obtain an economic guarantee, a pure formality. He left Salvatrice in charge of a family that migrated to Rochester. There she was befriended by Mrs. Vitale, wife of an Italian Protestant pastor serving the Methodist mission for Italian immigrants. Mrs. Vitale disliked the name Salvatrice because it sounded too Catholic and called my mother Maria instead, her name for the rest of her life. Maria lived with the pastor's family a short time, then met and married my father, a Protestant convert. Of their five children, I was the youngest.

Maria, quiet, religious, and energetic, determined that her children would be well educated whatever the cost. For her first child, George, born in 1904, that cost was high. Blond and blue-eyed like both his grandfathers, George was bright, restive, hard to control. He went to kindergarten a year late owing to injuries incurred by a fall down the 100-foot gorge of the Genesee River when he was supposed to be in Sunday School. The only Protestant child in a mostly Irish Catholic neighborhood, he got into fights with other boys. My father taught him to respond to Catholic taunts by calling them pagans, superstitious idol-worshippers. His Irish Catholic teachers, he claimed, humiliated and denigrated him. Although he was musically gifted and played the violin, the teachers failed him even in music. Mother's intercessions at school were no help. Unhappy in school, family and neighborhood, George ran away from home several times, finally joining the army in Panama where he served a three-year term playing French horn in the band. He continued to study the violin, read omnivorously, and completed several high school correspondence courses. I never really knew George until he returned from Panama in 1925 when I was seven. In tracing my family socialization, I begin with the period before he came back.

Work Ethic and Education

For Nancy, Arnold, and me home life was less tempestuous. We rarely had time to play. When not at school, we practiced our instruments, did our home work, and seemingly endless chores. Mother provided the example, at work before any of us awakened in the morning and until after we bedded at night. Obsessed with saving, she ran a self-sufficient household. She baked bread, planted a large vegetable garden, canned enormous quantities of fruits and vegetables, made clothes (including overcoats) for the entire family, made sheets, curtains, and pillow cases from flower sacks, washed clothes, painted and wallpapered the rooms of our apartment and the two apartments upstairs, and daily studied the newspapers for grocery savings. After dinner, she knitted and repaired garments, crocheted bedspreads and table-cloths and ornaments, and on and on.

As the children grew older, we assumed more household tasks like cleaning, painting, washing the walls, wall papering, weeding and watering the garden, shopping, canning fruit and vegetables, washing, ironing, and interminable cleaning and dusting. Home from school, our first obligation was to practice our instruments, next, do chores. After dinner we studied whether or not we had homework. On rare occasions, mother would rest for a few moments, read the Bible and sing hymns softly to herself. We prayed on arising in the morning, at every meal, and before bedtime, and we attended church twice on Sunday as well as the mid-week evening service. Working was a way of life, an endless automatic thing like breathing, a necessary contribution to the family and life itself. Cleaning, studying, making music, and religious participation were seamless family activities. Mother often said that the purpose of life was not to be happy, but to work, be good, and help others. Presumably, contentment would follow.

Before adolescence, we were unaware that mother kept a separate savings account for each child. The accounts grew steadily, eventually amounting to thousands of dollars. Whatever we earned we could not keep because she put the money into savings accounts for our education. It never occurred to her that we might not be bright enough to go to college or might not want to. It was our fate to go to college just as it was hers to make it happen. Self-denial was not to be threatened by leisure, travel, or going to the theater. The children's education and occupational success would be her pride and reward.

Learning Working-Class Culture and Politics

Father shared mother's passion for pinching pennies, working un-
ceasingly, and saving for the children's education. Upon returning from
work, mother had tasks lined up for him: repair the sidewalk, build a
fence, dig a cellar, wallpaper, paint. We owned another house that we
rented out. It too needed constant upkeep. On Saturdays, father cut our
hair, repaired our shoes, sawed wood for the stove, and worked for a
clothier collecting weekly payments from customers. Yet he sometimes felt that mother went a bit too far. He was gregarious while she
preferred solitude. Sometimes he had an urge to go to the theater, travel,
visit people, eat German food like pork and sauerkraut (a taste he developed serving in the Alps with the Italian army) and, on rare occasions, have a beer with his friends.

Father, a cabinetmaker, was very proud of his craft. For a long period he was a working foreman in the veneer department of a bedroom
furniture factory. A meticulous worker, he did the most difficult jobs,
taking great pains to match the grains of the veneer. Once, while finishing the back of a cabinet, a another worker asked him, "Why do you
fuss so much with it? After all, it'll go against the wall and no one will
see it." Father replied, "It's *my* work and *I* see it."

Father was also a carpenter. He added rooms to the house, repaired
windows and door frames, built storm shelters and sheds, replaced clap-
boards, shingled another house, and did carpenter chores for our relatives. Uncle Loreto once said, "You're a good carpenter, Tony. Where
did you learn it?" He replied, "Anything a carpenter can do, a cabinet
maker can do, but many things a cabinet maker does, a carpenter can't
do." He was proud of his skill and observed that most manual skills
require only a little training: painting, laying concrete, wall papering,
all of which he taught his boys.

In my working-class neighborhood, skilled workers were scarce.
Better educated than the others, they earned more, and interacted little
with their less-skilled neighbors. They took better care of their houses
and gardens, spoke better English, subscribed to newspapers, and discussed politics. I became aware of their higher status, a subject I later
examined in my research.

In church, father held the highest positions, played the major roles in
the dramatic society, gave the opening prayer at meetings of the Board
of Elders, was its Clerk of Session, and marching instructor of the church
band. He became Grand Master of the Odd Fellows lodge, wrote let-

ters for illiterate neighbors, was called to make peace in family quarrels, was consulted by neighbors about hiring lawyers, and engaged in electioneering. Serious, articulate, compassionate, a joiner, he was widely respected and bore his status confidently.

Father brought me to his factory to show me the kiln that dried the lumber, the power plant, his department, and the rest of the factory. I was impressed. On Sunday afternoons, he took me to the Labor Lyceum to listen to lectures on unions, working-class problems, and socialism. After the lectures, he always went to the platform, shook hands with the speaker, and asked questions. I was too young to know what was being discussed, but I tried to look attentive and felt grown up.

Father worked for another Odd Fellow, Mr. Stein, a Jewish merchant who operated a clothing store in the Arcade downtown. He sold suits to Italians on time and father collected their weekly payments on Saturday afternoons. When Mr. Stein visited our home on Saturday evenings to pick up the payments, he and father talked politics. Although he was a businessman, Mr. Stein was an ardent Socialist who quite convinced my parents to vote for that party, which they did for thirteen years, the only Socialists in the Ninth Ward. Mr. Stein was suspicious of the Boy Scouts who, he thought, were training boys to become soldiers. This seemed a bit far-fetched to my folks because our church sponsored the Boy Scout troop to which my brother Arnie belonged. Father eventually became a Republican as he thought them less corrupt than the Democrats. Untroubled by ideological inconsistency, father could espouse either Socialist or Republican values, depending on the issue. He saw the Democrats as the party of depression and the Republicans as the party of prosperity. He forsook the Republican Party in 1948 to vote for Henry Wallace who bolted the Democratic Party because he thought the country was heading for a nuclear war with the Soviet Union.

Father took our family to Convention Hall downtown one Sunday afternoon to attend a memorial service for the wrongly executed anarchists, Sacco and Vanzetti. Their portraits hung conspicuously on the stage, draped in black ribbon. The band played funeral music. As the speakers spoke, father, easily moved, wiped tears from his eyes. We walked home in silence. He was as passionate about politics as about Protestantism and brought up either topic on almost any occasion. He was violently antifascist because Mussolini persecuted Socialists, recognized the Vatican, and made Catholicism the state religion. He denounced Mussolini during the Italian-Ethiopian war, an unpopular stance in our neighborhood, and accurately predicted that he would be hung as a traitor. Father followed national and international events closely, often commenting on them at the supper table. His interest in foreign affairs made a lasting impression on me. I took as many courses in European history as I could and longed to go to Europe.

Kelly's shoe factory, a modern five-story structure, was only two blocks from home, right next to my Grammar School, Number 5. In warm weather the large windows were opened for ventilation. On the way to and from school, I would stare with fascination at the men working at their machines. Uncle Loreto, a Roman married to Aunt Giulia, had been apprenticed as a cobbler in Italy and he worked at Kelly's as a leather cutter, a highly skilled job. I was about eight when a union being formed at Kelly's held its first strike. Uncle Loreto, on picket duty every day, came to our home for lunch. One day when he accompanied me to school after lunch, we saw a number of policemen mounted on horses invading a crowd of workers who were trying to prevent strike breakers from entering the factory. Uncle Loreto rushed into the crowd as police made free with their billy clubs. Some workers were bleeding and being trampled by the horses. I was horrified. The union lost the strike and the factory closed in bankruptcy a few years later.

Uncle Joe and Uncle Frank worked as pressers at Hickey-Freeman men's clothing factory and their wives, aunt Grace and aunt Marietta were seamstresses at Stein's and at Bond Clothing. All tailor factories were organized by the Amalgamated Clothing Workers, most of whose officers were Jews who spoke no Italian. My relatives were strongly pro-union but had reservations about how their union officers collaborated with management. I grew up hearing about bargaining concessions on the part of the union, collusion between union and management, unsatisfactory working conditions, the severity of inspection, unfair piece rates, unfair distribution of overtime, promotion preferences, layoffs, and losses in pay when workers were sent home because of the heat.

Enter George

George returned from Panama when I was seven. He first worked in a factory then attended Mechanics Institute to become a radio technician. He proudly showed his parents a paper he wrote on Malthus for his economics instructor, who thought it exemplary. But after a month or two he dropped out of the Institute without telling his parents, spending his time in the library instead.

The folks may have wondered why George rarely discussed his classes at home, talking instead about *The Origin of Species* and evolution. George even wrote letters about its implications to the editor of the *Democrat and Chronicle*. A priest responded critically to one letter and an exchange went on for several rounds. The folks had few convictions about evolution, but they were proud of their son who, they thought, had bested a priest. George announced that he had become an agnostic and later, an atheist. Mother had her reservations but father kept an open mind.

George also talked about Marxism, Socialism, and the Soviet Union's experiments. The names and titles he cast about meant little to me then: Jack London's *The Iron Heel*, Marx's *Das Kapital*, and William Jennings Bryan and Clarence Darrow (his hero), both lawyers at the so-called monkey trial of the Tennessee teacher who taught evolution. He and father discussed the trial, and George lectured us in detail. While I understood little of his disquisitions, he brought into the family the ideas of the outside world, ideas that I later read about.

One day George brought home a crystal radio set and earphones. We took turns listening to barely audible voices on the airwaves. Later he bought a battery-operated radio and we heard music. Nancy was playing the piano at the time and occasionally father would toot his cornet. George always had a violin and mandolin handy, and he played regularly. When the Board of Education gave me a card that granted me the right to rent any musical instrument, George went to fetch it. He brought me a French horn, his instrument, rather than the flute I had requested. He then taught me to read music and play the horn. Within a week I was playing simple tunes. Brother Arnold also received permission to rent an instrument and George chose the oboe for him. Thenceforth, music became an integral part of family life.

Inevitably, the folks discovered that George was not attending classes at the Mechanics Institute. During one of the fights over his future, George agreed to become a pastor but, he claimed, the folks refused to pay for his room and board. One day without telling us, he left to join the army band at Fort DuPont in Delaware. As the band occupied only a few hours of the day, he had free hours to study biology, socialism, politics, and music. A year or two later he met Lydia Richards, married her, and returned to Rochester in 1929, Lydia with child.

As George's job prospects were dim, the folks didn't want to give him either of the upstairs apartments that brought in rent. Mother insisted that we add another room in back of the house next to the kitchen.

Father protested that it would cost too much. Mother brushed his objections aside. "Let's get started, zeen zeen zeen and it's done." Early next morning mother, Nancy, Arn, and I began digging the basement, putting the dirt in pails and piling it on the garden and side yard, raising their level two feet. The work was exhausting but mother drove us on. We finished digging in a week. Then father built molds, about three feet high, for the walls. All day long we mixed sand and cement, pouring it between the rocks in the molds, building up the walls about a foot or more a day. Each evening father inspected our work and raised the molds. Mr. Gaudino, carpenter and church friend, built the frame of the room, staying sober enough to finish the job in a week. George and Lydia lived in the room for about three years.

As the Depression deepened, jobs became more scarce. Finally, Stromberg Carlson hired George to build radios and play in the orchestra that broadcast concerts on the company radio station. The company also paid his tuition for night courses at Mechanics Institute where he resumed his study of radio. With a promising future in the company, George did well at the Institute.

Learning to build radios required about a year, an advanced skill, because workers had to learn how to build several types of radios in their entirety. Indeed, George built us a fine electric Stromberg Carlson radio by stealing a piece or two each day, carefully nesting them in his lunch pail. Along with other employees, he bribed a worker to open the storeroom on a Saturday so that they could appropriate large pieces like the transformer and cabinet. We became hooked on radio. One of mother's few pleasures was listening to the Metropolitan Opera. After George moved, he left his collection of librettos and mother even provided money to buy more.

George was eager to escape his parents' constant monitoring. Yet they helped him in many ways, most often by lending him money and forgiving the debts. When Stromberg Carlson was laying off workers, my parents gave George $400 to buy stock, thinking that this would help secure his job. They also gave him wine to present to his foreman at Christmas. Through wage cuts and job redesigns, George hung on to his job.

One Saturday, the day that family crises always occurred, George parked a black Model A Ford business coupe in front of the house. "Whose is it?" mother asked. "Mine," George replied. "How much did it cost?" After some verbal fencing, he said, "It's used; about $300." "Where did you get the money," mother asked. After more evasion, George finally admitted that he had sold the stock. Mother, normally taciturn even dour, could be a volcano, "Monci Beddu," as my father put it, Sicilian for Monte Bello (Mount Etna). Mother erupted, "What? How could you?" I don't remember the details of the exchange but mother finally calmed down enough to ask why he bought such a small car with room only for two, not enough to take the family for a drive in the country or for more than two people to go shopping. Lacking the sense to cool off, George screamed, "I bought it for MY family. What do you think I am, the driver of a CARAVAN," and he turned to go upstairs. But mother wasn't finished. Still out of breath from the angry shouting, she yelled, "So, we're a caravan. After all we've done for you, building the room, buying stocks to protect your job..." (Replays were called the Caravan Fight.) George and mother quickly patched their differences, something that father never learned to do, and George took mother shopping each week the next forty years.

Meanwhile, to cut costs, Stromberg Carlson began to introduce assembly lines, hiring women as semiskilled operators at lower rates of pay. Radio builders saw their occupation being de-skilled and their wages lowered. George decided that organizing a union was the only solution and began to talk about it to a few trusted friends. Father built benches in George's large garage for the first organizing meeting. Although all who attended were sworn to secrecy, an informer reported the details of the meeting and George's role in organizing it. He was called to the personnel office and asked about it, but he would not promise to discontinue his efforts which, he warned, were perfectly legal.

The company gradually reduced George's hours until he was working only one day a week. He was not fired. He had received commendations for his work; besides, federal law prohibited firing on grounds of organizing. The search for other jobs was fruitless because George was informally blacklisted as a trouble maker and labor organizer. Still in high school, I learned a great deal how companies and unions operate in labor disputes.

After George and his family went on welfare, the Works Progress Administration (WPA) gave him a job playing French horn in the WPA band. His life was now much as it had been in the army: two-hour rehearsals in the morning, a short rehearsal or an occasional concert in the afternoon, and plenty of free time to read or earn extra money. Attached to his rented home was a small shop with an entrance on the street. Hanging up a sign, Form's Radio Service, George was in business. He spent most of what he earned on the finest radio instruments available, building one of the best-equipped shops in the city.

In the midst of the depression an increasing number of radio repair-men competed in a limited market, resulting in cutthroat competition and lower fees. George again felt that the only appropriate response was to organize the radio repairmen into a Guild that would set mini-mum fees for visits and different kinds of repair. The Radio Technician's Guild with about fifty members was organized. The best trained and equipped technicians joined the organization, but their ability to main-tain the fee structure was eroded by amateurs who "creamed" the mar-ket by doing the simple jobs (replacing a tube) and bringing the few tough jobs to Guild members. The Guild had limited success.

In college at the time, Arn and I visited George weekly. We spent the time in his shop listening to the problems of the Guild and discussing national and international affairs. By this time, I knew enough about economics, history, and sociology to argue with some knowledge. But it was tough going because George was an impatient listener and de-fended his idealistic utopian views with great emotion. In an argument over Soviet policies where I firmly held my ground, George insisted that the crucial experiment of organizing a non-capitalist state had to be carried out whatever the temporary costs.

When I went off to graduate school in 1939 George was still playing in the WPA band. The approaching involvement of the United States in the War was beginning to stimulate industry. As unemployment rates fell, the WPA slimmed down. George applied for a position in Roches-ter Products Division of General Motors as a generator specialist, a job he knew well. A college chum of mine was the personnel officer and knew of George's history as a labor organizer. He tried to extract from George what at that time was illegal, a commitment not to engage in labor organizing. George was excellent at doubletalk, using enough vague words and phrases to be hired.

George discreetly helped to organize the plant, a task made easier by the fact that the United Auto Workers had already targeted the plant for organizing. The union was soon recognized and George became active in it. Full of idealism about what the union should do for workers, the working class, and society, he attended meetings and made a number of suggestions. Among those he pushed hardest were the establishing of college scholarships for children of workers (UAW members or not), cooperating with management to assure quality of production, limiting wage and profits to keep the industry competitive. He correctly pre-dicted that the Japanese would successfully invade the U.S. auto mar-ket if this not happen. The local turned down all his proposals.

George reported that only a few members attended the meetings, mostly the officers and a few who wanted to be. Their main idea was to get the meeting over as soon as possible. Whatever the officers proposed, their friends backed. They offered no ideas or suggestions of their own. They attended the convention in Miami with all expenses paid and had a good time. They didn't report on what went on and how they voted. The less they say, the earlier the meeting can adjourn and the more time they have at the bar across the street. Some members were more interested in the UAW bowling team than the interests of the workers or the well being of society. George said he stopped going to union meetings. It was a waste of time.

Each Christmas and every summer, I returned to Rochester for a week. George would report in detail what was going on at General Motors. He held jobs as an inspector in quality control, worked at electronics and production jobs, operated Brown and Sharpe machines, was a relief worker, and worked on all three shifts. Most of his jobs gave him mobility and opportunity to observe what was happening in different parts of the shop. He was not gregarious at work, never became one of the boys, took his work seriously, and yet earned the respect of fellow workers who consulted him on both technical and personal problems. A good reporter of shop events and politics, he loved an audience and would spend hours recounting goings-on in shop and union.

Although I never did factory work, I learned much about factory life from George that was later useful in my studies of workers, industry, and working-class politics. Most university professors have a relatively small reservoir of first hand experiences outside of academia, but I was fortunate to be socialized by family and kin who had a wide range of experiences which they shared in great detail, spurring a lifelong interest in work, politics, music, religion, and society.

3

The Accidental Apprentice[1]

Introduction

I grew up feeling deprived of everything I thought American children had: candy, new clothes, toys, a bicycle, roller skates, Boy Scouts, even streetcar fare. My parents, relentless penny pinchers, shared a blinding faith in education, but rarely told us children of their determination to send us to college. In the early 1930s, as the furniture industry began moving west and south, father's factory was struggling to survive. When I was in high school, dad worked part time. I was unaware that the folks had saved sizable sums for our education and their old age. We had rent from the two apartments in our house and from another house three miles away. Because mother didn't give me the things all the other neighborhood boys had, I thought that we were poor.

In 1934, in the depths of the Depression, I graduated from West High. I found no work that summer so mother pressed a man who peddled groceries from his truck to hire me. He said he couldn't afford it but to keep me off the streets mother urged him to take me on with no pay. Next day, he picked me up at dawn, drove to a farm on the city outskirts with two crates of strawberries he bought at the public market, and set up a table next to the highway. I became a farm boy selling fresh strawberries to passers by. He paid me only two or three dollars a week, but I had plenty of time to read.

When strawberry season was over I was out of work again. Mother, not one to see her children idle, occupied me with chores that I could escape only by reading. One August morning as I was painting the front porch, she asked me what I intended to do in the fall. I said I'd return to high school for courses in typing and shorthand as my brother

41

Arnie had done. Vetoing the idea, she announced that I would attend the University of Rochester.

I don't know why I didn't think of it myself. Both Nancy and Arn were enrolled at Rochester and my turn had come. Having been denied regular admission, they enrolled in the evening Extension Division held on the Women's Campus not far from the city center. (The Men's Campus along the Genesee River was three miles away.) Having done well by the end of the year, they were admitted as regular students. I expected to follow their route but mother insisted that I apply as a regular student. I said it was too late; the time to apply was January and I doubted that Rochester accepted late applications. Its touted ethnic quotas (2 percent for Italians, 3 for Jews) were surely filled.

But Mother insisted. As usual, she had her way. A few days after I applied, a letter invited me to see the freshman dean. When he asked what I had read recently, I told him about books I'd read that summer as a farm boy selling strawberries. I was asked to appear at freshman orientation camp the following week. As it would be embarrassing to sleep in my underwear, I convinced my mother to buy me my first set of pajamas.

Undergraduate Life

After three exciting days at camp, I eagerly anticipated pre-med classes. I entered a new world. College men dressed in suits, white shirts, and ties; women wore suits or dresses, silk hose, and heels. I felt ill-dressed in unmatched jacket and pants. We walked from one building to another for classes, all conducted as formal lectures. The professors treated students as adults. I was "Mr. Formicola." My first class, the History of Western Civilization, was in an auditorium that accommodated well over 100 students. Dr. Arthur May, tall, slim, and balding, strode to the platform and said, "Good morning, gentlemen. In the beginning, there was Adam . . . " As he spoke (an hour, without interruption), I was entranced. After giving us an assignment, he left the room. I went to my class in Introductory Biology. Again, about 100 of us listened to a brilliant lecture. The same thing happened in Introductory Chemistry. Rochester was a first-rate academic institution and the professors worked us hard. Classes in math, English, and German were smaller, but in lecture format. I was annoyed when students interrupted the flow of ideas with questions. For the first time I had to study methodically but I did well in both sciences and humanities.

Social life was limited. I went out for soccer and made the team as right wing, earning an R on a nice blue sweater that I wore constantly. When fraternity rushing began, I was invited to pledge an Italian one, the first in the nation; I pledged but knew I couldn't afford to join. I developed friendships with independents through soccer, intramural baseball and basketball, and studying with fraternity members. On soccer trips to other universities, I learned fraternity songs. Rochester was a friendly place and I had all the social interaction I needed.

As father legally changed our name to "Form" just before classes began in my sophomore year, university records were still unchanged. In my first class that fall, English Literature, the instructor for the first time in my life pronounced my surname Formicola rather than Formicola in calling the role. After class I told him about the name change. He was sorry but knew better than to ask why.

That fall I found a job in the library at fifteen cents an hour, financed by the National Youth Administration. With soccer, work, and studying I was very busy, but my grades improved even more. (When I appeared for work the following fall, I found that I had been fired for whistling while I worked in the stacks.) At the end of sophomore year, I had to declare a major. Although I did well in the pre-med courses, I decided not to become a doctor as it entailed graduate training and a heavy financial burden on my parents. Having three children in the university at the same time cost them $1,200 a year for tuition alone. Besides, they had never talked to me about a medical career and I didn't think they were serious. Since I was dating for the first time in my life, I thought that like others I would find a job after college, marry, and settle down.

I was drawn strongly to biology and history, but Nancy was a graduate student in biology and Arnie was majoring in history. I didn't want to follow in their footsteps and become a high school teacher. Then out of the blue, Arnie suggested sociology. I could be a probation officer like Mr. Argento, a distinguished member of the Italian Presbyterian Church we had attended as children. I didn't want to be a probation officer but I liked sociology as much as any other subject and decided to major in it and minor in psychology.

Mother eventually asked me about my major. I was evasive, she persisted. Distressed to hear that I had abandoned pre-med, she began what I knew would be unceasing pressure to change my mind. To extricate myself, I found myself saying, "What do you think, that there are only doctors in medicine? There are doctors in lots of things, even

sociology!" That settled things in her mind; I would become a "doctor" in sociology. But I never considered such an impossible dream.
After the B.A., the career issue would somehow resolve itself.

I took the required sociology and psychology courses and others I
liked, such as Renaissance and Reformation and Europe after 1870.
Department head Luther Fry, an inspiring lecturer and a nationally recognized scholar in the sociology of religion, had written the first text
on social research methods. He also conducted a vigorous urban research program. The more sociology courses I took, the more I liked
the field. As most majors were women, classes tended to be at the
Women's Campus with its engaging and well-dressed women. After
overcoming my shyness, I found they were friendly and even found me
attractive. I took courses in criminology, race and ethnic groups, family, theory, social psychology, and social research.

In my junior year Fry unexpectedly died. Raymond Victor Bowers,
a 1934 Minnesota Ph.D., became head. He later chaired the department and built a strong program at the University of Arizona. My senior year, he offered a seminar, Contemporary Periodical Sociological
Literature, using the *American Sociological Review* as text. I spent
hours studying the *ASR* with fellow major Carl Kujawski. We argued
in class that Merton's (1938) "Social Structure and Anomie" inad-
equately explained criminal and deviant behavior. While Carl and I
carried the discussion, the women silently took notes and, to our irrita-
tion, scored higher on the first test.

Because Rochester had been tracted by the U.S. Bureau of the Census, the local Council of Social Agencies had organized data on members by Census tract. Bowers (1938) used the data to test whether Burgess' ecological theory of concentric zones in Chicago held in Rochester,
discussing his research in our methods course. The first testable sociological theory I encountered, it sparked a long-term interest in human
ecology. My senior thesis would address the ecology of juvenile delin-
quency in the city.

As graduation neared in 1938, unemployment remained high and
job prospects dim. All sociology seniors were asked to apply for positions as social workers in local welfare agencies. All the women who
applied were offered posts but Carl Kujawski and I were not. Perhaps
we looked too immature or perhaps our ethnic backgrounds stood in
the way. Carl was of German descent but locals assumed he was Polish. We discussed our future with Oscar (Ockie) Holt, head of
Rochester's Council of Social Agencies. I asked him bluntly, "Will my

ethnicity bar me from social work?" He replied that growing up in "Dutchtown" he had experienced the same kind of discrimination currently afflicting Italians, Jews, and Poles. He advised us to persist. Society would change. The Italians would be accepted just as the Germans had been.

The Accidental M.A.

That left my immediate employment problem unsolved. I hadn't thought of applying to graduate schools. Just before graduation, Bowers called me to his office to offer me a graduate fellowship, perhaps learning that I was to be graduated *cum Laude*. It would pay $300 a year, cancel tuition of $400, and involve no work obligations. In a year I could complete the M.A. Hardly able to believe my good fortune, I accepted on the spot.

When the first monthly check arrived, I gave it to mother. As usual, she deposited it in my bank account and gave me a two-dollar monthly allowance. As the department's sole graduate student, I took the courses I wanted: race and nationality problems, educational statistics, municipal government and administration, psychiatric social work, and educational statistics. For the race course, I wrote a paper that Bowers liked on the assimilation of Chinese in America. I wanted to write an M.A. thesis on Rochester's Italian Protestant (Waldensian) Community, probably because my family was part of it. Although I had not read Weber, I wanted to test whether Italian Protestants were more upwardly mobile than Catholics. Passing up a rare opportunity to interview founding members of churches that lasted less than two generations, I yielded to Bowers's pressure to exploit Council of Social Agencies' Census tract data on the 30,000 members of constituent organizations. I liked the idea of doing another ecological study and putting my newly acquired statistical skills to work. I spent days running Hollerith cards through the IBM counter-sorter, eventually producing a dull master's thesis, "Demographic Characteristics of the Members of the Social Agencies of Rochester, New York."

Having completed all M.A. requirements by spring 1939, job prospects still dim, I cast about for graduate assistantships. I was accepted by a new Social Work Ph.D. program at the University of Pittsburgh but not awarded an assistantship, and by American University's new Ph.D. program in Social Security Administration but had filed too late for a fellowship. I would be first in line if anyone did not accept. When I reported this to Bowers, he casually handed me a mimeographed flier: the University of Maryland, launching a Ph.D. program in sociology, was offering fellowships. Reading it, I told him that I had nothing to lose by applying. He said that I could waste a year, one-fiftieth of my remaining life span. Although this unsettled me, I applied. If Maryland offered me the fellowship, I would be in the Washington area, in a good position for a fellowship at American University the next year. I asked Bowers and my criminology instructor, Alexander Radomski, for reference letters and within the month Maryland offered me a fellowship at $400 a year.

Going to Maryland

On a sparkling September afternoon in 1939 I packed my belongings into a large cardboard suitcase for a thirteen-hour trip to Washington. Father would send my books later in the handsome bookcase he built me. Mother decided not to see me off at the station. As she kissed me goodbye, she hid her emotions as usual and for once offered no parting word of advice. Father and I took the streetcar to the Pittsburgh, Baltimore, and Ohio Railroad Station and waited a silent hour for the train. I boarded it and sat by a window to wave goodbye. Father's eyes brimmed with tears. I smiled weakly, trying to maintain composure. The train moved slowly across the countryside for about thirty miles downstate where I de-boarded to wait for the Pennsylvania. It arrived at Mauch Chunk about midnight and our coach was hitched to a train bound for Washington. I couldn't sleep on the hard wooden benches and was glad when dawn broke as we entered Maryland.

The train finally arrived at Washington's Union Station. My suitcase was heavy as I carried it to the entrance. Leaning against an arch in the bright morning light, I stared at the Capitol with a sense of wonder and apprehension. A streetcar took me to the bus station where I waited impatiently for a bus to College Park. Passing through Anacostia, Bladensburg Crossing, Hyattsville, and Riverdale, it arrived at College Park about noon, dumping us by the curb on U.S. 1 beside a disorderly cluster of low buildings, a depressing sight in sharp contrast to the white colonial buildings of the University on a hill across the highway.

I had eaten nothing since leaving Rochester. Spotting a White Castle restaurant across the dusty lot next to Albrecht's Pharmacy, I bought a skimpy hamburger and a glass of milk, then lugged my increasingly heavy suitcase up the hill to find the Sociology Department. I introduced myself to the secretary, a very thin woman, young and blond, who spoke in the almost unintelligible accent of the Eastern shore. Anna Mudd told me that I was lucky: Dr. Joslyn, the department head, was in. He was cordial and pleasant. When I asked where I should go to rent a dormitory room, he replied that the university housed no graduate students. He'd no idea how I might find a room in town. Perhaps I should inquire at the local grocery store.

Still lugging my suitcase, I walked down the hill through town and several blocks past some fraternity houses to the streetcar tracks. Next to them stood the town's sole grocery, a small, dark, and messy place with a limited line of groceries. Luckily, the proprietor had a two-room apartment available next door. The living room contained three chairs, a wicker sofa, and a small table with a lamp. The bedroom had three cots, a closet, and one bureau. No kitchen. Even though I couldn't afford it, I rented the apartment hoping that incoming graduate students would be looking for roommates with whom they could share the rent. Within a week, Fred McBrien and Bo Woodworth moved in.

The arrangement didn't last. After two months Fred found a position as counselor in the District of Columbia School for Delinquent Boys as he needed more money. He got room and board and a small stipend. A day or two later, Bo Woodworth, busy teaching and dating, moved out. After Bo learned of my small savings account, I foolishly lent him a sizable chunk of it on his promise to repay within a month or two. Despite repeated requests, he never repaid a cent.

I found a room for $18 a month, almost half my stipend, at 6909 Dartmouth Road in College Park, home of Tom and Dottie Lane. I couldn't afford to date, have a beer, or see a movie. But the hospitable Lanes invited me to occasional meals and I sometimes played ping pong with Tom. On one occasion Archie Ward, fellow graduate student and pastor of the Towson Baptist Church in suburban Baltimore, invited Fred and me to his home. Drawing the shades, he served beer for an evening of poker.

I had little contact with graduate students out of class. Archie appeared on campus once a week for a seminar. Every night I dined at Albrecht's Pharmacy with a Lutheran pastor, also a graduate student in sociology. Poorly prepared, he was boring to boot. Our other dinner companion, a graduate student in political science, had surprisingly little interest in partisan politics and political ideology. His disquisitions on government organization and administration soon became tiresome.

Maryland's Department

World War II had just begun in Europe when I arrived at Maryland in 1939. In 1941 the United States would enter. In this brief interval, the department's social and intellectual life blossomed, then eroded. A year before I arrived, Carl S. Joslyn (Ph.D. Harvard, 1930), had become acting department head after the unexpected death of Theodore B. Manny, the previous head. Joslyn had come to Maryland in 1936 as an associate professor, was promoted to professor by 1939, and appointed head a year later. The university was encouraging the department to develop a Ph.D. program. The year I arrived, Joslyn had just hired Logan Wilson (Ph.D. 1939, Harvard), Clarence Hodge (Ph.D. 1938, American University), and Linden Dodson (Ph.D. 1932, Chicago), then at the Resettlement Administration in Washington. The payroll also listed J.E. Jacobi, instructor, who left the next year, and Harvey Clowes, of whom I recall nothing. Fred McBrien (M.A. Dartmouth) and I were the graduate fellows and Robert Woodworth, Ph.D. candidate at the University of North Carolina, an assistant instructor. In 1940, Joslyn hired John B. Holt (Ph.D. 1936, Heidelberg), then at the U.S. Department of Agriculture. In my first year at Maryland, graduate students enrolled in the hastily devised Ph.D. program included McBrien, the Lutheran minister, Archie Ward, myself, and two part timers.

One day while waiting in Joslyn's office to register for next term's courses, I noticed my open folder on his desk. After waiting impatiently for a few minutes, I impulsively examined it. With the transcript were Bowers and Radomski's letters. Like Bowers's letter, Radomski's letter was supportive, but closed by saying that "it should be noted that William Form is of Italian background." My anger surged. I had never hidden it from faculty or friends. Nor had I ever encountered prejudice or discrimination in academia.

Course Work

In my first year at Maryland Joslyn enrolled me in ten courses, five per semester. I do not recall that he later advised me to take other courses. Apparently the ten sufficed. If the department had formal requirements, I was unaware of them. Of course, the graduate school had requirements with regard to total credit hours, residence, and foreign languages. After the first year, I ceased going to Joslyn for advice and chose whatever courses I liked.

In the first semester, I enrolled in Joslyn's Systematic Sociology seminar, focused mostly on European theory. Joslyn was about forty years old, a pleasant, heavy-set man with a high and receding hair line who wore sparkling rimless glasses that emphasized his blue eyes. He always wore a navy blue serge suit, a tiepin, and a Phi Beta Kappa key dangling on a chain across his vest. Joslyn rarely made eye contact, but when he did, his expression was one of suppressing a smile. A man of modest physical and social skills, he depended on his wife Ida to make mundane daily decisions.

Although Joslyn left Harvard about a decade before I arrived at Maryland, he remained in touch with its faculty, especially Parsons, Homans, and L.J. Henderson. Taken up with Pareto's systems approach to theory, they were trying to make the discipline as rigorous as economics by constructing a theoretical system that would enable scholars to draw logical deductions from general propositions.

Joslyn's year-long seminar focused on nineteenth- and twentieth-century theorists. He would ask questions to ascertain whether we grasped the material, exposing us to a large literature, including the work of Sorokin, Durkheim, Pareto, and Henderson as well as Theodore Abel's (1929) evaluative summaries of German theorists Simmel, Vierkandt, von Wiese, and Weber. Joslyn concentrated on a theory's conceptual clarity, not its contribution to understanding how societies function.

We spent hours discussing Sorokin's (1937) logico-meaningful method of theory construction in volume 1 of *Social and Cultural Dynamics*. We also examined the clarity of his societal typology: sensate, idealistic, and ideational. We discussed Simmel's distinction between form and content, Vierkandt's empirical and phenomenological approaches, von Wiese's conceptual apparatus to systematize sociology, and Weber's *verstehen* and ideal type approaches to the discipline. In Durkheim's (1902, 1933) *Division of Labor* Joslyn again focused on the meaning and clarity of mechanical and organic solidarity. We read Henderson's (1935) and Homans's (1934) presentation of Pareto's (1923) *Trattato di Sociologia Generale*. For me, Pareto overemphasized concepts: logical and nonlogical action, derivations and residues. We compared Durkheim's mechanical and organic solidarity to Toennies's (1887, 1940) *Gemeinschaft* and *Gesellschaft*. Joslyn ignored Marx and American theorists except for Ellsworth Faris' (1937) *The Nature of Human Nature*. I was impressed by Faris' intelligence and ability to make sensible generalizations using logic combined with parsimonious references to data. Joslyn required written examinations but no papers.

Since Joslyn neglected a theory's substantive contribution, I read more of Sorokin and Durkheim. I was especially impressed with the institutional, historical, and comparative scope of Sorokin's (1927) *Social Mobility*. Even today, few sociologists have analyzed so systematically how institutions articulate to produce inequality and mobility. I eventually read all four volumes of his *Social and Cultural Dynamics* (1937-41). While not taken with his cyclical theory of societal change, I was awed by his historical erudition and ability to interrelate societal institutions. For the first time, I saw how economy, polity, architecture, religion, literature, science, art cohered as revealed by a comparative historical perspective. Durkheim's explanations of social change, anomie, and social facts and his use of empirical data also impressed me deeply. I read and reread his historical theory of occupational corporations in the second edition's preface of *The Division of Labor*.

In my first semester Joslyn advised me to enroll in Dodson's undergraduate course, Community Organization. Dodson, a tanned, handsome, muscular man of medium height, was in his mid-forties. His finely chiseled features rarely changed as he lectured in an even monotone, clinging closely to the text. Yet he communicated kindliness, sincerity, and concern for his students. He assigned us Sanderson and Polson's text (1939), *Rural Community Organization*. Finding the course pitched at too low a level for graduate students, I was shocked to receive a B on the first examination. Dodson apparently wanted students to recall the content of text and lectures rather than demonstrate how to integrate them. I adjusted quickly and gave him what he wanted.

An active researcher, Dodson involved Bo Woodworth and me in his projects. He asked me to adapt Galpin's (1915) methods to locate rural community boundaries in Washington and Frederick counties, a task that required mapping the residences of organization members and business customers. My maps were included in an Experiment Station Bulletin (Dodson et al. 1940). About 1941 Dodson also asked me to write an article, "Adult Education in Action," for a county extension bulletin. It was my first sociological publication, and in an area I knew little about. Fortunately, I have been unable to locate it.

In the first semester I also took Logan Wilson's seminar in criminology. With an undergraduate criminology course, I felt well prepared. In his early thirties, Wilson was a tall, lean, handsome Southerner. Like

Dodson, he spoke with a slight nasal Texas twang that lacked modulation. Although his bearing was patrician, he reached out to the graduate students. He invited me to his home in nearby Greenbelt, a federally constructed planned community. When he showed me his neat and orderly study, I was duly impressed. Wilson also asked me to read proofs of his paper, "Psychiatrists and the Messianic Complex," published in *Social Forces* (1940) and his manuscript, *The Academic Man* (1942).

Research-oriented, Wilson exposed us to the empirical literature, trying to teach us how to evaluate research and make it sociologically pertinent. Toward these ends, we studied Michael and Adler's (1932) *Crime, Law, and Social Science*, a fine critical analysis of the literature in the causation, treatment, and prevention of crime and of the criminal justice system. Demanding and well organized, his seminar represented a model to be emulated. I wrote a good paper for the course, but criminology did not appeal to me.

In my second semester, I took Hodge's seminar in American Regionalism. Hodge, a swarthy, slight young man with dark curly hair, was pleasant but tense and unsure of himself. He sat erectly on one side of the table while the students sat along the opposite side facing him. Although we read copiously from Odum's (1936) *Southern Regions*, we concentrated on Odum and Moore's (1938) fact-packed *American Regionalism*. Hodge tended to lecture but his comments lacked sociological depth. I didn't know then that he had been trained in political science, not sociology. Bo Woodworth, who had done research under Odum's direction at North Carolina, contributed modestly as a resource person. Although Odum didn't strike me as an ecological theorist, his work provided a regional perspective that supplemented urban ecology.

That semester, I also registered for Wilson's seminar on Comparative Sociology. Wilson worked us hard, showing us how to compare societies empirically and systematically. He asked us to read Hobhouse, Wheeler, and Ginsburg's (1930) pathbreaking work on the evolution of preliterate societies based on their subsistence technology. I was struck by it because it had an unstated ecological perspective that could apply to all societies, preliterate and literate; sociologists failed to build on this work until Lenski's (1966) ecological evolutionary theory. Wilson also had us read current anthropology.

Wilson's work on occupations stimulated me to write a paper on the shaman in preliterate societies. I didn't know then that the shaman is not an occupation as defined in market societies but a specialized status. The fifty-page paper was largely descriptive. I had dug deeply into the literature but didn't know how much more was available. Wilson liked it and suggested that I pursue the topic for a dissertation, which seemed to solve the distant task of selecting a dissertation topic.

When I arrived in Maryland I told Joslyn that I intended to study Social Security Administration at American University. Apparently, by the middle of the second semester, the faculty agreed that I was a good student. Strolling down the hill from campus into town on a spring afternoon, Joslyn asked me to abandon my plans and complete Maryland's program. I hadn't dreamed of attaining the godly status of professor, but I quickly agreed. I was heavily committed to sociology, subscribing to *ASR*, the *American Journal of Sociology*, and the *AAUP Bulletin*, and spending goodly sums (for me) to build my library. I would prove to Bowers and Radomski that I could make it.

That summer, I returned to Rochester to finish my master's thesis. In a few weeks I sent Bowers a draft of "The Demographic Characteristics of the Character Building Agencies of Rochester, New York," a descriptive thesis written in what I hoped was elegant prose. Bowers invited me to his home to talk about it. Sitting on the back porch steps, Bowers said plainly that it had to be rewritten. What was needed was a draft in clear precise prose. He offered no ideas of how I might improve the analysis. I drove home dispirited. When mother saw me she asked what was wrong. I said that Bowers didn't like the thesis and began to sob. She looked at me sympathetically for a moment then said, "Wash your face and get to work." I presented the revision in a few weeks. After the oral exam in Dean Gale's office, I had an M.A. (Form 1944).

In my second year at Maryland, 1940-1941, I enrolled in a methodology seminar and registered for research credits. The seminar was listed under Joslyn's name but John Holt handled it. I was the only student. Holt, a lean, tall young man with sparkling blue eyes, exuded warmth and good cheer. Putting formality aside, we quickly became colleagues. He would suggest things to read and when I felt the need I would stop by his office next to mine and chat about the material or about Holt's field experience at the Department of Agriculture. When Lundberg's (1942) text on research methods appeared the next year, Holt lent me his copy that I have to this day.

I was uncertain what other courses to take or how much time to devote to the dissertation. The $400 fellowship barely kept me alive. Then an auto accident abruptly worsened my money troubles. A university librarian who lived near Rochester invited me to share the driving on a trip home. As we approached Rochester, I was driving when the road became icy. Her signal to turn came too late and, turning impulsively, I skidded into a tree. I offered to pay $200 for the damages, $50 a month. But I earned only $40 a month and didn't want to ask my parents for money. Then, unexpectedly, Joslyn asked me whether I would like to teach a course in statistics at Hood College in Frederick, Maryland, fifty miles away. The instructor had resigned midterm to serve in the army. I agreed and bought a 1931 Chevrolet coupe that wiped out my savings. I taught twice a week and it went well, but I had nothing to do with the faculty there.

In the fall, Joslyn received a call from American University for an instructor to fill an unexpected vacancy. I agreed to teach five courses at their undergraduate campus: Introductory, Recent Social Trends, Race and Ethnicity, Criminology, and Sociological Theory. I was swamped preparing lectures, but things went fairly well. Again, although I went to the campus every day, I had absolutely no contact with other professors. I found little time to work on the dissertation but passed the French and German language examinations.

Maryland requires that candidates for Ph.D language examinations submit an appropriate book for approval; from it the language professor chooses a six- or seven-page passage to be translated in two hours with the aid of a dictionary. With three years of high school French, I felt confident of passing the exam. I selected Durkheim's *La division du travail social*, studied it two or three hours, and passed with no trouble. For the German examination, John Holt looked through his library and suggested I use Roberto Michels's (1930) *Italien von Heute*. I'd studied German for five semesters in college but had not kept up. To prepare, I chose three six-page passages at random, giving myself two hours to translate each. Although apprehensive, with luck I felt I could pass the exam on the first try.

Holding the book at arm's length without even glancing at a page, the German professor selected the six pages. I found myself looking up many, many words because the passage contrasted German and Italian bedding, mattresses, blankets, pillowcases, springs, sheets, and bed sizes. I was not sure I passed.

Two weeks later a letter summoned me to meet with the German professor. When I arrived at his office, he turned his back to me and muttered, "Well, Form, you barely passed but you passed." Relieved, I said, "That's great, but I could have done better if you'd selected a passage that dealt with sociological matters rather than bedding." Wheeling his swivel chair around, he shouted, "Form, you'd better get the hell out of here before I change my mind." I backed out of his office muttering, "Thank you, thank you, professor."

In my third year at Maryland, I finished the courses in my minor. At first, I had planned to minor in psychology and political science but after taking Experimental Social Psychology and Analysis of Propaganda, I became disenchanted with the field and dropped it. I kept political science as a minor even though I thought it lacked sociology's methodological and theoretical rigor. I had taken two political science courses in world politics with Professor George Steinmeyer in my first year. In the third year, I took his seminar in International Relations and Political Parties and Public Opinion with Professor Hugh A. Bone.

Steinmeyer's courses were unsystematic and his student expectations were modest. His lectures and readings provided no greater analytical depth than *New York Times* reports. In one course the final examination asked students to identify in a sentence or two 100 names and places of importance in world affairs. I finished in an hour. For his international relations seminar, which did not meet, I wrote a paper on the foreign affairs of Argentina, using mostly secondary sources. His only comment on the paper was "Very good." Hugh Bone's course in Political Parties was empirically oriented and he prepared his lectures with care. We used Odegard and Helms' (1938) excellent text, *American Politics* and Bone's pamphlet, *Smear Politics: An Analysis of the 1940 Campaign Literature.* Neither one had a theory of politics. Political science needed an infusion of sociological theory that Mills unexpectedly provided later.

Social life improved somewhat in my second year at Maryland. Joslyn invited me to dinners where I met Irene and Carl Taeuber, Douglas Ensminger, O.E. Baker, and other Washington area social scientists. John Holt and I shared an interest in the sociology of religion. Holt had recently done research on holiness cults in the South and had published an article on the topic in *ASR* (1940). Wilson invited me to his home and showed interest in my development. Dodson pulled me into his research project and we rode horseback on rare occasions when I could spare the money. Joslyn organized faculty seminars that I regularly attended.

I gradually grew closer to the Lanes. I loved doing things with Dottie and the children and Tom and I played ping pong nightly. An ardent anti-Roosevelt Republican and a strong New Dealer and socialist, we argued often, but neither of us yielded much. Tom Lane, Sam Gruber (another roomer), and I bought a small strip of land along the Patuxent

River in rural Maryland, spending weekends clearing land and cutting trees for the log cabin we intended to build. We barely recovered our investment when we had to sell the land within a year to the state, which planned to dam the river to make a reservoir.

In the spring of 1941, Joslyn claimed that he had hired the two best young scholars on the market, Wright Mills from Wisconsin and Peter Lejins from Chicago. Mills was the envy of Wisconsin graduate students. In a bad market and without a Ph.D., he was reumored to have been offered an associate professorship at $3,000 (Yinger 1994). Although the dissertation was unfinished, he had published two articles, one in the *ASR* (1939, 1940b) and one in the *American Journal of Sociology* (1940a). He would be promoted to associate professor when his dissertation was complete. Lejins, a Latvian emigré with a 1938 Chicago Ph.D., would enter as an instructor but would be soon promoted to assistant professor. He reputedly was the best read criminologist in the country because he knew both the American and the European literature.

I began spending days in the library of St. Elizabeth's, the federal psychiatric hospital in Washington, reading psychiatric anthropology for my dissertation on the shaman. In early summer, when I went to Rochester to visit my parents and girlfriend, I perused the psychiatric literature in the University's good library to learn about mental disease symptoms in order to recognize them in the ethnographies that dealt with shamans. The more I read, the more I became convinced that symptom descriptions were so vague and overlapping that they could not be usefully applied to available ethnographic accounts.

I decided to talk to anthropologists who knew more psychiatry and ethnology than I did. I drove to Harvard to talk to George Devereux (1939) who had studied mental illness in preliterate societies, then to Columbia to meet Ralph Linton who had started to work on that topic with Abraham Kardiner and others. Amazingly, in the early 1940s one could go to Harvard and Columbia, knock on a professor's door without an appointment, and be given an extended audience. Devereaux encouraged me to forge ahead and do the best I could with the material. Linton thought I needed more training in anthropology. I ignored Linton's advice and most of the psychiatric literature. I wanted to show how the shaman confronted deviants, tried to reintegrate them in society, or legitimated a separate place for them.

On returning to campus, Joslyn informed me that Wilson had accepted a position to succeed Robert Merton as department head at Tulane. I was stunned. Having invested considerable time on the dissertation, I did not want to abandon it. I asked Joslyn to direct it, but he insisted that neither he nor anyone on the faculty was competent enough.

My dissertation options were limited by faculty interests. Joslyn was interested in theory, Lejins in criminology, and Holt in migration and religion, areas that did not then attract me. Mills had not yet arrived. I still had some of the summer left to explore other topics. I had taken a course in Community Organization with Linden Dodson, who had tried to involve me in community research. We had attended services of a congregation of Friends in rural Maryland to explore leadership and decision-making in an unstructured environment but nothing came of it. Dodson, then living in Greenbelt, Maryland, a new federally planned suburb near College Park, occasionally suggested that I study town leaders. Recently opened for occupancy, the town had no traditions, organizations, or institutions. I should study emergent leadership. The idea had no appeal at first, but then I considered that Greenbelt was largely a town of government clerks and a study of that occupational stratum was appealing.

I had to master the leadership literature to work with Dodson. I spent a month or more at Holt's farm tending chickens and the goat while the family summered in New England. After a few weeks searching the literature, I wrote a long paper evaluating research that dealt mostly with leaders' personalities and styles of behavior. Most of it struck me as trivial and unsociological, even that of sociologist Pigors (1935), *Leadership or Domination*?

In fall of 1941, my Rochester classmate, Carl Kujawski, who had completed his master's degree at Columbia, came to Maryland for a Ph.D. We quickly resumed our old pattern of discussing everything we read. The Joslyns continued to invite faculty and students to dinners. (I never called him "Carl" as he never invited me to do so.) Because he had no manual skills, Joslyn asked me to do household repairs, even to the point of building a coal bin when he decided to support the war effort by switching from oil to coal. The Holts continued to invite faculty and students to their farm home. Elizabeth Holt, a professional art historian and gracious a hostess, made everyone feel at home. I had more social contacts than I needed.

Enter Mills

Lejins and Mills arrived that fall. The Lejins invited faculty and graduate students to tea and brunch. Mills, cordial toward graduate students, hosted an occasional party. Carl Kujawski and I, visiting him in Greenbelt, got to know him well. He would not be addressed by his first name, insisting on "Mills."

Lejins and Mills's arrival added spice to the social scene. They could not be more different. Lejins had a military bearing. Erect, slender, and fair, he dressed impeccably, spoke with a clipped accent, and was unfailingly stiff and polite. Mills was opposite: burly, in working-class garb, almost brutally direct in his exchanges with others. Their rivalry for status in the department and faculty seminars made life exciting (Form 1995a). Mills tried to dominate the interaction. Lejins politely but persistently disagreed and would not be squelched. He was friendly to graduate students, but I had little contact with Lejins because I had already taken Wilson's criminology seminar and was uninterested in the field.

Although Fred McBrien left in 1940 for the Royal Canadian Air Force and in 1941 Hodge, peripheral to the department, did not return and Wilson left for Tulane, the fall of 1941, was a brief high point in departmental life. In December, Japan bombed Pearl Harbor and we were in the war.

In January 1942, I took my only course with Mills, a seminar in sociological theory with four students. Mills was working on his dissertation's final chapters, which dealt with John Dewey's philosophy of pragmatism (Mills 1943a, chs. 15-20). He assigned Dewey's slim *Reconstruction in Philosophy* (1920) and Wilhelm Windelband's massive *History of Philosophy* (1893). We read half of the Dewey essays. In Windelband, we read a short section on science in the middle ages, a chapter on the rise of natural science in the Renaissance, and a chapter on the Enlightenment.

The seminar was unfocused. Mills didn't prepare for it and didn't work us hard. He would speak half an hour, ask a few questions, give an assignment, and dismiss us early. We read neither Charles Peirce nor William James, whose work Mills explicated in his dissertation, nor did we discuss George Herbert Mead, who influenced Dewey. However, Mills had us read Charles W. Morris' introduction to Mead's (1934) *Mind, Self, and Society*. Perhaps Mills felt that we could not acquire the necessary background quickly enough to engage him in serious discussion.

Because Mills had not yet worked through his own ideological analysis of pragmatism, his comments on Dewey were mostly positive and uncritical. He speculated that Dewey's small town upbringing in Vermont probably influenced his social philosophy. Dewey's method-ological advice he summarized as: "Put your hands in the mud but lift your eyes to the stars." Later, in his dissertation (1943a) Mills ad-vanced an analysis of pragmatism's ideology as individualistic, with a presentist orientation that supported dominant values, and an emphasis on *adaptation* that discouraged other political avenues, and faith in *in-telligence* rather than radical politics to solve society' social problems (Mills 1966, chs. 20, 21). With this seminar, I completed my formal course work at Maryland. Two years would pass before I would com-plete the dissertation.

Early in 1942, the department lost more graduate students and faculty. Assistant instructor Bo Woodworth married an undergradu-ate, became a Navy lieutenant, and left. The Draft Board classified me IV-F, unfit for service. I was devastated. Later I learned that I was rejected because a punctured eardrum made me vulnerable to poison gas. I tried unsuccessfully to join the Navy, then the Coast Guard. Carl Kujawski passed his physical examination, and while waiting to be drafted, married Randa Beaner, an undergraduate he was dating.

In March, Mildred Cotton of Rochester and I were married. Archie Ward, who had become a good friend, conducted the ceremony in his church at Towson. The Lanes, serving as witnesses, were the only oth-ers present. Randa and Carl hosted a reception attended by the entire faculty and the Lanes. Some time would pass before the entire faculty would attend another party.

Carl left in April, drafted into the Army as a warrant officer. Mills was exempted from service because of hypertension. Joslyn and Lejins were not drafted. I began to have sack lunches with Mills in his office. The Department of History was across the hall and its head, Wesley Gewehr, had recently hired three young assistant professors, Richard Hofstadter, Frank Freidel, and Kenneth Stampp, all of whom became outstanding scholars. They joined Mills and me for lunch, the high-light of the day.

In autumn 1942, no students entered the graduate program, leaving it all but dead. Dodson left for the government soon after. In 1943 Holt accepted a Navy commission, assigned to the State Department to work in the Germany section. At Heidelberg from 1931-1934, he had pub-lished two books on Germany. I took over Holt's Introductory Sociol-ogy in mid-quarter to the relief of the students, who found his rambling lectures hard to follow. After that, I was a full-time instructor.

The war nearly ended departmental social and intellectual life, including faculty seminars. Joslyn, inheriting a good-sized estate from his uncle, retired to become a gentleman farmer early in 1944. Only Mills, Lejins, and I were left. As these changes occurred, I spent more time with Mills. After my wife and I moved to Greenbelt in April 1942, Mills and I shared driving to campus. We invited Mills and his wife Freya to dinner. He had a prodigious appetite for food, drink, and lively conversation. After dinner Mills and I would take a walk or lie on the grass in front of our apartment, conversing until well after dark. When I left Maryland in August 1944, Mills and Lejins were the Department's only regular faculty.

Two Failed Dissertations and a Third

When Mills arrived in the fall of 1941 I was beginning my third year at Maryland, much worried about slow progress on the dissertation. That summer, abandoning my work under Wilson on the shaman's role in preliterate societies, I gave Dodson my paper evaluating the leadership literature. He liked it, offered no criticisms or suggestions, and advised that I attend meetings of Greenbelt's voluntary associations. After going to a few and interviewing some of the officers, I couldn't formulate a good research problem. I shared my concern with Dodson but he was unable or unwilling to communicate his vision of a sociological problem on leadership. Perhaps he thought I should come up with one on my own or that one would eventually appear.

I confided my doubts about the dissertation to Mills. In January 1942, I told Dodson I would not pursue a dissertation on leadership. I was strongly attracted to Mills, who resembled my brother George in his passion for politics, strong sense of social justice, and plethora of ideas. Like George, he talked nonstop, loved an audience, and had little patience with opposition because of his strong ideological commitments. As with George, I learned to listen, make oblique critical remarks, and ask questions. This learning technique worked well for me. More than two years would pass before my dissertation was finished, a dispiriting period of departmental decay, but for me a profitable period of informal training under Mills.

As a Greenbelt resident, Mills had some ideas of what was going on in the town. He thought that an occupational-community-stratification study of it could make an acceptable dissertation. I came up with a sketch on how to study workers' social origins, occupational and income mobility, organizational participation, and political beliefs. The research would combine the approaches of three studies I admired: Davidson and Anderson's (1937) intergenerational study of occupational mobility; Robert and Helen Lynd's (1937) organizational-institutional approach to community control in Middletown; and Alfred Winslow Jones's (1937) analysis of ideological beliefs of a community's occupational strata as revealed through constructed vignettes.

Mills accepted these ideas but didn't ask for a written proposal. He suggested that I write background essays on various topics. First was a paper combing the literature on social status, honor, and deference. I submitted a long one that he really liked but did not return with comments. He then suggested a study of residents' movie attendance, reading habits, and hobbies, which I resisted. He then asked for an historical analysis of the income and occupational status of American white-collar workers. I complied. In short, I submitted several papers and waited weeks, once three months, for a response. When he finally read the papers, he'd say that he liked them, give me a little feedback, and propose another topic. Although I was irritated by long waits and unending suggestions for new essays, I did not complain. Perhaps this was the way he conducted his research, probing different areas, writing pieces, and then stitching them into a coherent whole. I was unhappy with this approach, but it forced me to explore a vast literature I might otherwise have missed.

While waiting for Mills' responses to my papers, I waded through archives of the Farm Security Administration (FSA) in Washington, the agency responsible for building Greenbelt. The records enabled me to reconstruct Greenbelt employees' income and occupational careers. I interviewed FSA officials, read past issues of the town's weekly, *The Greenbelt Cooperator*, and interviewed officers of the voluntary associations. These materials were ultimately integrated into the dissertation.

When Mills arrived in the fall of 1941, he treated me as a student. When I began seeing him regularly, whatever he was working on became the main topic of our conversation. In time, we conversed more about my dissertation on white-collar workers until Mills became almost obsessed by them. An omnivorous reader, he often urged me to read things he had run across so that we could discuss them. For example, while he and Gerth were preparing a review of James Burnham's *The Managerial Revolution* (1941) for *Ethics* (1942), Mills studied two American authors who had struggled with the issue of managerial power under capitalism, Veblen's *Engineers and the Price System* (1933) and Alfred Bingham's *Insurgent America* (1935). My introduction to Veblen led me to cite *Absentee Ownership* (1938) and *The Instinct of Workmanship* (1943) in my dissertation.

Mills and Gerth argued that Burnham's thesis of managerial power was fatally flawed. Management had the knowledge to run industry, but didn't own it and therefore could not exploit the power of property to control government and political elites. Management also lacked the moral passion to bring about social justice. I argued that managers often controlled property decisions, especially when owners were uninvolved in making corporate policy. But Mills wanted to know whether managers could ever achieve political hegemony in national politics against property holders' interests. I argued, why should they?

Mills worked on several articles in which I was tangentially involved (see Form 1995a). The data for his (1943b) article, "The Professional Ideology of Social Pathologists," were derived from social problems texts. He and I carted about thirty of them from the library to his office to discuss their contents. He coded each text for the author's middle class bias and inability to grasp how capitalism had generated the social problems. Much of the documentation appeared in the eighty-three footnotes. I told Mills that before reading the text, I read all of the footnotes and got more from them than from the text. He beamed.

When Mills taught the undergraduate course in social research, he devoted no class discussion to various methods. In fact, the class didn't meet because he quickly organized the students to collect data from the *Dictionary of American Biography* for an article he planned. They coded entries for date and place of birth, migration, social class origins (father's occupation), sons' education and political activities. In "The American Business Elite: A Collective Portrait," (*Journal of Economic History*, 1945) he analyzed the data for seven generations, 1578 to 1879.

The students, who often worked together, got to know one another and pressed to have a sociology club. Thus, Mills was indirectly responsible for organizing it. Among Mills' students was Harold Sheppard, who later received a Ph.D. at the University of Wisconsin. Hal told me that when he designed his dissertation, he asked himself, "How would Mills criticize the ideology of Elton Mayo, founder of the human relations school of industrial sociology?" Hal thought that managers used warm human relations to make workers more productive and make them like it. Some of Mills' students who enrolled in my course, Techniques of Sociological Investigation, continued to collect data for Mills while I advised them.

Mills came to know Dwight Macdonald at the *Partisan Review* in New York. When Macdonald was starting a new journal of opinion, he told Mills that he was searching for an appropriate name. I suggested *Politics,* which Mills liked and forwarded to Macdonald, who adopted it. Mills' (1944) article, "The Powerless People: the Role of Intellectuals in Social Life," appeared in *Politics'* first issue. He used the theme that he and Gerth (1942) used to critique Burnham's (1941) *Managerial Revolution*: intellectuals have the knowledge to run society but do not and can not do it. I observed that knowledge did not and probably should not automatically grant people power. Mills agreed, but felt that intellectuals were morally obliged to seek social justice and make their knowledge accessible to liberals who would use it to influence political decisions.

During my first two years at Maryland, I had developed ideas about my interests: macroproblems and testable theories in ecology, work and occupations, and stratification. My two years with Mills helped me focus them more sharply. I learned from observing his pattern of research and even more from our informal conversations on what we were reading.

Faculty members at Maryland usually taught three courses but in January 1944, I was pressed me to teach "full time," five courses: Urban Sociology and four sections of Introductory. My anxiety over the unfinished dissertation became unbearable. I told Mills that I had to finish it by summer and would go on the job market. I still had to interview a representative sample of Greenbelt residents for data unavailable in archives. He liked the vignettes I had devised to plumb their occupational and political beliefs. We met at his home to sketch out the rest of the interview. I cleaned it up, returned it to him, and told him I wanted to start interviewing. He quickly approved it and I began the seemingly endless task of interviewing 150 workers, finishing by the end of spring.

I was scheduled to teach that summer, but decided I couldn't if I were to finish the dissertation. I met with Dean Levin Broughton to inform him of my decision. With a self-confident bearing, he sported a pince-nez with a black ribbon that fell to his coat. He stared at me coldly and declared that I must teach. When I insisted that I wouldn't, he said, "You will teach or I will terminate your appointment in the department." I resigned on the spot and told Mills that I needed a job in the fall. That summer I isolated myself and wrote the dissertation (Form 1944), but showed none of it to Mills.

The dissertation was much as I had planned, except that one-quarter of the residents turned out to be manual workers, so I broadened the study to compare white-collar and manual strata. I found some unexpected commonalities in family and occupational backgrounds. Examining their participation in community voluntary organizations, I uncovered a complex status structure. Finally, I compared their occupational aspirations and political beliefs which showed some persistent differences.

In early August I submitted the 456-page manuscript to Mills. He soon arranged a committee meeting for the oral defense but emitted no hint of what he thought of the dissertation. While waiting, I began to think about a job that fall. Joslyn had retired that spring and Mills didn't bestir himself to help me. I lacked the sense to inquire at local universities. One day I spotted an advertisement of the American College Bureau in the AAUP *Bulletin*. The Bureau collected information on positions available in various colleges; if hired, applicants paid the Bureau 5 percent of the first year's salary. I wrote the Bureau, which sent me three or four mimeographed postcards that described positions, mostly in small colleges. I made contact with three and waited.

My anxiety was high on the day of the defense. There was no feedback from committee members Lejins or Steinmeyer in Political Science, who was going blind but agreed to serve. When I arrived for the defense, Mills asked me to wait in the hall while the committee discussed procedures. After an eternity, he fetched me, looking grim. Then he put his arm around my shoulder and said, "Bill, they liked your thesis. You're in. You've nothing to worry about. Relax." I followed him into the seminar room, enormously relieved and very grateful. The examination went well until Lejins asked a question that stymied me. "Bill, what do you mean by 'the sociology of' in the title, "The Sociology of a White-Collar Suburb?" As I stumbled, Mills answered: "It's a common European expression that denotes a general study, with special concern for stratification and political matters." The dissertation was accepted without change. Maryland's Department of Sociology had awarded its first Ph.D.

The next day Mills told me that he thought the dissertation was good; two chapters, with modifications, were publishable. He then asked me to co-author *White Collar* (1951). He had already signed a contract with Oxford University Press. He gave me $250 of his advance, but didn't show me the contract. My first task was to assemble data on historical changes in the composition of white-collar occupations.

Gerth was visiting Mills as they were working on *Character and Social Structure* (see Oakes and Vidich 1999 for a sensitive account of the collaboration). Mills invited Millie and me to a party in Gerth's honor. As I chatted with Gerth, he asked me a question to which I replied, "I really don't know." Looking me straight in the eye, Gerth said, "Bill, now that you're a Ph.D. professor, you can't say that anymore. A professor has to have something to say about everything."

In the following week, Stephens, a junior college for women in Columbia, Missouri, offered me a position sight unseen. I accepted, wondering how would I deal with high status women at a finishing school. We moved to Columbia in early September and I quickly became involved in teaching and in the overorganized life of professors there. Mills wrote that it would be hard for us to collaborate on *White Collar* at such a distance but that I need not return the advance.

I had little contact with Mills thereafter. In 1958, fourteen years later, I bumped into him at the International Sociological Association meetings held in La Stresa, Italy. On a lovely afternoon we chatted for an hour about our lives since Maryland days. Mills said he was tired and somewhat depressed; he could not interest any agency or his department in supporting his research, even to the extent of providing a part-time secretary. That was the last time I saw him. In 1961-62, I spent a sabbatical year in Turin, launching my comparative study of autoworkers in Italy, United States, Argentina, and India. On 21 March 1962 my colleagues at the University of Turin and I went to Milan for a seminar that Alessandro Pizzorno had arranged for Talcott Parsons. After chatting with Parsons for a few minutes, we sat down to hear his remarks. He began by saying, "This morning I read in the *Herald Tribune* that Wright Mills died yesterday. Now, I have always disagreed with Wright Mills on an important point..."

An Accidental Apprenticeship

Before World War II, becoming a professor was like completing an apprenticeship: taking courses, passing examinations in various subfields, passing foreign language examinations, and writing a dissertation under a master's guidance. Looking back, my apprenticeship was accidental and unstructured. In the midst of the Depression, I was lucky to go to college and thought my education completed with a B.A. When

Rochester's department of sociology awarded its first graduate fellowship in 1938, I accepted for lack of other employment. There was no
graduate program and I took a random set of mostly undergraduate
courses.

The next year, Sociology at Maryland launched a doctoral program.
I accepted a fellowship with no thought of becoming a professor. Training was almost as unsystematic as Rochester's. World War II essentially terminated the program and once again I turned out to be sole
graduate student. I was unaware that I had ridden a wave of educational expansion that lasted up to World War II owing to increases in
high school completion rates and college enrollments, which reached a
high just before the war (Clark 1987, p. 150).

After completing the Ph.D., I didn't follow the normal occupational
path. I accepted a position at a junior college and by chance three years
later found myself at Michigan State, a small land grant college with a
tiny rural sociology graduate program which became a very large university nation with a large sociology department and graduate program.
When I arrived, I thought my Maryland training inferior to that of colleagues trained at Harvard, Columbia, Cornell, Minnesota, and Wisconsin, especially in methods and statistics, but I learned something
about them anyway, teaching them as a graduate student because of the
shortage of professors who were serving in World War II.

Yet my academic journey had some advantages. Course work and
graduate requirements at Maryland were no burden, so I had plenty of
time to read a larger literature than most of my peers elsewhere. My
training in theory was probably representative and my early exposure
to Max Weber under Mills gave me an early edge over peers. The two
dissertations that failed to materialize broadened my knowledge of sociology. For the first one on the shaman, I read widely in comparative
sociology, ethnology, and psychiatry. For the second, I covered the
literature on leadership and community. Both efforts helped me arrive
at a structural view of sociology, distinct from individually oriented
social psychology. In my third try at a dissertation, under Mills, I covered the literature in occupations, institutions, and stratification. In
addition, Mills' stimulated me to read in the area now called political
economy. Finally, teaching nine courses at three institutions while in
graduate school forced me to read even more widely and become a
generalist. Although later I focused on the economy and stratification,
I brought along themes present in political sociology, ecology, and comparative community analysis. Like Mills, I emphasized the connec-

tions between politics and stratification. While I admired Mills' ability to do this, I was not inclined toward his global qualitative critical analysis. I preferred a quantitative survey approach and usually gathered my own data, a proclivity originally stimulated by Raymond Bowers at Rochester. In his four years at Maryland and in early years at Columbia, Mills also generated data (Form 1995a), later shifting to the making of biting commentaries on modern capitalist society.

In the context of graduate departments at the time, Maryland had a small faculty, five at most. Yet, Roscoe Hinkle (1994:14) reported that as late as 1945, Chicago, Wisconsin, Minnesota, and Ohio State had only five or six tenured faculty. The Harvard and Columbia Sociology Departments were only about a decade old and their faculties barely larger. Parsons at Harvard was a young faculty member struggling against the towering Sorokin; Merton at Columbia was still an assistant professor. To be sure, sociological training was available at Harvard and Columbia before independent departments were established. Some land-grant universities had small sociology and rural sociology graduate programs: Cornell, Wisconsin, Minnesota, Louisiana, Penn State, and Ohio State among others.

William Sewell (1988a) reported that in the mid-1930s, Minnesota had no discernible structure in its graduate program. The department had seven faculty, only four of whom, tenured, could teach graduate courses. Only one seminar was regularly taught and no others were required for the full-time graduate students, no more than eight to twelve in number. Nor had the department any advanced statistics courses. After three years, students took a preliminary oral examination; professors asked whatever they wanted about sociology and the minor fields.

Yet important advances were being made in sociology. Ogburn, Burgess, Faris, and other Chicago notables pushed empirical research in several areas of the discipline. Stuart Chapin at Minnesota was striving to make measurement a mark of scientific sociology. Howard Becker at Wisconsin was pushing theory; Thomas McCormick, measurement; and Marshall Clinard, criminology. Howard Odum, Harry Moore, and Katherine Jocher at North Carolina were advancing research on Southern and American regionalism. While graduate students wrote dissertations in specialized areas, they were examined in the entire discipline. Not until after World War II did these departments establish large research organizations, like the National Opinion Research Corporation at Chicago, the Bureau of Social Research at Columbia, and the Institute for Social Research at Michigan.

Maryland's department had no such giants. Joslyn's monograph with Taussig, *American Business Leaders* (1932) was a promising start, but his research momentum sputtered and died. Wilson, fresh out of Harvard, had published *Academic Man* (1942) and would have become an outstanding scholar had he not gone into administration. Holt, well published for a young man, would also have become productive had he remained in academia. Lejins became well known in criminology and later established a school of criminal justice. Dodson was an above-average publisher in rural sociology but never attained general visibility. Mills showed the most promise but his stay at Maryland was brief. In short, Maryland's faculty was small, young, well trained, and active in research. It had the potential of becoming a strong department had the war not intervened.

In short, given the state of graduate training in sociology before World War II, students trained at distinguished institutions had formal training not so different from mine at Maryland, but they were in departments with traditions, with a core of graduate students and exposed to more distinguished scholars. Over the long haul, their superior training did not represent an enduring advantage.

Note

1.   This chapter is a revision of an article in *The American Sociologist* (Form 1997a). I am deeply indebted to John Pease of the Sociology Department, University of Maryland, for materials from department and university archives and for checking some of my recollections.

4

Journeyman Years

The Missouri Year

In the decade after receiving a Ph.D., I worked in three institutions, paralleling the ancient journeymen who moved from community to community before becoming established. Immediately after completing my apprentice at Maryland, we left for Stephens College in Missouri. Millie, Dottie Lane, her daughter Phyllis, and I drove to Columbia in a 1939 Plymouth bought from Arnie when he was drafted into the navy. Dottie wanted to explore Stephens for her daughter Phyllis, a high school senior. Stephens, an attractive junior college for women, had a reputation of being a good finishing school. Renting a bungalow sight unseen on Bass Street four blocks from campus, we slept on the floor that night. The furniture arrived the next day, and Dottie and Phyllis left two days later. It was a hard parting.

Columbia was a depressing rural town despite the presence of the University of Missouri and Stephens College, which was surrounded by a six-foot iron fence, perhaps to keep boys out. Retail stores were small, dingy, and poorly stocked. The biggest private business in town was the Missouri Book Exchange. The radio played nothing but Ozark hillbilly music, my first exposure to it. When we went for a walk at night, we could hear the crunch of the crickets as we stepped on them inadvertently. What were we doing here?

John Decker, head of the Social Science Department greeted me warmly and introduced me to the faculty: three sociologists, two psychologists, three historians, an economist, an educator, and two persons broadly trained in social science. About a third had Ph.D.s. No one was doing research. Everyone taught social problems and an introductory course in their own discipline, sociology, psychology, economics, history. The teaching load was fifteen hours a week in class, easy for me. Only two preparations.

All dormitories had a large, elegantly furnished reception room on the first floor. The campus had no classroom buildings as all classes were held in dormitory basements. Faculty had virtually no access to the departmental secretary who exclusively served the head. The ten faculty occupied small cubicles barely large enough to accommodate a desk and two chairs. To get to class, faculty and students walked through the Social Science Library, a room at the center of the basement that accessed four classrooms, which produced a traffic jam before and after each class period. Each classroom contained six round tables that seated five or six students. Thus some students had their backs to the teacher and blackboard in the front of the room. This arrangement was designed to encourage student interaction, a technique entirely alien to my lecture-centered style.

After classes began, my apprehension about teaching upper-status women vanished. Although the majority of students, called "Sussies," came from affluent families in the southwest, they appeared to be unsophisticated, naive, open, friendly, and without affectation. Some of them came to learn about making wedding plans, entertaining, home furnishing, grooming, riding, and flying airplanes. The college maintained a riding stable and a fleet of airplanes. A student once interrupted my Social Problems lecture to ask when we were going to talk about social problems like how to set a proper table. Even so, Stephens took teaching seriously and conducted an intensive faculty-training program to improve it. The administration also encouraged informal student-teacher interaction in and out of the classroom. Each faculty member, assigned about eight students to advise, was required to meet them every two or three weeks and to entertain them at home once a semester, at college expense.

I had never imagined living in a town like Columbia or teaching at a college like Stephens. A fish out of water, I would make the best of the situation for a time. Yet my colleagues were friendly and eager to integrate newcomers socially. The maelstrom of social life on and off campus was seductive at first. On most weekends we met in each others' homes for cocktail parties but I soon wearied of them. Getting high was not my idea of a good time and we couldn't afford to reciprocate invitations. The American College Bureau was extracting 5 percent of my first year's pay. Millie had registered for two courses at the University of Missouri but withdrew because we couldn't afford out-of-state tuition.

Teaching introductory sociology and social problems and spending week days with students and teacher training sessions and weekends in parties was for me a style of life that left little time for reading, reflection, and scholarly work. I could talk to Orden Smucker, a sociologist from Ohio State who was studying dormitory friendships for his dissertation. But he was interested in sociometry, family, and education, and I in occupations stratification, and politics. Our friendship was based primarily on our being reared in minority religious denominations, he, as a Swiss Mennonite, I, as a Waldensian. Toimi Kyllonen, a Ph.D. sociologist from Minnesota, was pleasant but so withdrawn that animated conversation was impossible.

I made contact with the Sociology Department at the University of Missouri. Professor Pihlbad, its head, invited me to give a paper. I met the faculty, but developed no close ties with any. I also met two European historians, Ralph Scholes and his wife Mary with Wisconsin degrees, intellectually stimulating and congenial. We soon became good friends. Pihlbad later told me that he would like me to join his faculty but had to delay an invitation to avoid giving an impression of raiding newcomers to Stephens. I learned later that he hired Toimi Kyllonen.

During the presidential campaign of 1944 the Department held a campus-wide assembly where faculty presented the platforms and views of the Republican, Democratic, and Socialist candidates: Thomas Dewey, Harry Truman, and Norman Thomas. As no one wanted to represent Thomas' position, I volunteered. Entering into the spirit of debate, I presented the socialist platform with passion, mocking prissy Dewey and aristocratic Roosevelt wielding his cigarette holder, and pounded out Thomas' platform that attacked both parties for disregarding the welfare of the working class and the poor. Immediately after the assembly, students predictably asked whether I was a socialist. I told them that I supported some features of the socialist program. In an evening lecture, noted journalist Dorothy Thomas presented her views on politics and the economy. Jumping up from my seat with perhaps too much passion, I was first to challenge some of her ideas, behaving somewhat like my brother George or Mills, a style not alien to my nature. This effectively spread my reputation on campus as a firebrand.

When it was time to invite my eight advisees to our home, we were concerned about buying enough supplies and the appearance of our home. Almost out of money by the third week of the month, we hadn't asked Stephens for an advance. Our living room furnishings consisted of a faux maple set—a sofa and two armchairs, all with wooden arm rests, two side tables with lamps, a coffee table, and a sisal rug. My study (the dining room) had a fiberboard desktop mounted on peach crates, a kitchen chair, and a board-and-brick bookcase. The kitchen had two chairs and a folding table; the bedroom, a bed on a two-by-four frame, a bureau, trunk, and small mirror. There were not enough chairs to accommodate everyone, and no one sat down. After serving coke and cookies in the kitchen, we took the Sussies on a tour of house and yard. Conversation was animated. The Sussies thought we had furnished the house creatively and seemed to have a good time.

In the spring, I took my Social Problems classes to Jefferson City to visit a prison. Lincoln University, a "Negro institution," was located there. I arranged with Oliver Cox, its sole sociologist, to hold a joint class on race relations on the same day. Cox (1948) was an early Marxist scholar who examined the relation of race and class. After the prison visit, we joined his class and had a profitable exchange of views and questions. Altogether, things went very well. Cox's students then invited my students to visit the girls' dormitory. For most of them, this was their first status-equal contact with Negroes and they were pleased with it.

Back at Columbia at our next class meeting, the Sussies proposed inviting Cox's class for another joint session; it was the courteous thing to do. Cox quickly accepted. But I found that Columbia restaurants were segregated and had to call Cox, who said that his students would eat a box lunch on the bus. Then I could find no place to hold the joint class meeting despite the fact that several comfortable rooms would be unoccupied on Friday afternoon. The administration finally assigned us a dingy basement room in its building. The students cleaned it up, brought in folding chairs and a table, and made it presentable. The class discussion went well as did the inspection of the dormitories.

A few days later, the president called me to his office. He had been a successful businessman with limited experience in education. He began by observing that he was not prejudiced against "Nigras." His grandmother had owned slaves and a "Nigra boy" had worked for him for forty years. But the Trustees were concerned about the College's public image. In the future, I must get explicit permission from him before inviting any guests to campus.

In June I was the only faculty member not to get a raise. I went to see Department head John Decker for an explanation. He liked me and had observed my teaching for a week, sitting in my class and trying to behave like a student. The Sussies had been aware I was being evaluated and came through with panache. Embarrassed, John confessed that, despite his having ranked me as the department's best teacher, the administration would not give me a raise. I should be patient and not worry, their opinion of me as a troublemaker, socialist, and integrationist would change; I had a bright future at Stephens. I could hardly contain my anger. I'd had a good year at Stephens, but wrote the American College Bureau the next day to say that I was on the job market. The first two-penny postcards I received described a position in sociology and political science at DePauw University in Greencastle, Indiana. It looked promising. With the war coming to a close, the job market was opening up. I applied and was summoned for an interview. The train stopped in the middle of a cornfield. The head of sociology, a trim old man, waited at the station. He was cordial and chatted uninterruptedly as we drove by miles of cornfields, then past a cluster of large attractive fraternity houses to the campus quadrangle with traditional ivy-covered buildings. Well-dressed students, mostly women (the war was still on), were strolling to class.

My interview with the chair lasted only a few minutes as he was eager for me to see the faculty search committee. Their questions were few and innocuous. Asked about my faith, I replied that I had been raised a Presbyterian which seemed to satisfy them. Then I met with the Harold Gosnell, head of political science whose work on Negro politicians and voting I knew (Gosnell 1935). The animated interview went very well. Then Gosnell introduced me to a young assistant professor who invited me home for lunch. His wife, greeting me warmly, asked whether I would like some wine. She pulled down the kitchen windowshade as she reached for the bottle. After lunch, when I commented on the semi-popular music on the piano, she began to play and we sang many songs in the album. I had a good time.

Before I left that day for the long train trip to Columbia, the head of sociology and I conferred in his office. He not only offered me the position but indicated that he would retire in a few years and I would likely replace him as "head" of a three-person department. On the train, I mulled over my decision. Columbia was about as small a town as I could endure and Greencastle, though more lovely, seemed even more rural and remote. Student affluence at DePauw was even more evident than at Stephens. DePauw was the birthplace of several fraternities and sororities which seemed as at Rochester to play an important part in campus life. While I had no concern about teaching at a college with a denominational affiliation, I wondered whether its ambience might be restrictive. By the time I arrived in Columbia, I decided to turn the offer down. At worst, I could stay at Stephens for another year.

While waiting to hear from the College Bureau, I worked on the articles based on my dissertation. Within a few days, I sent the first, "Status Stratification in a Planned Community," to the *ASR,* which quickly accepted it. It is possible that the editor, F. Stuart Chapin, didn't even send the article for review because he made no suggestions for change and I don't recall receiving reviewer comments. The article was published the same year, 1945. My second manuscript, "Toward an Occupational Social Psychology" was sent to the *Journal of Social Psychology.* Editor Carl Murchison accepted it, publishing it the next year. Again, no comments, but I had to pay for publishing the tables. Murchison, I discovered later, owned five journals that were independent of the American Psychological Association.

The Bureau's next postcard announced a vacancy in sociology and political science at Kent State University in northeast Ohio. I was invited for an interview at my expense. With gas rationing still in effect, I went again by train. Kent was a small and dirty industrial town six miles from Akron, but the university was situated on a lovely hill on the edge of town. Department head Jimmy Laing was a slight and trim white-haired gentleman who enunciated very precisely while continually smiling, exposing a fine set of teeth. The teaching load would be fifteen hours a week, three or four classes a quarter, one or two of them in political science.

Kent State's facilities were unimpressive. Historically, it had been a normal school and, though formally a university with a liberal arts curriculum, it still bore the marks of its origin. The practice school was situated near an administration building that connected to the two buildings that housed most of the faculty offices and classrooms. The small library down the hill faced Main Street. Bowman, the current president, had been a public school superintendent.

Kent aspired to enlarge its social science departments. Sociology and political science already had three members each and psychology had six. Laing had attracted some good sociologists in the past (Leonard Broom, John Cuber) and was scheduled to hire more. I would like living in an urban-industrial region with students of working-class background. Laing offered me a position at the salary I had received at Stephens, nothing for moving expenses. Few Ph.D.s had been awarded during the war; possibly I was the only candidate who had one. Both DePauw and Kent had offered me positions on the spot and I was in a favorable bargaining situation. Kent's offer was inferior to DePauw's but, eager to escape Stephens, I accepted it without bargaining, a pattern maintained during my entire career.

Kent State University

We drove to Kent in August just as World War II ended. Millie and I walked the streets for almost three days searching for a place to live, sleeping in the home of the vice president, Mr. Munzenmeyer. The housing shortage had resulted in high rents that we could not afford. The American College Bureau continued to extract 5 percent of my annual pay for informing me of the Kent State opening. We found an old uninsulated house heated by soft coal that daily produced a fresh layer of soot on all surfaces. We had two extra bedrooms that we rented to students who were desperate to find housing.

On campus, Sociology was housed in one room with four desks, a file cabinet for the head, no bookcases or secretary, and a typewriter. I began to work in a library that was barely adequate to prepare new courses. I was expected to teach any course in the catalogue to fill the fifteen-hour load. Over two years, I taught ten different courses, Introductory, Community, Urban Society, Techniques of Social Investigation, Anthropology, Ethnology, Industrial Sociology, Occupations, American Government, and National Constitutions. I didn't think the load excessive and enjoyed the teaching. Each quarter more World War II veterans enrolled. A serious, intelligent, and hard working lot, they were the best undergraduates I ever taught.

One day I wrote to a publisher for a text and asked Jimmy Laing for stamps. He selected a small key from his key ring to open the top drawer of his desk. From a sheet of stamps, he tore off a single one and handed it to me. I was stunned. The next time I needed stamps we went through the same ritual. Unable to contain myself, I blurted out, "Jimmy, do you mean that every time I need stamps, I have to ask you for one? Can't you tear out several, so I won't have to bother every time I mail a letter?" Stunned, he tore off six stamps, handed them to me, and left without a word.

Faculty mailboxes were incased in the wall of the atrium of the administration building where I met several faculty members with whom I walked to our offices in the attached building. They included an old

German professor, a young speech pathologist, and a couple of biologists. One afternoon, we converged in the hall to attend the first fall faculty meeting. I eagerly looked forward to attending my first one. Facing about sixty professors, President Bowman made a number of announcements and then read a speech about what was going in the state legislature and its impact on Kent. After an hour, he looked up from his notes, waved a hand toward us, and said, "Dismissed." That was it!

Rummaging in the library one day, I discovered that nearby Cleveland had an excellent collection of census tract data updated annually with local surveys. Without thinking about it, I put my dissertation aside, hardly beginning to exploit it for publications as I was eager to launch new research. I would plot the social class distribution of a major metropolitan area, residents' occupational, education, and income status. No one had done that before. I began the tedious job of organizing the data. Within a few months, I completed the task, including layouts of tables and maps. Then put it aside again and again (see below). In 1955 the Duncans (1955) published an article doing just what I had planned for Cleveland. Scooped, I unthinkingly tossed my laboriously gathered data into the trash.

A few recently hired assistant professors came to know one other because, heavy users, we ran across one other in the library. We represented sociology, psychology, political science, history, journalism, biology, and library science. Discovering a common interest in research, we organized a club that met regularly to discuss research in progress. Our families became a loosely knit circle. Almost every weekend Millie and I were invited to a dinner, picnic, or cocktails.

Delbert Miller, a Minnesota Ph. D., was part of that group. He left the War Labor Board to join sociology just before I came. While working for Sperry Gyroscope Corporation during the War, he developed a research interest in industry akin to my closely related interest in occupations and professions. Del suggested that we co-author a book in a new area, *Industrial Sociology*. Putting aside my Cleveland study temporarily, we prepared a twenty-page prospectus and sent it to F.S. Chapin, his mentor and editor at Harper and Brothers. Chapin immediately sent us a contract.

We planned a series of field studies to provide data for the book. Pressure to gather data and write articles with Del pushed my Cleveland research further into the background. The fieldwork was done mostly by our students, veterans from working- and middle- and lower-middle-class backgrounds, eager for field work experience. Our first study examined generational occupational careers in northeast Ohio, modeled after my mobility analysis of Greenbelt. Our students interviewed a sample of workers for their complete occupational histories, from part-time jobs while in school to retirement, including periods of unemployment.

The sample of 276 resembled Ohio's labor force in age, sex, and occupation. We divided the job histories in four stages: initial (before school completion), trial (five years post completion), the stable period thereafter, and retirement. The lifetime mobility patterns proved to be remarkably stratified from the initial jobs through to retirement. In the trial period, the highly educated with parents of high occupational and educational status moved quickly to professional and managerial jobs and stayed there. In contrast, with few exceptions, the least educated, moved aimlessly in short-term jobs for their entire lives and experienced frequent periods of unemployment. We published three articles based on the data, one that highlighted the use of career patterns as a sociological instrument to measure changes in stratification patterns (Form and Miller 1949).

In the fall of 1946, George Lundberg, head of sociology at the University of Washington, invited Del to teach Industrial Sociology in the winter semester. Sensing the possibility of a regular appointment, Del accepted and, as he predicted, was offered a position. He left Kent. The next year was a lonely intellectually interlude for me. I had published a few pieces and, within two years, in the spring of 1947, Kent promoted me to associate professor, apparently not unusual at the time. William Sewell (1998) reported that he was promoted to full professor at Oklahoma A & M four years after he completed the Ph. D.

Charles P. Loomis at Michigan State College in East Lansing, invited me to teach Industrial Sociology the summer of 1947 on the recommendation of my friend from Stephens, Orden Smucker, who had moved to Michigan State, I accepted at once. In his early forties, Loomis was a tall, lean, hard-driving person, with vacant blue eyes and little hair. Raised in rural New Mexico, he was proud of his ranching heritage and his ability to handle rope and horses like a true cowboy. He was open and friendly but socially clumsy and not very articulate. We quickly discovered common friends. A Harvard Ph.D., Loomis had earlier worked with Harvard classmates at the Department of Agriculture in Washington and had participated in the Strategic Bombing Survey in Germany after the War. He knew my Maryland professors, Carl

Joslyn, John Holt, and Linden Dodson and others whom I had met in Washington.

Eager to build a strong interdisciplinary department on the Harvard model (sociology-anthropology-social psychology), Loomis had recruited faculty from Harvard and rural sociologists trained at land-grant universities like Cornell, Wisconsin, Minnesota, and Louisiana. With its dozen full-time faculty and three adjuncts, the department dwarfed Maryland's at its peak. This, I thought, was a "real" department. The faculty held weekly seminars that summer and I gave a paper in Duane Gibson's home. The next day, I dropped by Loomis' office for a chat. He casually said, "Bill, I hope you like it here well enough to stay." Stunned, I asked, "Are you offering me a job?" He smiled and said I would come as an assistant professor. I told him to expect my decision in the morning.

I already had tenure at Kent and would lose it at Michigan State. Yet I dreaded returning to Kent's two-person department. Laing had found no replacement for Del Miller. I thought, why leave now? The market was opening up and there would be other opportunities. Already the University of Texas department had learned that I was doing ecological research in Cleveland and asked me to apply. Lansing, with its auto-motive factories (Oldsmobile, Fisher Body, Reo, and Motor Wheel), was an ideal research site for an industrial sociologist. Mainly, I fretted whether I was well enough trained to compete with Michigan State's faculty with degrees from first-rate universities. I decided that it was better to find out sooner than later and accepted the Loomis' offer, sending Kent a letter of resignation. President Bowman fired back an angry response complaining of the lateness of my decision. I apologetically explained that I found it hard to return to a virtually nonexistent department when I had an opportunity to join a strong one. To my surprise, he replied with a conciliatory note wishing me well. I went to Michigan State in the fall of 1947, downgraded to assistant professor with the same salary as at Kent, $4,200 per year.

Michigan State: Early Years

Life at Michigan State was to be full of surprises both for me and everyone there. When I arrived, the student body of 9,000 was growing as World War II veterans took advantage of the G.I. Bill of Rights. President John Hannah, an alumnus in Poultry Science, was determined to build a high quality institution that would rival the University of

Michigan (Hannah 1980). For decades after Michigan Agricultural College opened in 1855 as the first (with Penn State) land-grant college under the Morrill Act, it remained a small technical college. Later, its name became Michigan State College, but in 1947, the power plant smokestack still bore the white letters, MAC. About 1950, Hannah asked the legislature to change Michigan State College to Michigan State University, a move strongly resisted by the University of Michigan. Exploiting his contacts with the State Board of Agriculture and the state Extension Service, Hannah succeeded in the first of a series of moves opposed by the University of Michigan: joining the Big Ten, becoming a member of the American Association of Universities, rapid expansion of budgets, and the establishment of a College of Medicine (Hannah 1980: 86-119). By 1967, Michigan State had more students (40,000) and a larger budget than Michigan, and a victorious football team (Dressel 1987). Michigan State also successfully raised the quality of students and faculty. While all state institutions were expanding rapidly, Michigan State's growth was spectacular. From 1945 to 1970, graduate enrollments increased more than tenfold, from five to 25 percent of the student body, making the university the sixth largest national producer of Ph.D.s. Only three U.S. universities experienced larger increases in research funding (Geiger 1993: 216, 209).

This expansion was reflected in departmental growth. When Loomis arrived in 1944, Social Work split off, leaving Sociology with seven faculty members. Unlike most land-grant universities, Michigan State never had a Rural Sociology department because in fact it had a rural faculty and university policy precluded the formation of parallel departments in two colleges (Hannah 1980: 92). When the College of Arts and Sciences was formed, Sociology became part of it but retained formal ties with the Agricultural Experiment Station and Extension Service. Two decades after Loomis arrived, the department had about thirty full-time faculty and about 100 graduate students. The faculty teaching load had been reduced from four to two courses a quarter.

Loomis, like Hannah, dreamed of a strong research-oriented organization. With sufficient funds and dedicated faculty Loomis expected to compete with Michigan and other leading departments. His experiences before coming to Michigan State provided the organizational model. After receiving a Harvard Ph.D. in 1933 in the depths of the Great Depression he joined several talented sociologists in the Department of Agriculture. New Deal policy required the U.S. Department of Agriculture to set farm production quotas by size of farm, a task that

required gathering copious data. Government sociologists and economists were given staff and funds to conduct large-scale surveys, pio-
neering significant advances in sampling design, scale construction,
and attitude measurement. During World War II these advances were
applied to military surveys and after the war to large-scale surveys of
the effects of bombing on German and Japanese morale (Sewell 1989).

When these scholars returned to academia, they sought to conduct
research modeled after that in government and the military. This required formalizing the training of graduate students, building research
organizations with laboratories and staffs, and raising funds for large-
scale research. Only three departments (Michigan, Columbia, and Chicago) fully realized these objectives; others did so in part. On the curriculum level, courses in statistics, methods, and field research were
introduced, often made compulsory. Universities provided space for
laboratories, equipment such as calculators and IBM counter-sorters,
secretaries, and small funds for research. Primary funding was to come
from growing private foundations and government agencies.

Carnegie and Rockefeller, primary sources of social science funding
for elite universities before World War II, expanded social science funding (35 percent of Rockefeller's in 1950), much of it to state universities for international programs, especially in Latin America. By 1950,
the Ford Foundation was dispensing funds triple those of Carnegie and
Rockefeller combined, much of it for medical and health research (Geiger 1993: 40-50). The largest grants to study social aspects of health
came from the National Institute of Health and later, the National Institute of Mental Health. The U.S. Department of Agriculture expanded
Experiment Station funding so rapidly that it was available almost for
the asking. Finally, the National Science Foundation (NSF) expanded
its funding of basic research to include the social sciences. Having
developed contacts with all these funding sources, Loomis brought their
representatives to the department.

The rapid growth of higher education after the war spurred the demand for faculty and graduate students to handle the floodtide of undergraduates. Large graduate programs were an inexpensive way to
meet mounting instruction costs. For the first time, graduate students
began to teach post-introductory courses. Before the war, Michigan
State had half a dozen graduate students, a decade after the war, almost
100. By 1970, the lush expansive epoch was over.

When Loomis came to Michigan State in 1944, he immediately began to raise research money for faculty research. In the first decade, he

raised about a million dollars a year, about a quarter of it from the Experiment Station, the rest from Carnegie, Rockefeller, Ford, and federal agencies. Envious of Rensis Likert's Institute for Social Research and the Survey Research Center at Michigan, he established two parallel research units in the department: the Social Research Service with a research director and the Area Research Service for research in Latin America. The Experiment Station routinely funded half a dozen research assistants for the former and two for the latter. Other foundations provided funds for both services.

Every Wednesday the faculty lunched in a meeting room at Hunt's cafeteria near Morrill Hall, which housed Sociology. We reviewed routine departmental matters but the main agenda item was research. Every three weeks or so, Loomis brought a guest who represented a government agency or a research foundation. The faculty's task was to impress the visitor with appealing ideas that the agency might fund. Then the guest would be asked to respond to ideas we had generated. Loomis would close the meeting by informing the guest that his good ideas would be incorporated into a research proposal that he would soon receive. Loomis's contacts were largely with organizations dealing with rural life: schools, libraries, hospitals, and cooperatives. Except for me, all faculty members had rural backgrounds or interests. Seven of the faculty had Experiment Station or Extension appointments and the two anthropologists were interested in rural and small town life. Even Paul Honigsheim, a political refugee from Germany, had been on the Experiment Station payroll and had written manuscripts on Max Weber as a rural sociologist.

Loomis routinely went around the table, asking each of us to explain how our areas of expertise fitted the research interests of our guest's agency. As the lone person in industrial and urban sociology, I felt excruciatingly uncomfortable when my turn came. Indeed, Loomis sometimes was flummoxed about how to introduce me. Once, with a guest who was interested in rural Latin America, Loomis stuttered "F-F-Form is fluent in Romance languages and is eager to participate in research in Latin America. Bill, tell us about your ideas." As I slunk in my chair, I mumbled something incoherent.

Loomis constantly pressured us to participate in his funded projects. His own academic interest was to build a systems theory like that of Parsons and he took no major role in any of the research projects. He saw his mission as organizing research teams, monitoring their progress, and perhaps participating in publications. About six faculty and three graduate students typically were enticed to join a team and take part as equals in all phases of a project, from conception to final publication. A team's competence and composition mattered little. With hard work, Loomis thought, a good product would ensue.

My preoccupation was to keep up with Del Miller who was working exclusively on *Industrial Sociology*. My strategy with Loomis was to suggest useful ideas for his projects without committing myself to them. He knew that my publication record was better than most in the department and didn't punish me for not joining the research teams. But neither did he ease the pressure. While I escaped joining a project to study nurses, I could not evade a project to study high school students' occupational interests.

The Youth Project

Michigan Bell Telephone Company, experiencing difficulty in recruiting high school graduates to work in its expanding business, wanted to know why. Loomis proposed to study the occupational aspirations of senior high school students in the Detroit area, including, of course, their feelings towards occupations found in the telephone industry. Unable to argue that this was unrelated to occupational-industrial sociology, I reluctantly joined the research team.

Although I soon became restless with the project's endless meetings and slow progress, the team experience was good for me. I overcame fears that I might not be able to compete on equal terms with sociologists trained in the nation's best departments, and I learned a great deal about survey research from my colleagues. We gathered the data in less than a year, an opportune time for me to pull out. But Loomis convinced Michigan Bell to finance publication of a brochure to be sent to high school educators and vocational counselors.

Apparently, other committee members also wanted to leave the project, which delayed writing the brochure. Loomis called a meeting of the committee to get some action. After a long embarrassing silence, Duane Gibson and I agreed to write a first draft. Meeting daily at my home, we pounded it out in about two weeks. Finally, with six authors listed alphabetically (Brookover et al. 1949), The Social Research Service published a fifteen-page booklet, *Youth and the World of Work*. The brochure, with pretty drawings, summarized the main findings. The data and sample were good, but no one exploited the data for a professional journal publication. I resolved never again to join a team research project, even in my area.

Industrial Sociology

Teaching four courses a quarter, four different ones in the winter, I did little work on *Industrial Sociology* that first year at Michigan State. However, I immersed myself in the human relations literature, finding it much too social-psychological and applied for my taste as it focused on the climate of interpersonal relations between supervisors and workers. Apart from its managerial bias, it ignored labor unions, collective bargaining, technology, bureaucracy, stratification, and politics in and out of the work place, the drums to which I marched.

On the other hand, Miller was determined to build an applied sociology useful for solving worker-management problems in human relations that went beyond Elton Mayo's (1939) narrow clinical approach. His chapters focussed on applied sociology, the history of industrial sociology, the ideal training of industrial sociologists, and the adjustment problems that workers encountered from their first jobs while in school to retirement.

I found myself concentrating on the informal and formal organization of work groups, ecological and stratification analysis of large-scale organization, and industry-community relations. In sum, we reversed our original roles. He had been interested in work organization and I, in occupational sociology. In the book, he concentrated on the social psychology of occupational careers and applied human relations and I, on work organizations. As we wrote chapters independently, *Industrial Sociology* was in fact two books nicely stitched together.

Burleigh Gardner (1945) and Wilbert Moore (1946) had already published good texts on industry and work. Gardner combined micro-social systems analysis with human relations concerns and Moore integrated materials and frameworks from labor economics and social organization. I sought to develop a structural treatment that integrated contributions from ecology, social organization, politics, and social stratification (Miller and Form 1951, V-XII, XXI). This perspective differed from most approaches to industry, which were heavily social psychological, ethnographic, or syntheses of the two.

My main questions were, How do sub-organizations of large complex enterprises interlock in daily and long-term encounters in the enterprise's production or service outputs and in the problems they generate such as grievances, morale, and conflict? How do the special interests of the constituent sub-groups interact to produce various outcomes? In short, I developed an organizational framework that explained the political processes among sub-groups within enterprises that took into account their relations to groups external to the enterprise. The perspective viewed sub-organizations as engaging in a struggle to protect and advance their interests in a larger organizational field.

I first identified the small units that make up complex organizations, that is, employees under an immediate supervisor. The greater the number of such units in an organization, the greater is the potential for inter-unit cleavages, the more complex is the task of coordinating them, and the more complex are the outputs: channels of communication, accommodation, and bargaining.

The rising strength of organized labor after World War II pointed to a major cleavage in large-scale organizations that human relations scholars had neglected. Along with this major labor-management fault line, I identified other cleavages based on spatial separation, different functions, divisions of authority, social status, and other grounds. These cleavages were envisioned as transparencies overlaying one another. The more they coincided, the deeper the organizational segmentation, and the greater the resort to informal and formal bargaining, that is, political processes to resolve the issues.

The first "map" of an enterprise I portrayed was the physical ecology of work units from the factory floor to the top executive offices: plotting the location of walls, departments, offices, and technology. The second map depicted the flow of work and the vertical and horizontal lines of communication that integrated the organization's sub-units. The third depicted the functional and hierarchical divisions of the formal organization including the union and joint labor-management organizations. The fourth located the informal groups at *all* management levels, something neglected in human relations research that focused on the lowest level. Fifth, overlaying the four maps was the distribution of income, status, and power. Finally, I plotted linkages of formal and informal work groups to external community and national organizations, for example, business organizations, labor union federations, voluntary associations, and government.

These levels of analysis identified the major areas of stability, organizational cleavages, decision-making and bargaining. The task was to analyze the *inter-organizational* confrontations among functional divisions, between line and staff organizations (personnel, inspection, industrial relations), between levels of authority, and the strategies available to the component units to achieve their objectives. Unlike the human relations school, my approach was comprehensive and included segmentation within management, within labor unions, and between both at *all* levels, from grievances on the lowest level to informal and formal collective bargaining at the top, and with external institutions, such as education and government.

Unlike the human relations approach that exposed the informal organization of workers in terms of their customs, traditions, sub-cultures, and patterns of interpersonal encounters, I viewed it as an organizational response of *all* groups (including top management, office employees, workers, labor unions) to protect and advance their interests and as mechanisms to respond to their external organizational environment. As such, informal organizations were as rational and predictable as formal organizations and their study required no special analytic tools.

In short, I outlined a structural view of complex organizations that focussed an their internal segmentation and the resultant bargaining, anticipating later theories of organizational politics. Robert Presthus, a political science colleague at Michigan State, later editor of the *Administration Science Quarterly*, recognized my political view of organizations, and heartily approved of it. Finally, in December 1950, four years after its inspiration, we published *Industrial Sociology*, a book of 896 pages.

The book significantly affected our careers. Although it was a text, it contained much original research on work plants, unions, and occupational social psychology, defined a new field, and outlined a future research program. Within a few years, industrial sociology grew to be the largest specialty in the American Sociological Association (ASA). The book also attracted attention in business, labor, and government. It dominated the field for several years, slowing yielding to a broader specialty called complex organizations. Most scholars, unaware that Del and I were relative youngsters, probably attributed more wisdom to us than we deserved.

5

New Paths, Voluntary and Involuntary

Introduction

With the completion of *Industrial Sociology*, I had expected to focus more on my research program but events in the rapidly changing department and university altered my plans for almost a decade. Department growth brought in new colleagues who stimulated productive collaborative research in areas other than industrial sociology. Responding to pressure to engage in unwanted research resulted in frustration and wasteful distractions but also led to some surprisingly fruitful outcomes.

As Michigan State grew, departmental life changed. Soon after John Hannah became president in 1941, he created a Basic College that all freshmen would enter. Based on the advice of educator Floyd Reeves at the University of Chicago, the Basic College required all students, regardless of major, to complete four year-long courses covering the sciences, social sciences, humanities, and the arts and letters. Basic College departments would be independent of those in the upper division and courses would be taught by multidisciplinary faculty comparable in quality and pay to those in the upper division.

In the Department of Social Science, students enrolled in a year-long sequence (three quarters) that exposed them to an integrated approach to economics, sociology, political science, and social psychology. Although faculty were recruited from discrete disciplines, they were supposed to teach in an interdisciplinary fashion. As might be expected, the course content of each quarter centered around material drawn from the major disciplines, mainly sociology, economics, and political science. Since almost all Basic College faculty wanted to retain their disciplinary identity, they preferred teaching only courses that emphasized their own discipline. They would also offer to teach in the university's upper division departments. Because of their enormous teaching loads, the disciplinary departments willingly accepted them. In their introductory courses, the upper division faculty often found it hard to assess what students had learned about a discipline as taught in the Basic College. Departments sometimes considered dropping their introductory course but none of them ever did.

Sociologists in other university divisions also wanted to teach in the disciplinary departments. In sociology, at one time or another, these included faculty in Community Development (urban extension), the Effective Living and Social Science departments in the Basic College, the College of Education, Labor and Industrial Relations (LIR), Communications, Home Economics, and Criminal Justice. At the same time, some sociology faculty were given research appointments in other divisions of the university (e.g., Bureau of Educational Research, LIR, Community Development). At one point, adjunct or joint appointments in sociology were held by nearly half of the faculty, endangering the ability of full-time members to set department policies.

A Decade of Urban Research

After completing *Industrial Sociology*, I conducted research in three areas (urban, sociology of clothing, and disaster research) with faculty in three other departments. Each project had its unique complications.

The urban research began in 1950 when officemate J. Allan Beegle, a rural sociologist and demographer with an appointment in the Experiment Station, Sigmund Nosow, an instructor in the social science department, and I received a small grant from the Rockefeller Foundation for regional research, actually for any Michigan project. Having decided to study pathways to urban employment, we selected Lansing's Oldsmobile Division of General Motors as the site as it was recruiting workers from both rural and urban areas. At that time, labor economists were studying local labor markets (Myers and Shultz 1951; Reynolds 1951) but neglected sociological factors such as race, ethnicity, regional origin and industry characteristics that affect worker recruitment, placement, and earnings. In sum, what was lacking was Max Weber's analytical scheme that dealt with the social organization of markets.

We approached Oldsmobile management for permission to draw a sample of workers to interview, but were refused. Eli Chinoy, who had just completed fieldwork at Olds (published as *Automobile Workers and the American Dream* in 1955) had by-passed management and enlisted the cooperation of the United Automobile Workers (UAW), but his sample, as we found out later (see chapter 6), was badly skewed. We asked Professor Charles Killingsworth, a respected labor arbitrator in Michigan State's economics department to vouch for us at GM, but he also was unsuccessful. Researchers at Harvard, Yale, MIT, and Michigan routinely secured GM cooperation but Michigan State apparently lacked sufficient clout. We then decided to interview a random sample of Lansing workers, a fortunate step, as I explain later.

The data clearly showed that ascriptive factors (ethnicity, race), rural-urban origins, industrial and plant characteristics affected workers' job placement, income, mobility, and market behavior. Nosow used some of the data in his dissertation and a later publication (1956). I wanted to exploit the data further, using Max Weber's theoretical scheme on the social embeddedness of labor markets, but Nosow dallied and I turned to other projects. A decade would pass before I would try to apply Weber's insights in the new industrial sociology and labor market stratification.[1]

As enrollments continued to soar in the early 1950s, Loomis hired Gregory P. Stone who was completing his dissertation at the University of Chicago and Joel Smith who had just completed his at Northwestern. I was no longer the sole urban sociologist in a rural enclave. We instantly recognized a common interest in urban society and for six years became a productive research team. Stone had a half-time research appointment supported by an Experiment Station grant to the Department of Clothing, Textiles, and Related Arts in the College of Home Economics for a project that Loomis had generated. Stone was easily diverted from work on this project and on his dissertation by research opportunities closer to his heart.

Stone, Smith, and I decided to ask the cities of Lansing and East Lansing to finance a study to create a census tract plan for the metropolitan area. Conforming to departmental norms, a committee of eight faculty members and two graduate assistants was organized in 1952 to run the research. I chaired the project and the U.S. Bureau of the Census appointed me Key Census Tract Person. The committee quickly slimmed down to Stone, Smith, and Beegle, and me. Despite copious literature on "natural areas" in sociology, no systematic methodology had been devised to identify them. We decided to explore the extent that ecological, demographic, and social areas coincided to help us define the boundaries of sub-area, the bases of census tracts.

After identifying thirty-five ecological areas defined by physical features (land use, zoning, housing value, and racial segregation), we used Guttman scales based on seven characteristics of 139 Census enumeration districts (percent nonwhite, foreign-born, male, under twenty-one, over fifty-five, age and fertility ratios) to map contiguous areas that were demographically homogeneous (see Smith 1954). To identify areas based on social integration, we conducted 550 interviews of local family interaction (one in every other city block) and 200 interviews with businesses located outside the central business district to locate the areas they served. We identified six types of sub-areas based on an index of social intimacy: amount of interaction with neighbors, identification with the local area, use of local facilities, and the presence of formal and informal organizations, then prepared a map showing the contiguous areas of high, middle, and low social integration (Smith, Form, and Stone 1954). The three maps, compared for compatibility of their boundaries (Form et al. 1954), showed important deviations. Eventually, a "best fit" was made for the census tract boundaries. To my knowledge, no one since has so intensively analyzed urban sub-areas.

Soon after arriving at Michigan State, I began to keep track of land use changes in Lansing and became convinced that they did not conform to current ecological theories. Burgess's Chicago school adhered too closely to an impersonal competition model for land use while Hawley's (1944) biological niche model slighted purposive organizational behavior. Firey's (1945) cultural ecology theory had limited application because it dealt with the Boston Common and other areas of great historic or symbolic importance, areas that were almost nonexistent in the Midwest.

In 1952, I was elected president of the Ohio Valley (later, North Central) Sociological Association, the youngest president the Association had ever elected. Ed Schuler of our department probably engineered the nomination on the basis that Del and I had recently published *Industrial Sociology*. For my address, I organized my thoughts on ecological changes as I had studied them in Lansing, an attempt to improve ecological theory by making it more sociological. The theory emphasized interorganizational politics involved in urban land-use change in America (Form 1954). Essentially, it stated that four organizational sectors (real estate, large business, city government, and homeowners) were involved in most land-use changes. When, where, whether, and how they interacted (competed, fought, cooperated, bargained, or remained uninvolved) depended on issue salience, resources available, tactics used, and other variables. By studying zoning decisions over time, the dynamics of this political process could be revealed. I presented several cases that demonstrated the superiority of a structural political bargaining model over current ecological theories.

Published in 1954 in *Social Forces*, this article has been cited more frequently than any I have written. Later, several neo-Marxists (e. g., Moloch 1976; Feagin 1988) proposed a political model of land-use change, but they focused largely on downtown growth machines organized by big business and local government, neglected all other cases of land-use change over time, and ignored the notable failures in downtown development.

A productive urban research team broke up when Stone left for the University of Missouri as he hadn't completed his dissertation and Smith left for Duke because Loomis didn't like him.

During this decade of urban research, I sometimes fretted about neglecting industrial research. What bothered me even more was Loomis's incessant pressure to involve me in two research projects that I sought to avoid: the study of the social aspects of clothing and technological change in Latin America.

The Endless Clothing Project

Loomis had maintained his contacts with the Department of Agriculture in Washington after he arrived at Michigan State and had developed close ties with other departments in the College of Agriculture at the university. He learned that the department of Textiles, Clothing and Related Arts (TCRA) in the College of Home Economics aspired to grant a Ph.D. but its faculty was not eager to develop one oriented to economics, marketing, or fabric characteristics. Loomis encouraged Professor Hazel Strahan, head of TCRA, to require her graduate students to obtain Ph.D.s in sociology with minors in TCRA. Eventually, TCRA could develop its own Ph.D. program with its students minoring in sociology. He helped Strahan obtain a large five-year federal grant to conduct research on the social aspects of clothing. At the outset Loomis would furnish the personnel to design and coordinate the research, later, TCRA would assume the leadership and pioneer a new direction for home economics research.

Loomis hired Greg Stone half time on Experiment Station funds because the clothing project fitted neatly into his dissertation on the social aspects of shopping. An interdepartmental faculty committee was formed to plan and carry out the research project. It was chaired by John Useem, who had been recently hired as a "rural anthropologist," and Stone would coordinate research operations. A bulky committee of sociologists, TCRA faculty, and Milton Rokeach of the Psychology Department met regularly to hammer out a theoretical framework and design the fieldwork. Neither Useem nor Loomis could get the committee to focus. The committee could not even agree whether the project should deal exclusively with clothing. Why not add jewelry, makeup, or anything that affects appearance? We spent a frustrating afternoon discussing Milton Rokeach's proposal to include facial makeup and hairstyling along with clothing. Having launched the project, Loomis began skipping meetings.

Little happened the first year. Stone was more interested in working with Joel Smith and me on urban research, studying German to pass his Ph.D. language requirement, and thinking about how to apply symbolic interaction theory to the study of shopping in urban settings. The committee made one decision: the research would inventory *all* the clothing owned by all members of a representative set of families in a small town of 10,000 and the surrounding rural area in Michigan's corn belt.

I devised a plan to disengage myself from the project: skip every other meeting, make no comments on the ones I attended, and find excuses to avoid even the smallest task. Since others had devised similar strategies, Useem called fewer and fewer meetings until Loomis pressured him to action. I was in a bind: Loomis wanted me in the project, but I couldn't endure the meetings. Finally, I decided to extricate myself by submitting a small proposal tailored exclusively to my interests. If rejected, I could gracefully resign; if accepted, Stone would supervise the data collection and I would be free to pursue my research.

In two days, I designed a proposal to study the significance of clothing in men's occupational life based on interviews with a representative sample of male workers in the town. (Farmers would be ignored.) Since I was unaware of empirical research on the topic, I proposed to explore how workers in different occupational status levels regarded clothing, the kinds of clothes they were expected to wear at work, what happened when these expectations were violated, and whether clothing affected the way supervisors evaluated their job performance and promotion chances. I sketched a series of vignettes to probe how workers respond to disagreements on clothing norms in work situations: a wildcat strike over a compulsory dress code, a lawyer dressed inappropriately at court, a worker promoted because he dressed better than a more competent applicant, and the failure of a supervisor to conform to the dress code of other supervisors. I circulated the proposal and interview to the committee which quickly accepted both. Then I suggested that a parallel study be made on how women make clothing decisions when shopping for themselves, children, and husbands. I agreed to work with Stone on that interview and vignettes. The project now had enough focus to go into the field. With Stone responsible for fieldwork, I would disengage myself from the project. Together we eventually would write a report on my part of it, an easy task.

After a respite of about six months, Loomis called me to his office just before summer break, confiding that Stone had not begun the fieldwork and that the Experiment Station Director was pressing for publications on a project that was now more than two years old. Would I work for three weeks on the Station payroll to get the fieldwork started in Coldwater? I had never taught in the summer term because with a heavy teaching load, I needed summers for research and writing. He pleaded. I reluctantly agreed.

Stone and I went to Coldwater with a research team of graduate students, mostly women from TCRA, and lived in a dingy hotel for a month. The food was terrible. The fieldwork slowly got under way. My involvement in the project occupied most of the summer because we had to construct the town's occupational structure in order to select the sample. Then we pretested the interviews, trained the interviewers, checked interview quality, and made codes. Neglecting my own research, I felt I had had an unproductive summer. Finally, when the fall quarter started, I thought I had earned my freedom because Stone was still supervising field operations.

Stone hated working alone when he began to process data and would occasionally press me to work with him. That summer, we had asked a select sample of Coldwater residents at different status levels to rank the prestige levels of the main occupations in the community. We were mystified by wide variation in their rankings until we controlled for the ranker's social location in the community. We found that the assumption of a single status hierarchy in the community hid more than it revealed. In Coldwater, two parallel status systems had emerged, one for those oriented to and employed in the town's traditional economy. The other involved those employed in the town's large absentee-owned factory. Members of the two status systems had little contact with one another and used different criteria to bestow status in their respective systems. The largest disagreements appeared in the ranking of middle status occupations. Moreover, a score or more of long-distance truckers who lived in Coldwater because it was midway between Chicago and Detroit were ignorant of and indifferent to both status systems. In short, different status arrangements can emerge in heterogeneous changing communities. We published these findings in *The American Journal of Sociology* (Stone and Form 1953).

We then pursued the topic in a survey of Lansing residents (Form and Stone 1957), probing how people at different status levels arrive at status estimates of others in anonymous situations and the criteria they use to bestow status. We found that the signs and symbols used to identify and bestow status differ by status level. The results again challenged the assumptions of single hierarchical models of stratification. Failure of social scientists to take account of these ambiguities, variations, and contradictions helps to explain our inability to predict behavior. Unfortunately, we did not extend this promising line of research, nor have others taken it up.

Since I could not fully disengage myself from the clothing project, Stone and I eventually co-authored four Experiment Station Technical Bulletins and two journal articles on clothing. Only the Bulletin on occupational clothing (Form and Stone 1955) was relevant for my reference groups in sociology. We found that clothing had important symbolic significance at work, that clothing norms became more important yet more diffuse at higher occupational status levels, and that devices to enforce clothing norms become more indirect at higher levels. Few sociologists ever saw or referred to the Bulletin. Unfortunately, my involvement in the clothing project did not end with these publications. Graduate students from TCRA continued to do research on clothing and pressed me to direct their theses and sit on their committees.

In the spring of 1953, Loomis called me to his office and casually informed me that I was now an associate professor with tenure. I hadn't been asked to submit any documents and hadn't given the matter any thought. Perhaps tenure was easier to make then. Yet, in six years, with no time off for research and a teaching load of four courses a quarter, I had co-authored a book, nine articles, and two chapters. In the next few months, a number of unexpected and seemingly unrelated events determined my research activities for several years. I found myself thinking that people don't act; things happen to them.

Will Disasters Ever End?

On 8 June 1953, a violent tornado unexpectedly struck Beecher, a working-class suburb north of Flint, Michigan, killing 116 people, injuring 800, and partially or completely destroying more than 450 homes. Loomis, who had participated in the Bombing Survey in Germany, saw research possibilities in the catastrophe. The next day he called the faculty together and asked for volunteers to study the disaster. He had already made contact with the governor's office to get passes to visit the stricken area. On the following day, Loomis, Stone, Charles Westie (a sociologist in Community Development,[2] Duane Gibson, and I visited Beecher to inspect the damage and talk to residents and organizational personnel (police, firemen, Red Cross, Salvation Army). On the next day, Eli Marks and Raymond Gorden, experienced disaster researchers from the National Opinion Research Center, appeared on campus to help us devise interviews for survivors and organizations involved in the disaster. Five days after the tornado struck, a dozen faculty members and students were pretesting interviews in Beecher.

Predictably, faculty participation fell off as the study progressed. Stone, Westie, and I and three graduate students spent the summer interviewing over 200 victims and organizational personnel involved in rescue and rehabilitation efforts. Loomis obtained a small grant of $5,000 from the National Research Council to support the project, and I wrote a preliminary report on our research to the Council.

A seemingly unrelated incident occurred in the following spring. Loomis asked Stone and me to prepare a research proposal for the Rockefeller Foundation to study technological diffusion along the U.S.-Mexican border. Technological diffusion was high on the agenda of rural sociologists studying the economically less developed countries. Neither Stone nor I had studied that topic and we knew little about the U.S.- Mexican border. We demurred, but Loomis pressed us: "Just submit any ideas that come to mind. Any first thoughts will do. Use your imaginations." After mulling the topic for a day or two, Stone and I spent a day writing a brief and fatuous proposal and gave it to Loomis. He was grateful and that ended the matter, or so we thought.

In the fall and winter, the tornado project languished. Stone, Westie, and I, overextended, could spare little time to code data and prepare a report due to the National Research Council the following fall. In the summer, Sig Nosow in the social science department was hired on Council funds to process the data. I met with him regularly to review the coding, plan data analysis, and outline the report to the Council.

My cup was full, tying up loose ends on clothing and urban research in Lansing as well as a study of a UAW local I had launched in Lansing. I looked forward to a sabbatical year in Mexico City that fall to study the Mexican labor movement. Del Miller was planning a parallel study on his sabbatical in Bristol, England. We both assumed that organized labor would become an increasingly powerful player in community and national affairs in the United States and planned a monograph comparing labor movements in the United States, Britain, and Mexico. Living on a half-year's salary in Mexico would be difficult, but I thought we could make it. I had already arranged to rent an apartment in Mexico City.

One day as I passed Loomis in the hall, he invited me to his office for a chat. He casually mentioned that he had some unspent funds left over from his Carnegie grant for research in Costa Rica, just enough to cover my salary for three months on the U.S.- Mexican border. I could have it, no strings attached. Suspecting that he was trying to co-opt me in another of his projects, I pressed him to specify what he really wanted me to do. He replied pleasantly, "Nothing, Bill. Just do anything you like. Just so long as it is along the border. The money will have to be returned if you don't spend it. So, go down and do whatever you please." I agreed to think it over.

An additional three-months salary would make my income almost equal to my annual salary, greatly relieving my financial anxiety. In three months, I might be able to gather data for a comparative ecological study of El Paso and Ciudad Juarez. The cities were similar in size and geographic setting but their economic structures differed greatly, an ideal situation to test current ecological theory. Accepting Loomis's offer, I began to study Spanish. Three months on the border would give me time to hone my language skills.

By early September, the family was comfortably situated in El Paso and I began gathering data. True to his word, Loomis did not press me. I spent a glorious month taking hundreds of photographs of land use in all parts of the two cities, made contact with appropriate city officials, and collected areal maps and data on population, housing, and zoning. My Spanish was improving and I reworked Nosow's draft of our report to National Research Council on the Beecher tornado.

Then an unexpected letter arrived from Loomis: the proposal that Stone and I had sketched for research on the border had been funded by

Rockefeller Foundation to the tune of $250,000. William D'Antonio, an incoming graduate student who spoke Spanish, would be supported on the grant and would arrive soon in El Paso to gather data for his dissertation. I could supervise him. I was stunned.

D'Antonio had just that summer completed a master's degree in political science at the University of Wisconsin. Loomis had taught a seminar in Latin America there which D'Antonio had taken. He had been teaching Spanish at the Loomis School, an academy in Connecticut run by one of Charlie's distant relatives. Bill had almost no background in sociology. In line with his conviction that hard work overcomes all, Loomis had urged Bill to seek a Ph.D. at Michigan State. With a year's research assistantship to gather data for his dissertation on the border, he could spend the next year at Michigan State and complete all degree requirements.

With his wife and child (and another on the way), Bill soon arrived in El Paso. We located a house for them in my neighborhood but the rent was too high. While conversing with its owner, Bill discovered that he had known her brother as an undergraduate at Yale. Wanting to help Bill, she offered to lower the rent if he would make some repairs on the house. As I worked for my graduate assistant on plumbing, masonry, and carpentry chores, I found that his enthusiasm almost compensated for his modest manual skills.

Finally, we got down to business. Loomis had trapped me again. I could not complete my ecological research by my self-imposed deadline of January when I was due to leave for Mexico City. I had to devise a project that would meet Loomis's research goal to illuminate cross-border relationships and also build on Bill's political science training.

Del Miller and I had planned comparative studies of labor's community influence in preparation for a monograph. Labor in Mexico was part of the ruling PRI party (Partido Revolucionario Institucional), while labor in United States was independent of government. That thought inspired me to study community power in El Paso and Ciudad Juarez somewhat along the lines of Floyd Hunter's (1953) work on Atlanta. I would study the relations of labor, business, and government in each city, identifying the most influential leaders and tracing their role in local and cross border affairs. I sent the proposal to Loomis who asked the faculty to respond to it. Only Duane Gibson gave me detailed comments, mostly technical. We began to make contact with institutional leaders in both cities, drafted the interviews, pretested them, drew the samples, and outlined D'Antonio's work for the rest of the year.

In the midst of this work, a happy Charlie Loomis arrived with his new wife Zona and the three children they had recently adopted in Costa Rica. We took Charlie to the International Fair in Ciudad Juarez, introduced him to some local influentials, and showed him what we were doing. Although he had spent considerable time in Latin America, my Spanish was better than his. Charlie approved of our plans, offered no suggestions, and returned to East Lansing.

That fall heavy rains caused flash flooding along the Rio Grande, bringing death and destruction to downstream communities on both sides of the border. Loomis immediately saw the opportunity for comparative studies of how American and Mexican communities respond to disasters, their rescue and rehabilitation efforts, and how they cooperated. How fortunate that Bill Form, an experienced disaster researcher, was still on the border! Within a day or two, Spanish-speaking graduate students from Michigan State, mostly Mormons who had spent time in Mexico, appeared in El Paso to "help" me in my research. I quickly adapted some materials from the Flint-Beecher tornado studies and Bill, the graduate students, and I drove off to the twin border communities of Eagle Pass and Piedras Negras. This was my first unsought involvement in a series of studies on floods, hurricanes, and other disasters in Latin America. My students published much of this research, but I had lost interest in the area.

Early in January, satisfied that Bill D'Antonio could complete the interviewing without further direction, we left for Mexico City. I first made contact with the labor attaché at the American embassy and he directed me to labor officials he knew. My research plans were unfocussed because I felt I needed a better grasp of the Mexican labor movement before I could deal with issues of its influence in the ruling PRI party and local politics. The accounts I had read on the subject were worthless because they did not deal with issues. The agenda was huge, but I could get started and return later.

My Spanish was improving rapidly and I was making progress when, late in February I was stricken with paratyphoid fever. I was delirious, medical care was primitive. Recovery was very slow and I lost fifteen pounds. In the morning my fever was down, but every time I exerted myself, it returned. Weeks went by. The doctor attributed my slow recovery to the high altitude; be patient and slowly resume your work schedule. In mid-April, I abandoned the study. In two hours we could be at sea level at Tampico. Early one morning, as we drove toward the coast, the lower the altitude, the better I felt. I recovered quickly and gained a half-pound a day as we drove back to Michigan.

The Tornado Study

As the report on the Flint-Beecher tornado study was due at the National Research Council, I edited it before classes began that fall. Much of data still remained unanalyzed. Stone and Westie, overcommitted, had found no time to work on it. Although Nosow was no longer on the payroll, he continued to work on the project. We found that the data, coded question by question from the surveys, made little sense because they were not guided by a theory of action. We needed to know the *sequence* of activities on the part of Beecher residents (mothers, children, neighbors) and organizations (firemen, police, schools) when the tornado struck, immediately after, and still later. What did residents *outside* the area do right after they learned the tornado had struck, after that, and still later? What was the sequence of activities of the organizations mobilized outside the stricken area (State Police, Civil Defense, Red Cross)? In sum, who did what, when, and why?

I turned to the lonely and onerous task of recoding all the data according to a time frame (tornado impact, immediate post-impact, rescue, and the long rehabilitation phase) for individuals (victims, residents in the impact area and volunteers immediately outside it) and organizational personnel.

Nosow and I decided to apply role theory to help explain personal behavior. All interpersonal contacts were coded according to role relationships to victims and residents in the impact area. Signs of panic behavior were most evident among those who had family or relatives in the impact area, but who were outside the area at the time, and had no information about their family members. Uninjured residents in the impact area turned first to help family members, then neighbors, and then strangers. Theories that disasters disrupt social organization and create chaos were unsupported. On the contrary, behavior was predictable on the basis of role relationships at all stages of the disaster.

No comparable theory was available to explain organizational and interorganizational behavior. Almost all victims were rescued by residents and neighbors before organizations were mobilized. The first organizations to arrive at the impact area at best facilitated the work of spontaneously formed rescue groups. Organizational behavior in the immediate post-impact and later periods could be predicted on the basis of their structural characteristics. The State Police quickly cordoned off the area and monitored access to it and exits from it, provided information to incoming organizations, and expedited their work. Local organizations (volunteer firemen) contributed their skills to local rescue groups. External volunteer organizations (Salvation Army) functioned effectively if they had developed routines to meet immediate needs (provide food, clothing, money, transportation) without asking questions. External professional organizations (Red Cross) could not quickly mobilize their bureaucracies and volunteers for their wide range of services, provoking the ire of both residents and other organizations. Civil Defense did not achieve effective organizational cooperation because of poor planning and lack of experience. In short, social science theories were fairly robust in disproving panic theories of individual and organizational behavior in disasters. In 1956, these findings were communicated in the second report to National Research Council.

At the time Harper was publishing a series of short studies. The two reports submitted to the Council came to 250 pages. I edited them slightly to remove overlap, wrote a short introduction, and asked Harper of their interest in publishing a book based on the reports. To my surprise, they accepted the manuscript and proposed to publish it immediately. I replied that the text had to be completely rewritten and we would send a final draft as soon as possible. In a few months, the manuscript was submitted.

Having given no thought to authorship, I proposed that Form, Nosow, Stone, and Westie be listed alphabetically. Nosow objected strenuously on the grounds that he and I had framed the theoretical problem, and done most of the coding and writing. We agreed that the title page should read, Form and Nosow, with Stone and Westie (1958), and would write a preface that described everyone's contributions in detail. When we sent the manuscript to Stone at the University of Minnesota and to Westie at Central Michigan University, they objected strongly. Stone wanted to rewrite the entire manuscript and Westie thought he deserved equal recognition because he alone designed and gathered the data on organizational behavior. Nosow held firm. I was torn and wrote a letter to Stone and Westie explaining my dilemma and offered to withdraw from the project. In a very moving letter that I will always treasure, Westie responded with a compassionate letter; he appreciated my position and above all, treasured our friendship, wanted to preserve it, and would go along with any listing. Stone held firm, but finally agreed to go along. For a few years, at annual ASA meetings, he would harangue me on the incident until I lost patience and scolded him for being an undisciplined worker. Before he died he confessed that our friendship was too valuable to hold a grudge. I swore never to get myself into such a situation again.

Disengaging myself from disaster research proved difficult. Loomis pressed me to make trips to the border, supervise student theses, and publish with him (Form and Loomis 1956). On one field trip, I slipped on the bank of the Rio Grande as I was getting into a boat and was nearly swept away in the surging waters. But I could not bear the emotional toll of interviewing disaster survivors whose family and friends had been killed or injured. Despite its research promise, I abandoned the field and sent all the disaster data to Enrico Quarentelli at the Disaster Research Center then at Ohio State University.

Notes

1.   Almost a decade later I noted that the data set contained information on the occupations of worker's fathers and brothers. My student James Geschwender and I (1962) applied reference group theory to demonstrate that workers' job satisfaction was related to their fathers and brothers' occupational status; the higher the prestige of the worker's occuaption relative to that of their fathers and brothers, the higher their job satisfaction.
2.   Hannah established the Institute for Community Development as an urban parallel to the Extension Division of the Agricultural Experiment Station. At one time it employed three or four sociologists full-time.

6

Becoming My Own Master

Community Power

Paradoxically, by applying my sociological proclivities in Loomis' pet projects that I tried to escape, I ultimately was liberated to become my own master. Thus, forced to abandon my ecology project on the border for the study of institutional influentials in El Paso and Ciudad Juarez, I pioneered research in comparative community power structure. This experience, in turn, led me to novel research on the social organization of field methods. Just before our sabbaticals in 1954, Miller and I had sketched the outlines of a book that would parallel *Industrial Sociology*. We would extend the analysis of labor-business relations in the economic arena to their relations in the external community. Miller planned to study labor's community influence in Bristol, England and Seattle and I, in Mexico City and possibly Lansing or Detroit. It turned out that my work on the border better fitted the book than my original choices.

In the border study I changed Floyd Hunter's (1953) reputational technique for identifying key influentials in Atlanta's *Community Power Structure*. Since I was interested in an institutional rather than a reputational approach to community power, we first interviewed top officials in all major institutions of El Paso and Ciudad Juarez for their nominees of community and cross-border influentials. We interviewed officers in government, business, labor, education, mass media, religion, welfare, and health who, we assumed, would be able to identify those most influential in community issues that affected their sectors.

The influentials they named in city and cross-border affairs were then asked to identify those who were the most influential in community and cross-border projects and affairs. We found that the profound differences in institutional arrangements of the two cities affected the patterns of all decision-making, a matter heretofore unexplored. Ciudad Juarez displayed a bifurcated power structure between business and government, with each sector exhibiting a different set of ties to local and national institutions, while the El Paso sectors displayed a more consensual structure. The use of this technique in later studies of American and Latin American cities exposed variations in institutional power and community decision-making, an insight not revealed by Hunter's or other approaches.

Six years after planning *Industry, Labor, and the Community*, we published it (Form and Miller 1960) as a monograph. It traced how the economy of a community shapes its ecology, stratification system, and institutions; how the institutional structure impacts local union-management relations; how business and labor articulate with community institutions (government, mass communication, education, welfare, religion, and the family), and finally, the place of business and labor in the community decision-making in the United States, England, and Mexico. These studies pioneered cross-national and comparative research on community power structure.

D'Antonio continued to visit the border for the next seven years to trace changes in community and cross-border affairs. The patterns found in the original fieldwork remained stable. In El Paso, business aligned itself with different local factions on different issues. Sometimes business was not involved in major issues. Even when united, business did not always win; when it lost, the long-term outcomes did not necessarily work against business. Thus, factionalism was sometimes more symbolic than predictive of gains or losses.

In Ciudad Juarez, cleavages between business and government elites were so solidified that even when no disagreements existed on issues, institutional cooperation was impossible. Conflict had become its own end. Even greater structural ambiguity appeared in alliances and alignments on border issues. In sum, the coordinated power elite that many sociologists proposed with such conviction existed in neither city nor in cross-border affairs.

These findings appeared in a monograph (D'Antonio and Form 1965), *Influentials in Two Border Cities,* and in six articles dealing with other communities (see, for example, D'Antonio, Form, Loomis, Erickson 1961). Inexplicably, just as sociologists were making fundamental strides in the study of community power, interest in the field waned. Later, neo-Marxists uncovered conspiracies between government and business elites in promoting central city growth that they called "growth machines" (Molotch 1976; Feagin and Parkers 1989), ignoring the research of earlier decades. How can we explain this? Perhaps they ignored disconfirming evidence when it failed to support their ideological preferences (Hamilton 1996, ch. 7).

My experience in comparative research on the border led me to suspect the validity of some American fieldwork practices. At the end of a long and candid interview with a business influential in Ciudad Juarez, we thanked him for his cooperation and promised him anonymity in publishing our findings. We were shocked when he heatedly replied, "I don't want anonymity. I want the world to know how I and my associates feel about these issues. If what we tell you is buried in an anonymous report, you have wasted my time." Neither did any government informant in Ciudad Juarez ask for anonymity. In contrast, the elites we interviewed in El Paso were very guarded and asked for anonymity before agreeing to be interviewed.

Another research assumption that was challenged was the idea that knowledgeables and influentials are part of a single system of community influence. Agreements were rare in Ciudad Juarez. Elites in different institutional sectors, especially business and government, reported having no contact with influentials in other sectors. They even denied the existence of informal and indirect inter-institutional contacts, and said that they sought no support for their positions on issues. Governmental elites felt no obligation to consult business which, in turn, did not expect to influence government. These observations on field methods were later supplemented and generalized to a larger population of field studies (see chapter 8).

Assessing My Involvement in Loomis' Projects

After serving sixteen years as department head, Loomis resigned in 1957. He confided in me that he had only the thirteen years before he retired to get elected president of the ASA. He saw his first task as helping to mobilize a campaign to elect Sorokin. Parsons, Sorokin's junior, had been elected in the late 1940s. The late 1950s witnessed the election of three Harvard graduates in a row, Robert Merton, Robin Williams, and Kingsley Davis so it was high time that the old man be recognized, Loomis said. As it turned out, the late 1960s witnessed the election of four Harvard faculty members or graduates: Homans in 1964, Sorokin in 1965, Wilbert Moore in 1966, and Loomis 1967.

Charlie showed me his presidential address before delivering it. I warned him that his endorsement of the demand by some militant blacks for a separate state might land him in a fracas, but he decided not to change that section of the paper (Loomis 1967). Predictably, the media focussed on that section as did many sociologists who favored racial integration. Charlie was dismayed and angry at the reception his address received.

Loomis' efforts to involve me in his projects lasted about a decade, 1947-1957. In my first two years, I was involved only in the Youth Study of Michigan Bell, but thereafter I was entangled in two or more of his projects and directed theses related to them after my participation. Yet, I found time to conduct other research, including the urban studies with Stone and Smith, independent research on labor unions, and two books with Del Miller on industrial sociology and comparative community power structures. My feelings about serving in Loomis' projects remain mixed. On the positive side, he gave me freedom to do what I wished on his projects and did not insist on being a co-author. The Youth project resulted in a trivial monograph, but it helped me overcome fears that my Maryland training incapacitated me to work with colleagues trained in first-rate departments. I co-authored four monographs and articles on the Clothing project, but all but one was peripheral to my research interests. Yet, Greg Stone was a bright colleague from whom I learned a great deal and we managed to exploit some of the findings for articles on urban and stratification issues in *ASR* and the *American Journal of Sociology* (1953, 1957).

I willingly joined the Flint-Beecher Disaster study, which resulted in a monograph and an *ASR* article. While I had to abandon my study in the comparative ecology of El Paso and Ciudad Juarez, the substitute study fitted into my research program on labor-management involvement in community decision-making and resulted in two co-authored monographs and seven articles. Yet, Loomis kept me working on disaster research on the border and Latin America long after I lost enthusiasm for that area.

Charlie probably pressed me harder than others to work on his projects. While the pressure was irksome, I was fond of him because he was bright, charming, and appreciative. Once I got to work, I did not resent the day-to-day demands of the projects. Although Charlie found it difficult to build intimate interpersonal relations (with the possible exception of Al Beegle, his constant co-author), I knew he regarded me as a trusted friend. Not only did he treat me well with respect to promotions and raises, he had more confidence in me than I had in myself. As a generalist, he read widely in sociology and we had stimulating conversations, something I rarely had with most department members.

One night he dropped by my home without first calling. He followed me into the kitchen as I went to fetch him a beer. As I was pouring it into his glass he said, "Bill, if you want to do me a real favor, put in a shot of bourbon." We sat at the kitchen table and drank and talked sociology far, far into the night.

On My Own with the Autoworkers

After Loomis resigned as chair in 1957, I began to plan my own research program. A dozen years had passed since the end of World War II and sociologists were becoming increasingly involved in research abroad with the aid of Fulbright grants. Ever since high school, I had yearned to go abroad and my first opportunity came on my first sabbatical in 1954 when I went to Mexico. In my Lansing research on autoworkers and their union (UAW), I observed the striking political differences between the American and European labor movements, the persistent problem of accounting for American exceptionalism. I went to Mexico because that was what I could afford and it didn't occurred to me to apply for a grant to go elsewhere.

As my second sabbatical approached in 1961, I decided to go to Europe now that funds for international research were becoming increasingly available. Right after World War II, economists began to engage in research on economic development. They were soon joined by political scientists and others to study modernization. Rural sociologists were the first to study the diffusion of technological innovations in underdeveloped societies. Other sociologists later launched studies on development, modernization, and change.

In retrospect, my inability to execute a study of the Mexican labor movement was not tragic. Its labor movement had been absorbed into the ruling party and was dependent on it. Since it was not a free labor movement, I was better off studying European movements associated with multiparty systems. Parisian autoworkers, reputed to be the most radical in Europe, would make an ideal comparison with Lansing's conservative workers. I had decent command of French and could build on Georges Friedmann's (1955) work on the French auto industry.

My Lansing studies led me to reconsider the preconceived ideas on labor that I had earlier shared with most sociologists. We seemed to have been projecting our own values on the working class rather than examining what workers thought and felt. Eli Chinoy's research on the UAW exemplified the distortion. He had studied autoworkers in the Oldsmobile factory in Lansing in 1946, the year before I arrived at Michigan State. His *Automobile Workers and the American Dream* appeared almost a decade later (1955). With an Introduction by David Riesman and acknowledgements to Robert Lynd and Robert Merton, the book received wide acclaim. Its theme was that autoworkers, socialized to believe in the American dream of upward mobility, had become alienated from work by the dehumanizing routines of the assembly line. Unable to realize their aspirations, they were trapped into a pattern of consumerism that their high wages made possible. They had been bribed to trade fulfilling work for an unceasing and unsatisfying chase for material goods. Many dreamed of becoming small businessmen or farmers, but they were fated to endure meaningless work lives until retirement.

Like most liberal sociologists, I had shared Chinoy's views, but the three Lansing studies planted seeds of doubt. The first, with Nosow (1946), sampled a wide range of manual workers. The second (Form and Dansereau 1957) involved a UAW local that included several small plants. In the third, my student Heinz Bloch (1965) interviewed employees of GM's Fisher Body plant. None of the study findings supported Chinoy's conclusions. In all three, only a minority of UAW workers worked on the assembly line and most of them were content with their jobs, the company, and the union. Contrary to popular belief (at least, among sociologists), jobs in the auto industry involved considerable diversity in skills and wages. Most autoworkers took low-skilled jobs when first hired, but if they remained in the industry, they gradually moved to better ones. They intended to remain in their jobs until retirement and rarely reported dreams of becoming small businessmen or farmers. Finally, they had conservative political views and a low sense of class awareness.

A close reading of Chinoy (1955, ch. 3) explained why he had arrived at different conclusions. First, since the union membership roll did not adequately represent Oldsmobile's labor force, he decided to interview a sample of union and non-union workers. The union helped him identify the sixty-two workers he interviewed: nine worked on the assembly line, fifteen were skilled, twenty nonskilled, and eighteen were not engaged in production. Ten were or had been union stewards. All lived in Lansing.

Clearly, the UAW had helped Chinoy to select an unrepresentative sample. My studies consistently showed that half of Lansing's autoworkers lived outside the city. One-sixth of Chinoy's informants were or had been union stewards and he met with them in the union hall. His sample was too small to reliably portray the range of beliefs among any of the sub-groups of workers, and he selected quotations that supported the received wisdom. All four of my subsequent studies of autoworkers based on large representative samples provided contrary evidence for every major point that Chinoy had made.[1]

I wondered whether European scholars, even more ideologically driven than Americans, would have similar biases. I decided to find out. In 1958, I attended the meetings of the International Sociological Association in La Stresa, Italy and made contact with French sociologists there. After meeting with several who were somewhat diffident and surprisingly uninformed about empirical research on the working class, I met Franco Ferraroti and Emilio Pellizi who were working in industrial sociology in Italy. One of their students, Paolo Ammassari, had recently been graduated from the University of Florence and was eager to study in the United States. I asked him to apply at Michigan State and succeeded in getting him funded.

After Paolo arrived, I decided to go to Turin instead of Paris for my comparative study. FIAT had built automobiles in Turin since 1899, as long as Oldsmobile had in Lansing. FIAT employed 100,000 autoworkers and Turin had a strong and continuing radical party and labor union tradition. Dominated by the auto industry, Turin was a closer fit to the domination of the auto industry in Lansing than was Paris. Lansing and Turin unions represented opposite ideologies; Lansing, mildly liberal and Turin, communist and socialist, a good contrast for studying how ideology, technology, and alienation might be related.

Turin also attracted me because my maternal grandfather had been born nearby and reared as a Protestant in a Waldensian valleys near the French border, but all of that was no help when it came to handling Italian. While I understood some kitchen Italian, I could not utter a coherent Italian sentence. Ammassari offered to tutor me, but that didn't work out because he was too preoccupied with mastering English. Although a middle-aged professor in an undergraduate class attracted more attention then than it would now, I enrolled in a beginning course in Italian, did all the assignments and took the examinations. Learning foreign languages comes easily to me, but clearly it came more easily to some of the students. I discretely hid from classmates my tests covered with red-pencilled corrections that Professor Sirianni had made. My Italian accent was beautiful, but I found it difficult to master the many exceptions to rules and the archaic elegance of the language. Yet, by the end of the year, I could carry on a simple and grammatically correct conversation.

Funding my project was relatively easy. I applied for a research Fulbright for the fall of 1961 and I submitted proposals to the Social Science Research Council and the National Science Foundation (NSF). My proposals hypothesized that workers exposed to a common technology in different countries would share a wide range of beliefs, ideology, and behaviors. As a structuralist, I posited that local culture and ideology would have little effect on workers' adaptation to industry. My limited observations in Mexico and in the United States led me to suspect that factory jobs with good wages were highly prized by workers who accommodated quickly to factory discipline.

In my proposal to NSF, I leaned heavily on Inkeles' (1960) article, "Industrial Man," in the *American Journal of Sociology* and Kerr et al. (1960) *Industrialism and Industrial Man*. Stripped of details, Inkeles argued that regardless of culture and level of economic development, factory workers the world over display modern attitudes and that the factory is as much a school for modernity as education. Labor economists Kerr and his associates presented the institutional side of this argument. The spread of industry shatters traditional cultures by bringing about accommodating structures in the form of labor markets, factory organization, labor unions, occupational training, dispute settlement, pay hierarchies, and institutional accommodations in families, neighborhoods, communities, and the nation. This thesis has often been misrepresented. Nowhere did Kerr and his co-workers state that all societies had to converge into a single pattern. On the contrary, they offered several alternatives themselves and their theory permitted others.

I proposed to test the hypotheses systematically in a comparative study that tightly controlled for technology (automobile production), stratification (skill level), and level of economic development (United States and Italy). I predicted that differences between American and Italian autoworkers would be minimal in all major areas: work adjustment, union ideology, and social integration into work group, neighborhood, community, and society. Moreover, variations within both countries would be explained largely by occupational skill level and extent of exposures to complex technology. National politics might be an exception, as work-related factors might have little bearing on political beliefs at that level. I called this approach, the industrialism-convergence hypothesis. Awarded grants from Fulbright, the Social Science Research Council, and NSF, I went to Turin on the first leg of a comparative study that ultimately included 1,000 interviews with autoworkers in four countries.

I kept to my resolution never to speak a word of English to my Italian colleagues. After a first dispiriting presentation in Italian, my language skills improved rapidly. By the time I left, I managed quite well. The most serious obstacle in the endeavor was to gain cooperation from the four unions at FIAT (communist, socialist, liberal, and a company union) which, except for the company union, were mutually antagonistic and hostile toward FIAT management. Management was also skeptical about cooperating with the unions and a foreign scholar. Its experience with scholars was that all of them were critical of FIAT management. After many meetings with all parties, we finally gained enough cooperation to interview 306 employees. Fortunately, I kept a detailed diary of our encounters with seven parties (four unions, FIAT, my university sponsors, and the interviewing team of social workers). I continued the practice of maintaining a diary in the three other research sites (see Form 1976, appendix).

Upon returning from Italy, we launched the Oldsmobile phase of the study, completing the data gathering by 1964. Obtaining cooperation from GM and the UAW involved many meetings with representatives in Lansing and Detroit, Once that was secured, Steven Deutsch was able to interview 249 Olds employees. Although administrative duties impeded my research momentum for the next three years, I was able to broaden the research. In pursuing the analysis of Olds-FIAT comparison, it soon became clear that the two plants and nations were more similar than I had anticipated. A better test of the industrialism-convergence hypothesis required adding cases in less economically developed countries.

Del Miller, who was then expanding his comparative study of community power, had conducted research in Lima, Peru and Cordoba, Argentina. When he described Cordoba's auto plant to me, I decided that it would make a good case for my comparative research. The cornucopia for funding of international research was at its peak then, in the middle 1960s. The Ford Foundation had given several universities sizable grants to administer research proposals in order to reduce the Foundation's burden of processing them. Michigan State had received such a grant. I submitted a short proposal for expanding my research to Cordoba. To my surprise, the funding was approved within a few weeks.

Cordoba turned out to be a good choice. The American Kaiser Auto Corporation had organized IKA (Industrias Kaiser Argentina) in Cordoba and sent IKA the machinery it had used to build the outmoded Rambler. The plant was being run by Argentine managers who had recruited workers, most of whom had no experience with industry. The plant was relatively small but its workers represented the range of skill levels required for the research. In the summer of 1966, I went to Cordoba to help my graduate assistant, Richard Gale, gain cooperation from a reluctant management and labor union, by far the biggest stumbling block in all of my automobile studies. My Spanish was still good enough to get by. Ultimately, we gained the necessary cooperation to select the sample, translate the interview, and train the interviewers. Gale successfully supervised the gathering of 275 interviews.

In the following year, I asked the Ford Foundation's Michigan State committee to fund a study in India. Premier Auto Limited (PAL) had bought machines to build an outmoded FIAT model in Bombay. PAL represented the ideal extreme of a plant whose workers had little or no previous contact with manufacturing in a country at a low level of economic development. The local managers were running a factory that for India had relatively advanced technology. If its workers responded much like those in the United States, Italy, and Argentina, the industrialism-convergence hypotheses would be supported. My graduate assistant, Baldev Sharma, a mature and wise scholar, overcame the resistance to the study and successfully supervised the interviewing of 263 workers.

In 1969, when my administrative tour as department chair was finished, data gathering on the four-nations project was complete. My third sabbatical was due. I spent it trying to make the data on the four nations comparable and trying to overcome endless computer problems. Finally, I was far enough along to write although I didn't complete the project for another two years after moving to the University of Illinois. The articles I wrote in this period were eventually consolidated into *Blue-Collar Stratification* (Form 1976).

The results strongly supported my hypothesis. Workers from rural and urban backgrounds in all countries adapted equally well to industrial and urban life. Country differences were small. The quantity and quality of social interaction in social systems extending from the plant floor to society was relatively high in all four countries. In "Autoworkers and Their Machines," (Form 1973b) I reported that most autoworkers were satisfied with their jobs, machines, and contacts with workmates in and out of the factory. They did not seek to escape factory work and found it preferable to farming. Even assembly workers complained little about job monotony. I tried ten different ways to gauge workers' satisfaction with their job, but none of them confirmed Chinoy's (1955) description of the alienated worker. Contrary to Marxist theories, workers in countries at higher levels of industrialization were less alienated toward their jobs and factory life than workers in less industrialized countries.

Surprisingly, regardless of union ideology or personal politics, workers everywhere preferred job-conscious to political unionism. Contrary to Marxist theory, neither skill nor relation to technology bore on workers' union militancy or preference for political unionism. Skilled workers everywhere dominated union affairs, tending to influence them in a conservative direction. In support of the industrialism hypothesis, workers everywhere were similarly involved in work groups, union, community, and national affairs. Union members everywhere failed to link their activities in the local union to party politics. Nowhere were workers solidary; they were consistently stratified by skill level and participation in social systems inside and outside of the factory. Although the skilled were more cohesive socially than the less skilled everywhere, the more developed the society, the greater the skill differences in pay, system involvement, and politics, contrary to the thesis that working-class solidarity increased with societal industrialization. On the contrary, the working class became more heterogeneous and stratified.

Some scholars suggested that my findings, limited to countries under Western influence, would not hold for Asia. However, when the auto study was later replicated in Korea, the research results there strongly confirmed those of the four-nation study (Form and Bae 1988). An important by-product of the four-nation research was a series of articles on the social organization of social research on which I report later.

Note

1.   In 1991, the editor of a university press asked for my recommendation about republishing Chinoy's book. Although I pointed out the problems, he went ahead. The guarded but positive blurb I wrote upon his invitation was not used.

7

Shop Politics at Michigan State

Introduction

Sociologists have scrutinized fights in business, on the factory floor, in labor unions, government bureaus, and political parties, but they hesitate to write about the politics of their own shops, the departments. Yet the ubiquitous intellectual disputes in the daily life of a department spill over into its social and political life. The sorting out of intellectual and personal differences within the faculty results in cliques or factions with opinions on whom to hire, release or promote, what to require in the curriculum, and many other decisions. Sometimes the divisions result in formal splits, breakups, or even departmental dissolution. Conflict between a department and the university administration may speed faculty turnover and clique realignments. Shifting student enrollments in response to changes in the economy lead to struggles over departmental downsizing or expansion. I do not, probably can not, analyze the politics of my Michigan State shop in detail. I simply report recollections of some events, issues, and conflicts as I perceived them over my twenty-four years there, from assistant professor to department chair, to departure.

When I arrived at Michigan State, department heads, deans, and university administrators made all major decisions. Over time, department and university governance became more responsive to the faculty, although administrators continued to make major decisions. At the department level, much depended on how the head or chair wanted to function. While I was at Michigan State, sociology had four: Charlie Loomis, John Useem, myself, and Bill Faunce in that order. Charlie was a head; the rest of us were chairs. Each of us faced different problems and operated differently. All four wanted to be seen as democratic. Loomis was least likely to reveal his policies or share decision making. With varying degrees of success, Useem, Faunce, and I tried to run a more open department.

Loomis was head from 1944 to 1957, Useem was chair from 1957 to 1965, I from 1965 to 1968. Faunce was still chair when I left in 1971. Loomis's regime was the longest and the one most responsible for departmental growth and development. He was head in the years immediately after World War II when enrollments were exploding in response to the invasion of veterans, an era that lasted to about 1952 when the rate of increase in student number began to ebb. During this era, university and external research funding sources were plentiful and Loomis successfully tapped them, enlarging the faculty and providing it with many research opportunities.

In the 1950s sociology was heavily influenced by social psychology and anthropology. When Loomis arrived, social psychology courses were taught only in Sociology and he wanted to keep it that way. Following the Harvard model, he wanted to build an interdisciplinary department in sociology, anthropology, and social psychology but never consulted the faculty on this strategy. All in-house publications bore a shield, each of whose three corners was named for one of the areas. Loomis apparently thought that the department had enough sociologists but needed more anthropologists and social psychologists. I was unconvinced that we needed an interdisciplinary department. Most graduate students had a feeble grasp of the basics of sociology and were ignorant of a structural-organizational framework for the study of society.

As anthropologists were added to the department, they pressed for more required seminars in the graduate curriculum. Useem, who thought of himself as an anthropologist when he succeeded Loomis as head in 1957, was sympathetic to their growth. The growing number of social psychologists also pressed Loomis to require more training in statistics, which I backed although I was concerned that they rarely used sociological, structural, or organizational materials in their teaching. Meanwhile, the Department of Psychology had been hiring social psychologists who were permitted to teach in Sociology. Over time Psychology added social psychology courses under different rubrics, ending with a more coherent program than Sociology's.

By the time Useem took over in 1957, external research resources had stabilized or even declined relative to enrollment. Sociology was subject to a hiring freeze. Anthropology was pressing to become a separate department. A newly established College of Communications was mostly hiring social psychologists. This period of relative stasis lasted until the postwar baby boomers began to enter college in the mid-sixties.

When I became chair, enrollments were rising rapidly with the entry of the baby boomers. Predictably, legislative lag in funding increased teaching loads, but some progress was made in hiring more faculty. Disagreements among sociologists, anthropologists, and social psychologists decreased somewhat. This prosperous era lasted almost a decade.

Department Politics Under Loomis

Loomis dominated departmental politics for sixteen years. He wanted to operate democratically but was incapable of restraining his urge to control outcomes. For example, when I first arrived at Michigan State, faculty were squeezed three or four to an office on the first floor of Morrill Hall. Overcrowding became even more severe as the department grew. Finally, Sociology was given two more rooms on the first floor and four in the semi-basement. We could now disperse two to an office and also have a needed laboratory. Charlie asked me to bring him a plan as to who should share offices. I demurred on the grounds that the task should go to a more senior person, but he insisted that I do it because, he said, I was the department's sociometric leader and knew the most about informal faculty ties. I did not believe him as I thought that his knowledge of interpersonal relations was limited. Using Charlie's favorite sociometric research tool, I paired people who liked one another and had common interests and asked them to respond to my paring proposals. In general, people preferred office mates who came to Michigan State at about the same time. I gave Charlie my plan, but in the final allocations, he reversed my sociometric pattern by pairing people who had little in common. The only exception was his pairing of me with Al Beegle, his collaborator and my closest friend. We shared a passion for Bach and human ecology and an unspoken empathy for a somewhat parallel religious upbringing. My sociometric plan would have strengthened bonds and alliances in decision-making; Charlie's weakened them. He paired anthropologists and sociologists, new and old arrivals, activists and conformers, conservatives and liberals. Perhaps he hoped to promote interdisciplinary cooperation and social solidarity by minimizing cleavages. If so, he never succeeded.

At one point Charlie hired Edgar Schuler, an old friend and Harvard classmate who had worked with him in the Department of Agriculture in Washington. He was to direct the department's Social Research Service and was given a small budget, responsibility for raising funds, supervising laboratory staff, assigning graduate students to research projects, and guiding the department's research thrust. Schuler assumed that he had independent authority, but Charlie closely monitored all of his decisions. Schuler was so open, honest, and friendly that he quickly developed stronger personal ties to the faculty than did Charlie, which Charlie may have seen as a threat.

I jointly taught a class with Schuler on Public Opinion and Attitude Measurement. His social psychological, atheoretical, pragmatic, unstructured approach almost incapacitated my teaching because I couldn't publicly disagree with him.[1] As my senior by more than a decade, I respected him for his obvious honesty and humility. Schuler was not confrontational but he insisted on his prerogatives as Director of the lab. Yet he failed to satisfy Charlie's expectations for raising research funds and assuming research leadership. The struggle so undermined their long-term friendship that Schuler decided to leave.

Wayne State University in Detroit invited him to head its Sociology Department. Over the years, I had come to know its faculty well, a feisty, contentious, and confrontational crew, pro-active in departmental and university politics, who relished conflict and were highly suspicious of administrators. Ed was tense and deliberate in dealing with others, quiet but firm in his convictions, yet willing to listen and work out compromises. When people became confrontational, he would withdraw without revealing his feelings.

Ed consulted me about taking the job. We had become good friends, playing regularly in the department's informal poker club. Expressing my reservations, I advised him not to go. The Wayne faculty came from ethnic working-class neighborhoods in metropolitan areas. Ed would face a rambunctious crew who would challenge his ability to survive the rough and tumble political climate of department and university. They would look askance at a rural sociologist as head.

Ed didn't share his disagreements with Loomis with anyone, but apparently they sufficed to persuade him to accept the offer. Predictably, the Wayne State faculty found him seclusive, naive, and incapable of enjoying a good fight. The contentious atmosphere gradually wore him down and he left for Washington DC. In 1965, about ten years later, Ed returned to Michigan State, this time in the College of Education. Charlie undoubtedly played a role in getting him back, their friendship renewed.

Indeed, Charlie remembered his friends and was influential in getting them to Michigan State. John Holt, my professor at Maryland, remained in the U.S. State Department for twenty-five years. Charlie played a part in Holt's taking a position in Michigan State's Justin Morrill College to teach international relations.

Charlie gave Al Beegle responsibility of supervising the clerical staff of the Social Research Service but reserved authority to make policy decisions. He continued to bring in millions of research dollars, especially in the medical area where federal, state, and private funds were widely available. Only one of his projects attained his ideal of a group of scholars working together on a project from conception to final publication. Toward the end of his regime four faculty members assisted by eight others published *Community Involvement* (Sower et al. 1957), a study of a community self-survey of health conditions and needs.

Loomis could rely on Al Beegle to work conscientiously to carry rural research projects to completion, including their many joint publications. But most of the huge research grants generated little more than reports to funding agencies. While graduate students who took part in these projects profited from good field training, even the best dissertations rarely generated articles in the major journals.

Loomis took little responsibility for personally supervising research, and pressed the faculty with only modest success to publish the findings. He did not even advise students who worked in his own area of interest: systems theory. John McKinney, who taught in the Department of Social Science, was writing a Ph.D. dissertation in systems theory under Charlie, a work that paralleled Parson's (1937) *Structure of Social Action*. Charlie asked me to direct it, a request that I stoutly resisted because I was not up to it and liked neither the topic nor the research approach. Charlie wouldn't hear of it and McKinney completed his dissertation under my direction. This sort of thing happened to me about six times.

McKinney had published a couple of pieces with Loomis that applied Loomis's categories for analyzing social systems. Loomis brought McKinney to the attention of Robert Merton at Columbia, who saw the young man as a rising star in theory. Merton recommended McKinney as the new chair of sociology at Duke, where he had a strong administrative career.

Selecting a Department Head

Although Sociology was attached to both the College of Arts and Sciences and the College of Agriculture, there was no doubt about Loomis's primary loyalty to Agriculture. When he decided to retire as head in 1957 after serving sixteen years, Loomis quietly backed Ed Moe, a rural extension sociologist, for the position. John Useem was asked to chair a department meeting to assess faculty preferences for chair. Calling a meeting, he asked us to list the most important attributes a chair should have, writing each one on the blackboard. When the list approached twenty, I blurted out, "Hell, John, we don't want a human being, maybe a superman, Jesus Christ."

The meeting never got around to discussing candidates. That was done among friends and cliques. Most faculty felt that Ed Moe had done little research and publishing in sociology. A very decent human being, Ed was virtually unknown outside of rural circles. He could have satisfactorily chaired a small rural department, but by this time more than half of the faculty were non-rural sociologists or anthropologists.

Al Beegle and I, recent full professors since 1953, were the department's most productive scholars but Al made it abundantly clear that under no circumstance would he serve as chair. I emitted similar noises although I might have accepted the position had it been offered. Wilbur Brookover, promoted to professor with Al and me in 1953, was a half dozen years older, a productive educational sociologist with joint appointments in Social Science, Education, and Sociology. A recognized scholar, he owned a farm in Indiana and would work well with the College of Agriculture, which made him a good choice.

Several department members thought John Useem the best choice even though a bizarre rumor had it that the Dean of Agriculture doubted that a Jew would have had enough exposure to rural problems to be able to monitor rural programs, which indicates, whatever else, the gap between the social sciences and Agriculture. John was widely recognized on campus as a dynamic lecturer and an intellectual. He was a full professor, almost seven years older than Beegle and I. He had studied sociology at Harvard and Wisconsin, and had a master's degree in anthropology from Columbia. He had supervised research in Palau while serving in the Pacific theater as a navy commander during World War II and edited several monographs on the area. Loomis had hired him as a rural anthropologist, for when Useem was at South Dakota, he, Pierre

Tangent, and Ruth Underhill Useem (1942) published an article about stratification in a prairie town in the *ASR*.

Several faculty spoke up bluntly, saying that they did not want Moe who was often upstate on extension business and took little part in department life. Brookover was clearly qualified but several considered him to be more identified with Social Science and Education than Sociology. His rural farm background had no appeal for younger faculty who resented Agriculture's role in selecting a new chair. The results of a faculty poll were not made public, but Useem was finally appointed by the dean.

Useem's Regime

Times were unfavorable to Useem's plans for departmental growth. Not only was the administration sluggish in providing positions to meet the department's expanding teaching needs, the anthropologists were restive to have their own department. Archie Haller, trained at Wisconsin, was Charlie's best recent appointment in the rural program. An ardent social psychologist well trained in statistics, Haller launched a research program in individual social mobility, regularly publishing his work in good journals. He and Jay Artis, another rural sociologist interested in methodology, urged Useem to hire Frank Camilleri, who was interested in social psychology (small groups) and had strong quantitative skills. Camilleri, then in the California State system, had previously been at Stanford. Frank said that he had resigned himself to living out his life in a department without a strong graduate program, but he was finally persuaded to come to Michigan State. I was uncertain about hiring him, not because of his strong quantitative orientation, which I liked, but because of his small group-social psychological orientation. I wanted the department to take a more macro-organizational direction.

Frank was a very bright, articulate, and cordial colleague who, though he never became department chair, exerted strong influence on department policy decisions. Soon after arriving, he announced that he would not teach advanced statistics unless students first took more mathematics courses, especially calculus. Haller then encouraged some of the graduate students to enroll in the statistics courses offered by social psychologists in the College of Communications. I was ambivalent about this because I felt that statistics training by social psychologists worked to the disadvantage of students who were learning to think like sociologists.

Haller, seeking to build a campus-wide social psychology program, urged Useem to grant the Communications faculty a joint appointment in Sociology. Communications had recently hired Everett Rogers, a noted rural sociologist who had a million-dollar grant from the Agency for International Development to study the diffusion of agricultural practices in third world countries. Useem consulted a small group in the department to discuss the issue. Although there was strong support for a joint appointment, Loomis and rural sociologist Sheldon Lowry opposed it. The offer was not extended. Neither the meeting nor its outcome was made public. Had I known of it, I would have been conflicted, but probably would have backed Rogers. Haller knew of the meeting, a fact that may have influenced his later decision to leave.

In short, I felt alone in insisting that graduate students be exposed more to a consistent structural framework in their training, including statistics. I used this framework in my upper division course in industrial sociology in which some graduate students enrolled just to learn the perspective. Although I had opposed co-equal status with anthropology, I thought it might work if all students were required to take a seminar in structural sociology in addition to theory, methods, social psychology and two, later three seminars in anthropology and the other required courses.

In 1963 the proposal was accepted without opposition, creating a niche for my seminar in General Social Organization. It focused on how to apply a structural framework to most major sub-areas of the discipline, demography, ecology, criminology, community, social institutions (economy, polity, family, education), social stratification, social movements, and even social psychology and research design. The seminar, intended to give students a coherent sense of sociology as a distinct discipline, became the most influential course I ever taught. However, even today, most students lack this approach to sociology.

I asked Al Beegle to co-teach sessions that stressed the integration of demography and ecology into a sociological structural framework, Jim McKee for a session on social movements, and others, for lectures in their specialties. I dispensed with guest lecturers the following year because, except for Beegle, they were unable to explicate a structural perspective.

Ironically, because they were well aware that the combined curriculum barred their own expansion, two anthropologists urged their students to take my seminar. Richard Adams was dedicated to a materialist ecological-evolutionary perspective and Moreau Maxwell was a hard-nosed physical anthropologist.

Five years later John Useem presided over the breakup of the joint department. Sympathetic to Anthropology (he had a master's degree in it from Columbia), he was at first undecided as to which department he would join. He remained in Sociology. Anthropology had not asked him to chair their department, and he may have sensed that they did not really see him as a card-carrying anthropologist. While graduate students could still get combined sociology-anthropology degree, few chose that option after the split, and the joint program eventually died.

Not a fundraiser, Useem thought that faculty should bring in their own grants. The cornucopia of outside funding was shrinking while teaching demands remained high. Funding an expanding program in Anthropology, the administration kept Sociology at bay. Comparative sociology was becoming a popular area, perhaps in response to anthropology's rising popularity and the nationwide growth of separate anthropology departments.

John wanted to develop a departmental program in comparative research that would include training in the sociology of language (which turned out to be a fad). In 1964, he arranged a retreat at Gull Lake and asked me to prepare a position paper on plans for the department's future. I thought that this would be one of a series for the faculty to consider, but he called for no others. Among other things, I proposed that we establish field stations in Mexico, Quebec, and the United States. We would build exchange relationships with nearby universities and engage in joint research on urban-industrial and rural issues. John thought that was splendid.

That year, he made contact with Karl Schuessler at Indiana University to establish an Institute for Comparative Sociology that would involve Northwestern and Wisconsin and, later, other Midwest institutions. Bill Faunce and I went to Monterrey, Mexico's Pittsburgh, to arrange an exchange program with its university and a field station. I told John I would go to Quebec to do the same but he did not pursue the idea. Neither did he try to get continuous funding for the comparative program even though the university was still funding two research assistantships that Loomis had obtained for Costa Rican graduate students to study in our department while he and other faculty did rural research in Turrialba. I had already done comparative research in Mexico, Italy, and the United States and was participating in the annual meetings of the Mid-West Consortium of Comparative Sociology along with John Useem, Fred Waisenan, and Peter Manning (see Armer and Grimshaw 1973). At the time, no others besides Loomis were launching systematic comparative studies. The comparative program remained largely a paper plan.

Joint appointments were becoming an increasing problem. Under Loomis and Useem, they were an inexpensive way to meet the department's mounting teaching needs. Sociologists in the Basic College, Education, Community Development, Communications, and elsewhere, not wanting to lose disciplinary identification, pressed their units to release them to teach in sociology. Joint appointments, who voted in the department, increased in number until they represented almost half of the faculty. This bothered me, for the department could not then be master of its own fate.

Mostly Administration, 1959-1969

Without thinking much about it, I took on an increasing number of administrative responsibilities, eroding my research progress. In the decade after World War II, organized labor had become a growing political force in Michigan, which the universities recognized. The University of Michigan had established an Institute of Labor and Industrial Relations to sponsor research on labor and help train union members in parliamentary procedure, grievance bargaining, labor history, and contract administration. In order not to appear captured by labor, Michigan's Institute also taught courses in supervisory training and the handling of grievances to personnel in lower management and small business. President John Hanna, who had been using Michigan State's Agricultural Extension Service network (four agents in each county) to generate support for the university's agricultural programs, envisioned building a parallel network in urban areas. He began to involve the university in urban programs including those of organized labor and business.

Hannah asked Charles Killingsworth, a former head of Economics, to organize a Labor and Industrial Relations Center (LIRC) for research and extension. Teaching and conducting research on labor would take place in the departments; extension courses would be taught primarily by LIRC personnel. Killingsworth invited me to become a research associate in the Center. I would have a research assistant, reduced teaching, and access to clerical services. Killingsworth organized the Center, directed it for three or four years, resigned, and was rewarded a research professorship with no departmental duties, a bonanza that stunned the faculty. But we shrugged, concluding that Hannah was probably unsophisticated in academic affairs. With a masters' degree in Poultry

Science, he had married the president's daughter, become secretary of the Board of Trustees, and was then named president. At the same time, however, we well knew that Hannah was an unusually talented administrator who had built a large if not yet a great university.

When Killingsworth resigned, he recommended Jack Stieber, LIRC's associate director of research and planning, as a replacement. Jack was a young, bright, productive Harvard-trained labor economist. Appointed director in 1959, he asked me to serve as associate director. Although inexperienced in administration, Jack ran the Center efficiently and remained a very productive scholar. My tasks were to obtain research funding, supervise the school's reprint series, arrange colloquia, recommend research appointments, make salary recommendations, and prepare the research budget. With the position came a full-time secretary.

I found myself swamped with responsibilities in two departments. I enjoyed my LIRC contacts with economists, historians, and the business and labor extension staffs. I brought in some research funds and co-edited several books based on the lecture series I had arranged, and supervised LIRC's publication series. Nonetheless, I soon found myself in Ed Schuler's position. Stieber monitored my activities so closely that I had little independent authority. While he never was unpleasant, he gave me little latitude in spending the budget, preparing the reprint series, and other duties. When I left on sabbatical in Italy in 1961, I decided to retain the joint appointment with the Center but not to return to administration.

When I returned, Useem, fearing that I was tempted to leave the university, asked what he could do to make me happier. I was not unhappy but my automatic response was that I wanted a position like those in the Experiment Station, nothing more, nothing less: half-time research, half-time teaching, a little research money, and secretarial help. Within a month, I was appointed research professor with a half-time teaching load, some secretarial help, but no research support or summer appointment.

I had little opportunity to enjoy my bonanza. Within the year, Jack Stieber took sabbatical leave and asked me to take over as acting director. I did not want to give up teaching general social organization and chairing the Ph.D. qualifying examinations committee in Sociology. The director's job would be more demanding than chairing an academic department because it involved dealing with labor and business leaders statewide. Progress on the comparative automobile study would be slowed. Yet, I owed the Center something in return for past support, so

I agreed to fill in for Jack. I discovered that with the authority to act, I enjoyed administration.

The Center's autonomy was short lived. the *Detroit Free Press* exposed a labor extension specialist at the University of Michigan's Industrial Relations Institute who was advocating a Marxist line in his classes. The business community charged the Institute with a labor and radical bias, demanding that the instructor be fired, and the Institute dismantled. Sensing the possibility of a similar attack at Michigan State, President Hannah recommended that LIRC be shifted from the provost's office to the College of Social Science, asked to develop a graduate teaching program, widen its extension activities, and be renamed School of Labor and Industrial Relations (SLIR). I warned the dean, without much support from colleagues, that within a few years, SLIR would develop separate degrees, hire its own teaching and research faculty, and loosen departmental ties, all of which happened even more rapidly than I predicted.

In 1965, I received the Distinguished Professor Award, with a check of $2,000. When it was announced to the department, Frank Camilleri said, "Great, now you can invite us to a nice dinner." I said, "You're on." Faculty and spouses gathered that weekend at a downtown restaurant for dinner and drinks. On the next day at dinner, I observed that there was still award money left over after the departmental affair. Daughter Cathy, then seventeen, cheered, "That's great. Let's get out of the cold and go to Puerto Rico for spring break." We did but, as I expected, the award money fell far short of the cost of the vacation. Nonetheless, 1965 was to be the high point of my academic life at Michigan State.

It began in 1964 when John Useem announced he would resign as chair. Realizing that I might be nominated to succeed him, I announced at once that I would not serve under any circumstance. I had served as an administrator for three years in SLIR and wanted to concentrate on my auto study. Al Beegle would have been the obvious choice because he had an exemplary research record, was a splendid teacher, was in the Experiment Station, and had the full confidence of all faculty. But Al was as adamant in refusing to run as I. I decided to throw my support to Jay Artis, a rural sociologist who taught methodology and was respected academically. Although his research record was slim, he had the confidence of the dean of Social Science, had administrative experience as assistant dean, and still held an appointment in the Experiment Station.

Louis McQuitty, dean of Social Science, announced that no one could withdraw from consideration as department chair. He would interview everyone and reserved the right to persuade the best candidate to accept. Al Beegle would never accept. I talked things over with Jay, who said he would accept were an offer made. If the dean chose me, I would refuse and support Jay, the position I took in my interview with him. Eventually, McQuitty called a department meeting to announce his decision. He talked on and on and I impatiently asked him to tell us his choice. He continued to speak in vagaries. Again I interrupted, asking for his decision. He looked at me squarely and said, "Well, Bill, I've been waiting for an opportune time to announce that you are the department's unanimous choice." Everyone applauded and left the room leaving me breathing hard, staring at McQuitty.

The next day I met with him and bluntly told him I would not accept and that he should appoint Jay. McQuitty knew I was serious because, asked to be a candidate for his position as dean, I had refused to be considered. He simply said, "Bill, I have already offered Jay the position of associate dean of the college and he has accepted. I have no choice but you." My anger surged because I thought that Jay, a good friend, had not leveled with me.

Launching Programs

I needed time to think things over. Things were not going well at home. I finally decided to tell McQuitty that I would be chair for three years if he would reduce the number of part-time faculty, provide several new appointments, and build research laboratories. McQuitty promised that he would to do all he could to help build a strong department and he expected me to serve a full five-year term. As I left, I said, "Three years!" He replied, "Come on Bill, you'll like the job and you'll change your mind."

I disliked the separation of the rural sociologists from the rest of the department. The rural group had offices and a small research room in a corner of the fourth floor of Berkey Hall, its own duplicating equipment, secretaries, and control of research funds and graduate assistants. And, of course, each member of the as yet all male department had his own research budget from Agriculture plus equipment and travel funds. Over the years, their salaries had been reduced so that they were in fact underpaid for an eleven-month appointment. Ideally, their budget should part of the department's and the chair should be able to shift people on and off the Experiment Station lines, depending on individual ability to contribute to the research program.

As chair, the first thing I did was to consolidate all secretarial services, equipment, and supplies, erasing differential accessibility, and assigning one person to keep track of expenses. I distributed the savings as seed money for research, which increased the output of the few productive faculty. Gradually the salaries of the rural staff were raised to better reflect eleven-month appointments. And I got rid of incompetent secretaries.

Soon after I became chair, Frank Camilleri proposed that the department build a strong program in small group research like Stanford's. He also pushed for strengthening training in statistics, but still would not teach advanced statistics to poorly prepared students. They should take courses in the mathematics department to qualify for his courses. As the department did not approve of this, some students sought advanced statistics training in other departments.

Frank claimed the department needed two small group laboratories to be productive. Although not keen about this research area, I obtained funds from the dean to build labs according to Camilleri's specifications. Then the department needed well-trained faculty, preferably from Stanford. We eventually hired three. First was Tom Connor, a new Stanford Ph.D. who earned the distinction of being the department's sole Republican. Tom and Frank played chess for an hour or so at lunchtime in Frank's office. Tom taught statistics and social psychology, but did little small group research.

Bo Anderson, an assistant professor at Stanford, had published some things, and Frank considered him the most promising candidate on the market. We found that Bo was legally blind, scarcely able to see people within a few feet of him. Nonetheless he created a favorable impression on the social psychologists and we offered him an associate professorship with tenure. To assure that he would come, Frank urged me to offer him a full professorship. Overstepping my prerogatives as chair, I did so, which several of the faculty resented. Showing little interest in small group research, Anderson became preoccupied with social stratification and problems of equity. Whatever his specialty, he was somewhat less visible than we had hoped as his work appeared mostly in Swedish outlets.

Finally, Frank urged us to hire Hans Lee, a young Stanford Ph.D. with strong mathematics and computer skills. Bright and cheerful, Hans was disorganized and somewhat of a misfit in academia. He juggled numbers dexterously but evinced much less interest in teaching and research than we had hoped.

Frank argued that his own and the department's productivity was low because the teaching load was too high. Over the years the load had been reduced from four to two courses a quarter. Frank complained that that still was too high. As at Stanford, it should be one five-hour course per quarter. He raised his courses' credits, almost achieving his goal. Although Frank did not publish often, he insisted that its quality was so high that it was more widely recognized than the work of more productive faculty. His occasional articles were indeed excellent.

My major concern as chair was to recruit talented faculty. In a booming job market it was not easy to attract the most able and motivated candidates to a department that seemed perhaps overly dominated by the College of Agriculture. Recruiting was made more difficult or at least less pleasant by the fact that one faculty member relentlessly bombarded candidates with tough questions that too often left them incoherent or silent. In my memory, only two candidates sustained a defense stout enough to silence their tormenter. Herbert Karp from Brown University would not be cowed, snapping back until the questioning eased up. Philip Marcus, then at the University of Michigan, adroitly manoeuvered the faculty member into areas where he had little substantive knowledge. After I discussed matters with the provoker, he agreed to ease up on candidates and did so to an extent. Still, the quality of our appointments did not improve appreciably.

I almost succeeded in building a program in human ecology along the lines proposed in Duncan's POET model, integrating the study of *P*opulation, *O*rganization, *E*nvironment, and *T*echnology. I reasoned that if there was anything distinctive about rural sociology, it dealt or should deal with the physical *environment* (land) as a major variable. Al Beegle was an expert on *population*, rural ecology and sociology. The industrial sociologists, Bill Faunce and myself, who emphasized the importance of *technology* in social organization, could apply our expertise. Phil Marcus, Faunce, I and others studied social *organization*. We should be able to merge the complementary interests of demographers, human ecologists, industrial sociologists, and students of social organization, thus erasing barriers between rural and general sociology.

The department needed ecologists interested in *both* urban and rural social organization. We hired four. Harvey Choldin, trained in demography and urban sociology at Chicago, was currently studying rural development in Bangladesh. We hired him in the Experiment Station sight unseen. We also convinced Herb Karp, broadly trained in human ecology at Brown, to accept an Experiment Station appointment. Kevin Kelly, trained at the University of Washington, wrote a dissertation on urban ecology, and Peter Manning from Duke had studied it under Joel Smith.

Karp and Kelly soon found common interests and merged their dissertations into a book. But Herb developed cancer of the kidneys and soon died, ending a very promising career. Kelly lost his research momentum, taught criminology, and ceased doing urban research. Choldin's interest in rural development and population waned as he turned increasingly toward urban sociology, finally accepting an appointment at the University of Illinois in Urbana-Champaign. Manning's interest in urban sociology was temporary and he accepted a joint appointment in the medical school, concentrating entirely on symbolic interaction and qualitative analysis.

I was determined to launch an ecology laboratory, equipped with drawing boards, calculators, and Census materials. Adjacent to the departmental library, it would become the research center of the department. Michigan State had at that time a centralized computer facility to which John Gullahorn and Hans Lee had joint appointments. Yet, it was difficult to penetrate the computer bureaucracy and get data analysis done quickly. I proposed that the department hire computer expert Frank Sim, one of the department's doctoral products, and make him head of the lab and liaison between faculty and computer center. John Gullahorn resisted the idea and said in a public meeting, "Bill, you only want Frank to do your computer shit work." In truth, I had spent a fruitless year with a competent assistant trying to get complex tables from the computer laboratory. I had hoped for strong departmental support for my program but only Al Beegle provided it. Most of the faculty, making no heavy demands on the computer laboratory, did not share my vision of a focused departmental research program. The POET research program collapsed for lack of support and my failure to pursue it with more vigor and imagination.

The quality of graduate training during the 1960s was good and student morale was high. They were required to complete a core curriculum before taking a qualifying examination in theory, methodology (research design and the logic of inquiry), social psychology, and social organization. The qualifying examinations were tough because they required students to integrate the four areas. Seminars were well taught and students worked hard. Occasionally, I would drop by the department on Saturday night and find graduate students at work in the small but excellent departmental library. On Monday mornings, I accosted some students and remonstrated them gently on their absence. They were amused at my teasing. Later, I learned that some of them referred to me as "Uncle Bill." Years later, when I met students of that era at ASA meetings, they told me that they felt better trained than their colleagues.

An unusual administrative arrangement at Michigan State made the sociology department a member of three colleges, Agriculture, Medicine, and Social Science with joint faculty appointments in each. The arrangement was costly in administrative time. Most of the various steps in recruitment and promotion had to be agreed to by an extra-departmental hierarchy and in addition the chair was obliged to attend dean's meetings in three colleges.

At the time, Peter Manning, who already had a very promising research record, held the department's only joint appointment in medicine, whose dean actually welcomed social science input. Medicine strongly supported the appointment financially and required Peter to teach only one seminar a year jointly with a member of the medical faculty. He was given funds for a full-time secretary, an equipment budget, and sizable research funding. He fully equipped his office in the first year and could scarcely spend his equipment budget the second year. The department relieved him of this burden. Research funds helped him build a substantial library. He hired graduate research assistants and kept his secretary busy with routine research tasks. With more resources than even Experiment Station faculty, he was the envy of everyone.

The joint appointments made for a very uneven ratio of benefits across the department. Full-time faculty taught full loads for nine months furnished only with a typewriter, paper, mailing privileges, some clerical help, and small sums to attend professional meetings. Faculty in Agricultural Extension taught nothing on campus and those in the Experiment Station taught half time during the academic year and were on full-time research in the summers. They received research funding as well as full expenses for professional meetings. The sole member in the College of Medicine had it best: less teaching, better funding for equipment and research, a secretary, and full travel expenses.

Apparently, the dean of Agriculture and the rural sociologists must have decided that I was an acceptable chair of sociology. I had authored four Experiment Station Bulletins and had been on its payroll one summer. I had been at Michigan State for eighteen years and knew the system so well that I truly had no new experiences as chair, except for dealing with Agriculture. In the dean's first meeting with department chairs, I made sure to arrive on time at 8:00 A.M. I entered the meeting room as the campus bell tower tolled eight. All other department chairs were already seated at the table and the dean was greeting them, "Good morning." Silence until I was seated. The meeting proceeded with a series of announcements. No policy issues were raised and no questions were asked. Then we were dismissed. In contrast, in meetings of the Social Science College, the dean was constantly challenged to amplify and justify his position.

Every four or five years, a reviewer from the Department of Agriculture in Washington appeared on campus to review the work of Experiment Station and Extension Division personnel. Faculty were asked to submit their reports beforehand and answer the reviewer's questions at a meeting. One reviewer was a biologist who knew little or no social science. His task was to report on the progress individual faculty members had made on their five-year plans. No special knowledge was required to conclude that some of our faculty who had made little or no progress had mastered a marvelously obfuscatory style to answer the inspector's questions. The reviewer neither met with me to evaluate individual achievement nor did I ever see his reports to the dean or the Department of Agriculture.

In my reports to the dean, I recommended that he cease supporting unproductive faculty. This meant that the department would have to assume their salaries and increase their teaching loads. In one case, this meant giving a very poor teacher more courses to teach. But the dean never released anyone. I put steady pressure on the worst offender to publish, but to no avail. He maintained the facade of an active scholar engaged in cutting-edge research in organizations. His office contained so many files that there was hardly room for a visitor to sit. The less productive the professor, the greater the physical display of research. When he retired, I commented that we wouldn't miss him; he retired the first day he arrived on campus, thirty years ago.

My productivity suffered during my tenure as chair, publication slowed to a trickle although I managed to expand the comparative auto study to include Argentina and India. In the first faculty meeting in my third year as chair, I announced my resignation effective July 1968. William Faunce, trained as an industrial sociologist at Wayne State, had a productive research record and was then serving as Associate

Director of the School of Labor and Industrial Relations in the position I had vacated. I considered him the best candidate for chair to maintain pressure to improve the department's research record. Inappropriately, I revealed my feelings to others. The next year was my sabbatical and I had the sense not to appear at departmental meetings or affairs. Two years later, I retired from Michigan State after 24 years of service.

Summing Up

The year after I returned from my Italian sabbatical in 1962, just as we were completing the interviewing of Olds autoworkers, I was pressed to be acting Director of the Labor and Industrial Relations Center. Then I chaired sociology for three years. I took the job too seriously, not delegating enough responsibility. I was irked by faculty who continually allowed students to delay fulfilling departmental requirements, so I monitored all student programs. I continued to teach and supervise graduate qualifying examinations. Recruiting also took much time as did attending deans' meetings in three colleges. I extended field research on the automobile project to Argentina and India, but got little writing done. After my last year as chair, a sabbatical leave was due. The dean did not want a second term and I was pressed to succeed him. While I enjoyed administration, it distracted me too much from my research. When the provost called me to consider the position, I flatly refused. My marriage was collapsing and I needed to turn to research and writing, my refuge.

I was chair in prosperous times and the dean lived up to his promises. My term began with fifteen full-time faculty equivalents and ended with 27.5. Yet, most programs that I initiated were not realized. I partly succeeded in erasing distinctions between the rural and other segments of the department. I was able to encourage research by scrounging money from the dean and from the department budget to help the most productive researchers.

Yet, I did not attain my main goal of significantly improving faculty research productivity nor, with a few exceptions, did I succeed in hiring productive faculty. The launching of the small group laboratories had only modest results and I failed to establish a program and laboratory in human ecology along the lines of the POET model. I should have tried harder to fund it and started pilot research projects. The comparative research program improved marginally and I brought in more research fellowships from the U.S. Department of Labor than anyone nationwide save for John Dunlop at Harvard. At SLIR, I brought in research money, organized speaker series, and edited two books. I stayed on at Michigan State despite attractive offers from Penn State and Wisconsin. Michigan State had treated me well and I thought, perhaps mistakenly, that moving would not significantly improve the quality of my ideas or my productivity.

Asked what I had achieved as chair, I jokingly said that I was the only one of three department chairs able to rid the department of a particularly incompetent secretary who had Civil Service status. A fawning person, she had tried to ingratiate herself to faculty by devising special favors. Gaining access to my office before I arrived on my birthday, she left a birthday card and two glazed doughnuts on my desk. I hate doughnuts. I began a search to transfer her, finally locating an old codger who wanted a secretary to do his shopping and attend to his personal needs. They were made for each other.

Bill Faunce became chair in 1968, the year of my sabbatical leave. I resolved not to engage in departmental affairs to give him room to establish himself. The festering Vietnam War was ushering a period of student unrest, activist campus politics, and the hiring of professors who aimed to develop a curriculum in political activism. Campus disturbances were mild at Michigan State compared to those in other Big Ten universities. I disapproved of the war from its inception, but I could not stomach student deification of Mao and crude Marxist sloganizing. The following year, the core curriculum for the qualifying examinations that had served students so well was disestablished, permitting another curriculum in Social Problems and Change (read political activism). Useem, Faunce, Waisanen, and Bo Anderson, all of whom had research experience abroad, attempted to revitalize the comparative program. The department hired Barrie Thorne to teach the sociology of language, and planned a field station in the Upper Peninsula where Fred Waisanen had contact with various ethnic groups. But Thorne became more interested in gender studies and the field station never materialized.

My last two years at Michigan State were difficult. My marriage had broken up and with it, my involvement in departmental social life. I was rarely invited to social gatherings. Three colleagues invited me to their homes for dinner with their families. On one occasion, I was invited to dinner with four other divorced or widowed men. Three of my colleagues invited to bowl with them weekly, but I soon tired of that. Phil Marcus, Sig Nosow, and the Useems were gracious and supportive.

Just before I left for Illinois, I attended a department party in my honor. I insisted on an ordinary party with only the briefest ceremony. Bill Faunce expressed the department's gratitude and gave me a globe as a parting gift. The day before I left the shop, I cleared my office and discovered that I had directed forty-three dissertations and theses in twenty-four years, but only a few resulted in publications in visible journals.

Note

1.   My experience with Dr. Hoffer, a rural sociologist and the department's most senior member, was more painful. Hoffer had isolated himself from general sociology for many years. Loomis asked us to team-teach a graduate seminar in social psychology. Sitting at the end of a long table, Hoffer recited what he remembered about the field half a century ago. I made a few comments; he nodded agreement. Loomis probably expected me to take leadership but that would have violated my sense of propriety in dealing with Dr. Hoffer, who addressed me as "Form."

8

Confronting Ideologies

Introduction

In 1971 Joan Huber and I were married. She had been teaching at Notre Dame for four years and liked it. We wanted to be together. Bill Liu, chair at Notre Dame, offered me a named chair, but we preferred a university new to both of us. Charlie Loomis had told Fritz Fliegel, chair of Sociology at the University of Illinois at Urbana, that we were available. Fritz had formerly chaired Rural Sociology. When asked to chair Sociology because its internal turmoil prevented consensus on a new chair, like a good marine (his words) he responded to the request as if it were an order, agreeing to serve for a time at least. Fritz invited us for interviews.

Joan had written several things with Charlie that he considered first rate. Charlie told Fliegel, "She's as good as he is and you ought to hire them both." Bernie Karsh, an old friend whom I had tried to hire at Michigan State, held a joint appointment in Sociology and the Institute of Labor and Industrial Relations (ILIR). He urged Fliegel and Melvin Rothbaum, then the director of the Institute, to hire me. Joan was offered a position when she went for an interview. My interview was a formality. I visited briefly with Fritz, lunched with four faculty, two from each unit, and was offered a joint appointment.

Illinois: First Impressions

We moved to Champaign-Urbana in June and settled in. The campus was less attractive than Michigan State's, spreading as it did into two cities with the boundary line running through the campus. Yet, I immediately sensed the university's strong tradition of scholarship. The library was magnificent, second only to Berkeley among state universities. The computer facilities were excellent; all my computer problems were solved quickly, a relief after struggling for a year at Michigan State's computer and getting only a small useable output. Although sciences and engineering dominated the university, the quality of the social science departments was above those at Michigan State. Psychology was outstanding. ILIR's faculty was second only to that of Cornell, and ILIR's excellent library just fifteen paces from my office. Anthropology and Political Science were good. Illinois' International Studies programs were more highly developed than Michigan State's, and the Comparative Research section regularly funded faculty research. Sociology had formal links to the university's Survey Research Center, which funded half-time faculty positions in Sociology and an annual state-wide survey. Illinois took quality research seriously and rewarded it. I was eager to go to work.

My first seminar in Sociology was on community power and decision making. Having taught it a number of times, I expected the twenty graduate students to perform better than those at Michigan State. To my surprise, they worked less hard yet expected A's. Participation and term papers were generally weak. I gave a half of the students a grade of C, in effect, a failing grade. While I anticipated an unfavorable reception, even those who received B's protested that I undervalued their work. Grading standards had been relaxed since the early student protests of the Vietnam War. (One faculty member reported giving many A's in a large introductory course because it helped students by increasing their self-esteem.) Within the year most of the students who performed poorly dropped the program. I had always assumed that students regarded me as a decent guy but for a few years they defined me as a tough SOB. No one chose me to direct their work. Eventually, this changed.

In the early 1970s, student protests over the Vietnam became nationwide. In 1971 when Nixon ordered the armed forces to invade Laos and mine North Vietnamese ports, Illinois students trashed several stores near campus. The camera store of my neighbor who opposed the war and supported the students was trashed a second time. With military installations not far away, the trashing of local stores seemed senseless symbolic gestures.

One evening when Joan and I hosted faculty and students at our home for a colloquium, two faculty members explained to students how best to vandalize property and distract the police. Although eager for the armed forces to withdraw from Vietnam, I could not stomach the inability of some faculty to separate science and politics in dealing with students. Departmental cleavage on this issue had far-reaching consequences in department life (see below). By contrast, ILIR students, serious and hardworking, did not engage in disruptive political activism, perhaps typical of students planning to work for corporations, government, and organized labor.

I was not fully aware at the time that the discipline was entering a difficult era. Social science research funding, especially in sociology, was beginning to decline as was the ability of the discipline to attract highly qualified students. Increasingly, they entered occupations that offered more opportunity, such as business and law. Sociology was also attracting students who thought it should advance political reform over science. As the job market for Ph.D.s declined, the number of graduate students recruited remained constant, perhaps to cut costs of undergraduate teaching. These trends eroded the discipline and the professional organizations for years.

Income and Ideology

Despite these disturbing trends, the first years at Illinois were productive in advancing two research projects, one with Joan and the other the continuing four-nation automobile study. Joan had written a dazzling dissertation on stratification in Muskegon, Michigan. We had already published an article or two on it. I set the auto study aside for a year to help finish *Income and Ideology* (Huber and Form 1973).

While most studies of stratification beliefs (ideology), based on probability samples, had too few rich, poor, or minority respondents to justify analysis, thereby obscuring variation from middle-class views, we designed a community study that overcame this problem to an extent. We oversampled rich, poor, and blacks to enable us to compare their beliefs with those of middle-strata whites. All statements were worded in either-or form to avoid response bias (Campbell et al., 1960: 510-15). Respondents were asked, for example, whether young people of high ability do or do not have fairly equal opportunity to attend college, and whether young people whose parents are poor are or are not just as likely to go in college as those whose families can help them. In the political arena, we asked which of three descriptions of how government functions best fit the facts: Riesman's (1953) model of pluralism,

Mills's (1956) power elite model (big business, military, top government officials), and a Marxist model positing that big business makes all major decisions. Respondents also ranked twelve major interest groups for their influence on Congress.

We found that income and racial strata clearly differ in their stratification beliefs. Upper strata tended to endorse the pluralism model; lower strata, the elite or business dominance models. Privileged respondents tended to explain success as a result of merit, which legitimizes privileged status. Blacks especially tended to endorse structural explanations of mobility and stratification. Later, other scholars who followed this line of investigation confirmed that stratification ideologies vary by income and even more by race. While these findings are now routinely accepted, they were novel when we first published them.

The Four-Nation Study and Its Dissenters

I worked on the comparative study of automobile workers for another three years, writing a dozen articles later consolidated along with new material into *Blue-Collar Stratification* (1976). The study had two major consequences, an extended debate on its main findings and an unanticipated methodological contribution on comparative research. I comment on each in turn.

Study findings strongly supported the industrialism-convergence theory: workers from rural and urban backgrounds in countries varying in economic development adapt well to urban life and industrial discipline, with small differences by country. The quantity and quality of interaction in social systems from the plant floor to neighborhood, community, and society was relatively high in all four countries. A myth-smashing article, "Auto Workers and Their Machines," reported that most auto workers were satisfied with their jobs, machines, and contacts with workmates in and out of the factory (Form 1973). They did not seek to escape factory work and preferred it to farm work. Even assembly workers complained little about job monotony. I tried ten different ways to gauge job satisfaction. Not one confirmed Chinoy's (1955) description of the alienated worker. Contrary to Marxist and other theories, workers in the more industrialized countries were not more dissatisfied with their jobs and factory life.

Surprisingly, regardless of union ideology or personal politics, workers everywhere preferred job-conscious to political unionism. Contrary to Marxist theory, neither skill nor relation to technology affected the level of union militancy or preference for political unionism. Regardless of level of development, skilled workers in all countries dominated union affairs and tended to exert a conservative influence on them. In support of the industrialism-convergence hypothesis, workers everywhere became similarly involved in work groups, union, community, and national affairs. Nowhere did union members link official union political ideology to their own political behavior.

Autoworkers everywhere were a heterogeneous lot, stratified by skill level and the extent of social system participation inside and outside the factory. Although the skilled everywhere were the most socially cohesive, the more industrially advanced the society, the greater was the gap between them and the less skilled in pay, system involvement, and politics, a finding directly contrary to Marxist theory of increasing class proletarianization and solidarity. In sum, industrialization increasingly stratified the working class.

Stratification of the Working Class: First Phase

The gist of these findings appeared earlier in an *ASR* article, "The Internal Stratification of the Working Class: System Involvements of Auto Workers in Four Countries" (Form 1973a). I did not then know that the next two decades would be devoted to defending and extending the position that industrialization stratified rather than homogenized the working class, as Marxists claimed.

First to object were Petras and Rhodes (1974) who charged that I failed to consider the political context of autoworkers in Argentina who, soon after my fieldwork, displayed solidarity in a series of protests against a conservative regime. They cited two Argentine studies documenting autoworkers' solidarity in political demonstrations and general strikes and also singled out a few findings in my eleven tables that did not support the association of industrialization with working-class stratification.

In reply, I quoted a section from my article that Petras and Rhodes ignored: namely, that the skilled had provided leadership in aligning with the Peronista unions that were demanding recognition in the political system, that the unskilled were politically isolated, and that the socialist-communist wings of the Peronista movement lacked influence. Fortunately, the magnificent Illinois library had both of the Argentine volumes that Petras and Rhodes had cited and both volumes supported my position. The first author reported that the earliest political outbreak was backed by a broad spectrum of manual *and* white-collar groups; that union participants were *not* among the most combative, and that they were severely *divided* by ideology. The second author supported my contention that most Cordoba union members wanted a *traditional* union movement that rejected the Marxist political line. Moreover, the Argentine labor movement as a whole was torn by class, ideological, and regional conflicts. The Peronista right wingers seemed to be strongest because they had ousted a left-wing Peronista governor. Finally, I commented that although my critics rejected survey research methods, they scrutinized my data to find two non-supportive pieces of evidence, ignoring 200 pieces that did.

The next year, 1974, Kenneth Spenner, then a graduate student at the University of Wisconsin, informed me that he had used my *ASR* data for a seminar paper in Professor Robert Hauser's seminar on loglinear methods. Spenner's methods suggested that my hypothesis might not hold. As the data were insufficient to lead to reliable conclusions, could I provide more data? This task took two or three days, but I sent him all the data he requested. In 1975 Morris Zelditch, editor of *ASR*, sent me proofs of Spenner's article "The Internal Stratification of the Working Class: A Reanalysis," and invited me to comment.

I was irked because Spenner did not tell me he had sent his paper to *ASR*. I would have gladly collaborated with him on a reanalysis of my data. His paper held that my main proposition (increasingly differentiated social involvement by skill level) was not supported; loglinear models showed that level of industrialization was the more powerful explanatory variable.

Since my statistical training was limited, I had to learn loglinear methods from Ken Land and Fred Pampel to comment on Spenner's paper. I found that he had misinterpreted some of his findings because he was unfamiliar with the logic of comparative research, nor was he knowledgeable of the societal context of the four nations needed to interpret the findings. He had also ignored some of the data I had given him that supported my hypotheses. The larger data set clearly supported my hypothesis. Then Zelditch gave Spenner the opportunity to respond to my comment in a subsequent issue, asking that I provide Spenner with the additional data he needed to do this. Moreover, I was not permitted to respond to Spenner's comment because he authored the original *ASR* paper. This struck me as unfair, given that I had provided the data for both critiques. I objected strongly and Zelditch finally relented with the proviso that this exchange would be final.

As often happens, the second exchange did little to change our positions. Spenner (1976) analyzed the larger data set and introduced new statistical techniques to interpret the findings. Again, I was pressed to learn the new techniques and scrutinize their applicability. The exchange became even more complex when we analyzed results from both my random and purposive samples (I had oversampled skilled workers to get a number large enough for statistical analysis).

Again, I found that Spenner had analyzed only some of the data that I had given him, but even there the majority of his findings supported my skill-industrialization hypothesis. When I analyzed the purposive sample, a majority of the tests supported my hypotheses (Form 1976). Again, Spenner's unfamiliarity with the logic of comparative analysis led him to erroneous judgments on where significant effects should and should *not* be expected. Finally, I discovered that his confidence in Goodman's techniques was equivocal, given Goodman's assumptions that Spenner had not considered. In sum, Spenner was a talented critic who made me expand my statistical knowledge, very useful in later research.

The Sociology of Social Research

Thumbing through my research diary on FIAT soon after returning from Italy, I was struck by the differences in my American, Italian, and Mexican fieldwork experiences. I began to compare systematically the problems confronted in each nation to see what could be learned. In the immediate post-World War II era, like many researchers, I gathered many of my own data, largely by survey research. For example, in our studies of neighborhood integration in Lansing, we knocked on doors and asked permission for an interview. While I did not enjoy doing this, turn-downs were relatively infrequent and rapport was quickly established. But when I tried to gain research access to organizations like Oldsmobile, a labor union (UAW), a government bureau (State Police), or a disaster organization (Red Cross), I encountered varying levels of resistance and refusals. Research methods texts provided few guideposts on how to gain access into different kinds of organization and field situations.

Obtaining interviews from top business leaders in El Paso on the Border Project had been especially trying because, I thought, we lacked local sponsors to vouch for us. Being professors from a Midwestern university doing research funded by the Carnegie Foundation carried little weight in Texas. Also, using the same techniques to get research cooperation from top officials in parallel positions on both sides of the border did not work, forcing us to reconsider and revise our approach to respondents. Matters came to a head when we tried to arrange interview appointments in Mexico. Respondents preferred late afternoon, about our suppertime. Even so, when we arrived, we often had to wait an hour or two, never the case in El Paso.

This national difference was trivial compared to those encountered later. We were on the border to learn about national institutional and cultural differences, yet we needed that knowledge beforehand to gain informant cooperation. We had to improvise both in Texas where we had no social capital or sponsor as well as in Mexico where we lacked both sponsorship and knowledge of how to behave in research situations.

In El Paso, we gradually learned that obtaining an interview in one community sector (government) gave us no social capital to get an interview in another sector (business). Gaining rapport with university professors was easy, but that did not help us get cooperation from government or business leaders who didn't know one another. Cooperation of the Executive Director of the Chamber of Commerce opened no doors to most of the business elite we wanted to interview. Cooperation from one business executive did not necessarily make it easier to gain cooperation from others.

In Ciudad Juarez, the opposite was true both in business and government. When we finally earned the confidence of the President of the Chamber of Commerce, access to individual business executives was easy. The President gave us his calling card with a handwritten note: "Please help these professors." That was enough. The same pattern held in the governmental sector. In El Paso, interviewees responded cautiously to our questions and we promised them anonymity, a standard practice. Moreover, they answered each question without elaborating. The reverse held in Ciudad Juarez. Respondents quickly grasped the intent of the questions and freely elaborated on related areas, which resulted in a free flowing conversation. In El Paso, some business executives, government officials, and party officials had worked with one another in community projects; in Ciudad Juarez, inter-institutional contacts were almost non-existent. Thus, in the process of gaining access to informants, we learned a great deal about the institutions and culture of the two cities and how to adapt our research strategy to those differences (D'Antonio and Form 1965, appendix).

On my Italian sabbatical in 1961, research access was even more complex and difficult. Contrary to my American experiences, my first interview in the ideologically charged Italian culture revealed that I could not avoid answering questions about my own political views when I asked informants about theirs. I could gain nuanced information only by engaging in an exchange. Arguing gently with respondents elicited more candid and fuller responses than simply asking questions ad seriatim. When I informed respondents about the kinds of information I was getting about their organizations from other interviews, I received fuller and more contextualized information. Moreover, Paolo Ammassari, my research assistant and I discovered that we had to assume that when we held an interview with one respondent, it might well be communicated to others we had interviewed or might eventually interview. Thus, we found that an informal communications network existed among FIAT's four competing unions. Moreover, management had informants in all four unions. With moles so endemic, we were obliged to visit all unions within a week after we visited any of them. Failure to do so risked being denied further access and information.

Getting these mutually antagonistic groups in labor and management to cooperate in the research enterprise called for bargaining, enhanced sponsorship, intervention by influential parties, and even threats. As in the case of the border research, the lessons learned from gaining research access provided important data on the subject of our research. In short, the rules of investigation I had been taught had to be violated both in Mexico and Italy.

In my first article on the auto workers (1963), I tried to systematize what I had learned about gaining research access in Turin. The process was described as building a social system or network that included researchers, sponsors (university and government), hosts (four unions and FIAT management), and external groups (municipal bureaus). Building the system was analyzed as a pattern of bargaining within and among the groups, a system of exchanges that finally produced a fragile structure that permitted the research to go forward.

Returning to Lansing to launch the Olds phase of the comparative study, I needed the cooperation of both GM and the UAW. Failing three times earlier to bring it about, I was forced to change the research topic each time. Now I had to have their cooperation or abandon the comparative study. Applying some lessons from the FIAT experience, I was partially successful. When I gained access to GM officials in Detroit and pointed out that in my three studies in Lansing I did not embarrass

GM in any way, it promised not to oppose the study, thus assuring us that they would refrain from warning Olds workers not to cooperate. When we informed UAW officers in Detroit of this, they finally allowed the Olds local in Lansing to furnish us the seniority list needed to select a sample. In short, both management and labor agreed to violate a contract clause that prohibited either party from releasing the seniority list to any outsider.

When my assistant Richard Gale went to Cordoba, Argentina to study the auto factory there (IKA), he experienced difficulties in obtaining union-management cooperation. When I arrived, I found that the parties had strong ideological differences, not unlike the situation at FIAT. Moreover, the top officials in both management and the unions avoided meeting us. We decided to make contact with second tier officers on both sides and consulted them several times on secondary issues involved in our research. Over time, they appeared to gain status and self-esteem from advising high status professors and eventually secured appointments for us with their superiors. In a relatively short time, we obtained the kind of sponsorship we needed and the trade-offs that the parties needed: monitored symbiotic cooperation. In comparing my experiences in the three countries, I began to think of them as a natural experiment: the research objective in all countries was the same as were methods and sampling, the researchers, the two sponsors (Michigan State and the local university), and union and management antagonisms. The main variable was the changing incentives of labor unions and management to cooperate when confronted with the shifting definitions of the situation thrust upon them by researchers and sponsors.

Before Baldev Sharma went to Bombay to study Premier Autos Limited (PAL), I spent hours teaching him the field lessons learned from FIAT, Olds, and IKA. A mature person reared in India, he knew what to expect. Before he left, we made contacts with potential Indian research sponsors in academia, industry, and government, and I provided him with impressive set of American and Indian documents. Through a high status Bombay influential, he succeeded in getting cooperation from management. Labor, which was in a precarious situation, had to go along to maintain a semblance of coequal status with management.

I assembled my conclusions from the early Lansing studies, the border, and the four-nation research in an essay, "The Sociology of Social Research" (Form 1973c). In the early Lansing studies, I emphasized the reasons for failing to gain cooperation from management and labor. For the border research, I emphasized the political sophistication of the

Mexican informants and the ideological cleavage between business and government, in contrast with the ideological agreement between business and government informants in the United States and their concern for anonymity. In India, gaining the sponsorship of high status influentials was critical for gaining access; in Argentina, developing rapport with second-tier bureaucrats in business and unions; in Italy, constant bargaining with the parties and introducing external pressures on them; in the United States, establishing the researchers' ideological trustworthiness.

To be sure, these observations were grounded in a limited set of studies and had limited applicability. Yet, sociologists should be able to apply their knowledge of social organization to improve understanding of the research process. I attacked the task in an essay on the sociology of social research (Form 1971). First, I proposed that all research methods be examined as social systems that involve researchers, sponsors, and hosts, namely those being studied, and others. Then, I described a range of possible reciprocal role sets among system participants, pointing to systematic differences when researchers are individuals (as in a craft model of research) or organizations (as in a research institute model). In the former case, social psychological principles dominate; in the latter, principles of inter-organizational relations. Then I described how relationships among participants, individuals or organizations, are complicated when the research examines problems of power, ideology, and conflict. Finally, I proposed a research program for systematic study of the research social system, which no one has pursued.

Working-Class Stratification: A Problem that Wouldn't Go Away

With the termination of the four-nation auto study, I turned my attention to occupational power, a problem that Joan and I (Form and Huber 1976) had explored earlier, showing how different occupational groups confront the factors that affect their income and status. Then, when Lew Coser was elected president of the ASA in 1975, he chose as his program theme "The Uses of Controversy in Sociology" and asked me to prepare a paper for a thematic session. With my *ASR* controversies on working-class stratification fresh on my mind, I decided to examine three commonly accepted ideas in sociology about skilled workers, labor's aristocrats: that industrialization eroded the need for skills, that industrial unions (which press for wage equalization) erode the earnings advantages of the skilled over the less skilled, and that the growth of industrial unions erodes craft unions' political influence, resulting in a more politically liberal working class.

My paper showed that even a superficial survey of U.S. occupational trends revealed a trend almost opposite to that of the received wisdom. Census data showed that for more than fifty years the proportion of skilled workers in the labor force had not declined but remained constant in manufacturing and had increased in other sectors. A systematic search of the labor economics literature revealed that wage differentials between skilled and unskilled workers had remained constant for over a century. In lifetime earnings, not including their superior fringe benefits, the skilled earned half as much again as the unskilled. Earnings differentials were similar in nations at different level of economic development. In fact, the annual earnings of U.S. skilled workers and foremen were surpassed only by those of managers, officials, and proprietors. Historically, the skilled in both union and nonunion shops had protected their advantages over the less skilled. Most attempts of industrial unions like the UAW to lower the wage differentials had failed. Finally, throughout their history, the skilled had successfully excluded women and blacks from their ranks.

In the political arena, all available surveys of presidential elections revealed that the skilled were more politically active, more independent and more conservative than the less skilled. Industrial unions had had little impact on the political divide between the skilled and less skilled of the working class. Finally, the available literature on social values, life-styles, social participation, and occupational aspirations revealed persistent differences between the skilled and other manual workers.

I did not realize that this paper (Form 1976b) would lead to two decades of research on working-class stratification. But I was now convinced that social scientists were ideologically biased about the stratification of the working class. They disliked the idea and ignored it, preferring instead to believe in historical myths that fit their ideology of increasing working-class economic, social, and political homogeneity. Perhaps my findings in *Blue-Collar Stratification* (1976a) were not the chance result of having selecting autoworkers for study, but a general reflection of working-class stratification.

I began to examine current popular studies of the working class. Marglin (1974) had proposed that the division of labor in the West since the industrial revolution was driven neither by technological change nor the drive to increase productive efficiency and profit. Workers' skills could have been preserved but capitalists and managers designed machinery and industrial organization that would divide and weaken the working class. The technology and factory organization associated with the industrial revolution was not inevitable, but a capitalist program to control the working class.

Three years later, Braverman (1974) proposed a parallel thesis that became so popular that the Marxist Section of the ASA established an annual prize in his honor. Braverman averred that twentieth century capitalists had conspired to simplify skills and degrade work. With Marglin, he held that skill degradation was part of a managerial program to wrest control of production from skilled workers, concentrate it in management, and divide the working class. This process had accelerated most in the United States, bastion of capitalist hegemony.

For the annual meeting in 1979, Tad Blalock's presidential theme was "Sociological Theory and Research: A Critical Approach." Invited to participate in a thematic session, I submitted a paper on resolving ideological issues on the division of labor (Form 1980). I asked whether it is possible to reduce ideological disputes in sociology by gathering comprehensive data that adversaries would accept as valid and reliable. For this, I gathered evidence on the Marglin and Braverman theses. Marglin's thesis held nowhere. All historical and cross-national evidence pointed to close correspondence between technological sophistication, division of labor, and productivity. Everywhere, technological innovation primarily reduced the need for unskilled labor by substituting for it semi-skilled machine operatives. Everywhere the proportion of skilled workers increased , as did the complexity of work in the white-collar sector. In short, the historical evidence supported a trend toward rising occupational heterogeneity and complexity for the labor force as a whole.

It also showed that the Soviets had once embraced the arguments of Marglin and Braverman, which were, in fact, earlier formulated by Marxists. All of the Soviet Union's experiments to wrest power from bourgeois managers, engineers, and the educated in order to shift it to the proletariat had failed, with disastrous productivity reductions. The Soviets were then forced to train engineers and workers much as in the West. Once given control over production, engineers created occupational structures like the West's. Communist China's similar experiments in the Great Leap Forward also failed. All the data I found on experiments in worker participation in management in capitalist, socialist, and Soviet countries showed no basic departure from Western-style technology and division of labor. Comparative studies of the same industry in East and West, in capitalist and socialist societies, showed similar occupational profiles.

Nor did I find credible evidence to support Braverman's thesis. Apprentice training for skilled work from medieval to modern times was available only to a minority of workers. Most of our ancestors engaged in low-skilled work in manufacturing and farming. The ten studies I found of pre-nineteenth-century urban occupational structures revealed that the large majority of manual and service workers were unskilled. Census data of industrializing countries in the nineteenth and twentieth centuries revealed no decline in the skill levels of the labor force. On the contrary, they showed declines in unskilled and domestic labor and increase in white-collar occupations that required more training for complex skills. Although I did not pursue the matter in depth at the time, when I reviewed the literature in my four-nation study of automobile workers, I found little support of the idea that the shift from agricultural to industrial work increased job dissatisfaction and work alienation. On the contrary.

Tom Steiger, an Illinois graduate student, chose to study the construction industry for his dissertation. As his father had been part of it, Tom knew quite a bit from first-hand experience. The literature averred that the industry's ancient craft tradition was being buffeted by changes that threatened craft control of work. Manufactured parts in factories were being shipped to construction sites, power tools were dumbing down skills, large bureaucratic firms were replacing independent artisans in residential and public construction, solo builders were eliminated by large firms who hired them as subcontractors. These trends increased outside managers' administrative authority and undermined craft work control. Moreover, similar changes were allegedly taking place in the professional services that had many structural features similar to the crafts. Combined, the building crafts and their professional services comprised about a quarter of the labor force. Our research was designed to discover whether these allegations were true.

Since past case studies of construction rarely represented the entire industry, we decided to interview (1) self-employed workers in trades; (2) employees, supervisors, and owners of firms that had two levels of supervision; and (3) workers in firms with three or more levels. A large unionized governmental agency with full-time construction workers was also selected. Using unionization and number of supervisory levels as factors for selecting firms produced five types of organization: solo operators, union and nonunion firms with two supervisory levels, and union and nonunion firms with three or more levels.

A theme common to the interviews dealt with the degree of control and responsibility for work at the construction site. Our conclusion was clear: in all types of work sites, even in the largest bureaucratic union and nonunion firms, control of work and responsibility for it remained with individual workers (Steiger and Form 1991). Subcontracting by large firms tended to decentralize administrative control to craft workers, who preserved their traditional authority and responsibility for work. Subcontractors, often craft workers themselves, were reluctant to monitor their employees closely. Subcontracting, in fact, tended to augment system inefficiencies as administrators could not precisely define the responsibility of each subcontractor. Individual workers and subcontractors freely selected tools for the job as long as they conformed to the craft expectations. In short, craft traditions pervaded in all types of construction sites because they regulated work pace, job techniques, choice of appropriate tools, and responsibility. Here again, research failed to support generalizations about skill degradation in construction.

I systematically brought my thoughts together in an essay on the degradation of skills (Form 1987). I found that most sociologists had not examined the historical record of occupational change in different industries. Thus, Marglin's (1974) skill degradation hypothesis was based on what presumably had happened in Britain's early textile industry. But historical records of the industry pointed to a more complex pattern: managers had preserved some old skills, created new ones, and routinized others. Studies of mechanization of the steel industry showed that technological change did not homogenize skills. Some were preserved, other eliminated, and unskilled labor was largely replaced by semiskilled machine operators.

Moreover, the growth of new industries (chemical, electronic, others) in the West created more skills than were lost by the declining traditional industries. Scientific management and Fordism, innovations that allegedly degraded skills, were never widely adopted, not even in mass production industries. Everywhere industrialization increased the demand for literate and more educated workers to fill occupations that required longer training than traditional apprenticeships. The shift from blue-collar to white-collar clerical, professional, and administrative occupations everywhere called for more skill and training.

Social scientists had learned little from studying mechanization because they made the same mistakes about skill degradation when they analyzed the effects of automation. I concluded that many ideological disputes in sociology are resolvable only if the parties agree to accept evidence from comprehensive historical empirical research.

Labor Market Stratification

Since my early concern with organizational stratification in *Industrial Sociology* (1951), I was intrigued by the problem of how, under widely different circumstances, certain occupations successfully maintained their earnings and other advantages over others. The opportunity to examine this question arose in 1971 when Robert Dubin (1976) asked Joan Huber and me to write a chapter for his *Handbook of Work, Organizations, and Society*, letting us pick a topic from a list of chapters he proposed. We chose occupational power.

Max Weber (1920, 1947, section II) early pointed out that labor markets are rarely free; all occupations are affected by such social factors as laws, traditions, social status, material resources, and the nature of their formal organizations. Our task was to discover how and the extent these factors affect the control that occupations exert in their environment.

Our survey of the sociological literature confirmed that few contemporary occupations function in free labor markets. In *Industrial Sociology* (1964, ch. 11), I had proposed that owners, managers, and directors of large firms operate in self-controlled markets, setting their own salaries and benefits regardless of performance. In traditional markets, independent professionals and some artisans adapt fee structures to the client's social status and wealth. On the other hand, governmental bodies create administered markets (e.g., the military) that fix occupational salaries, set step increases in salaries, and specify the measures to gain promotion in the organization. In contested markets, organized labor and management bargain to set wages and benefits for occupations over extended periods. Only the wages of powerless, low-skilled, and marginal workers are set in free and unstructured markets.

We concluded that some easily identified social factors affect occupational earnings. Thus, union members earn more than the unorganized. Ascriptive characteristics of workers like gender, ethnicity, and race influence occupational placement and earnings even when educational qualifications are identical. Human capital in the form of education and training do not explain all earnings differences between licensed and unlicensed occupational groups. Industry characteristics more than employee productivity help explain earnings inequality of similar occupations. Totalitarian governments, within limits, control the relative earnings of occupational groups. In short, we tried to systematize a structural theory of earnings.

Later, my students and I engaged in three labor market studies to test the theory: a national study of American manual workers' earnings; factory workers' earnings in India and Korea. In the early 1970s, sociologists at Wisconsin had proposed a theory of male occupational income attainment based on individual education, age, work experience, and father's education and occupation. Meanwhile, some economists proposed a theory much like those of institutional economists in the 1950s (e.g., Reynolds 1951), noting that workers of equal qualification earned higher wages in capital intensive core industries than in labor intensive peripheral industries, which indicated a dual (later tripartite) labor market. They also noted that industries and occupations in metropolitan centers paid higher wages than those in small communities. Other industries paid low wages by crowding, recruiting women, blacks, and others whose unemployment rates were high. These observations neatly fitted into our structural theory of labor stratification based on ascriptive (gender, race), organizational (union-nonunion), control (skill monopoly, licensing), and other characteristics.

Bob Bibb and I (1977) put together a data set that contained indicators of our structural model (sex, union membership, firm size, industrial sector, community size, skill) and of the status attainment and human capital models (individual education, job or vocational training, work experience, tenure). Multiple regression analysis revealed that the structural variables explained three times the variance in earnings than did the attainment and human capital variables. Combining the models explained only slightly more than the structural. Gender, community size, and union membership contributed most to the structural explanation; vocational training, the most for the human capital explanation. Comparing earnings by gender, the structural model was more powerful for women than men; the reverse was true in the human capital model.

This article was among the earliest social structural studies of labor market outcomes. Widely cited, it provided a coherent theory and method for the "new structuralism" in the sociological study of labor markets (Baron and Bielby 1980). Yet, the "new" structuralism was hardly new. Young sociologists seemed unaware of Weber's work and that of earlier sociologists and institutional economists. To be sure, it was new for those addicted to the status attainment approach of the 1960s.

The second labor market study focussed on anomalous findings in my study of Indian automobile workers. Contrary to other countries, Indian skilled workers exhibited no earnings advantages over the less skilled. I discovered that my skills classification disagreed with management's in 47 percent of the cases, the correlation being only 0.389. But management's classification correlated more highly with wages. I had earlier presented a paper on this anomaly at the Institute for Comparative Sociology at Bloomington in 1971, but had tucked it away. When I later uncovered it, I asked my student Fred Pampel to help reanalyze the data with more sophisticated statistics (Form and Pampel 1978).

We regressed researchers' and managers' skill classifications on all variables that might effect job placement: background (fathers' occupation, caste, community of origin), training (education, job training and experience), and work history (previous occupations, previous employment sector experience, and years worked). The researchers' skill classification confirmed that workers from advantaged backgrounds, with more education, training, sector and occupational experience were in fact performing higher skilled work. Management's classification conformed to a pattern wherein skill designation was determined largely by age, tenure, rural background, and moderate job training. Since management made earnings and job titles commensurate, many employees with low skills who earned more than some with higher skills, were defined as skilled.

Since this statistical analysis did not explain management's behavior, we searched for an explanation. Managers maintained that they hired and promoted employees on universalistic grounds and opposed particularism and paternalism. An examination of historical changes in plant technology, its internal organization, and a chain of political events provided a proximate explanation. When the factory first opened as an assembly operation, management needed relatively low-skilled workers. In its drive to economize, it hired lower caste rural migrants to Bombay who had little education and industrial experience. As the plant expanded and began to manufacture automobile parts, it recruited semi- and skilled workers who came from more privileged backgrounds: higher caste, urban residence, more education, more job training, and more industrial sector experience. In the midst of these changes, the union launched a strike that lasted 110 days. Finally, the union, defeated, was replaced by a more conciliatory one whose officers were "intellectuals and politicos" with little industrial experience.

Officials of the new union were reluctant to strike, yet they needed to demonstrate, especially for the most active unionists, their ability to wrest concessions from management. The activists were largely older employees who had strong ties with their fellow workers. The more recent and more skilled employees had little experiences with unions; only a few of them engaged in plant floor politics. To keep the loyalty of the older activists, union officials pressed management to award them "productivity" raises. To avoid a showdown, management succumbed. Moreover, over the years, a series of national government decrees to raise wages across the board further weakened the relation between job titles and earnings. The rising disjunction between earnings and skill titles created a pool of cynical workers and lower managers.

In the third study, my student Kyu Han Bae proposed to replicate my four-nation study in Korea. I asked him to obtain detailed earnings data on the internal labor market of the auto industry. Korean factory managers, socialized in the Confucian code that stressed homage to authority, order, and hierarchy, were also aware of Japan's Nenko system of rewarding job security in exchange for lifetime guaranteed employment. They also were aware of the advantages of American personnel practices that tuned wages to human capital: training, skill, and experience.

Allegedly in line with Confucian heritage, government policy had severely restricted labor union autonomy in favor of familistic labor-management councils that presumably would monitor and resolve all disputes. Since personnel practices at Hyundai represented a mixture of three personnel systems, we sought to gather data on indicators of each one: the Nenko system associated with social status (seniority, age, tenure, marital status, family obligations); the human capital system based on formal education, skill training, and experience, and the Confucian system with its emphasis on labor-management collaboration and mutual obligations.

The Confucian system was least operative. While both managers and employees claimed to honored Confucian principles, neither side thought the other side did so. Management would not totally embrace the Japanese Nenko system because it considered the labor market too turbulent to guarantee workers lifetime employment and technical training. Yet to maintain as stable a labor force as possible, it manipulated rewards for different skill groups.

Entering wage rates were based on education and vocational training, not on skill. Because seniority and overtime pay rates were the same for all workers, they tended to equalize earnings. The major source of variation in earnings resulted from changes in the employee's standard hourly rate, based largely on supervisory evaluation of individual performance. If wage rates were based on productivity, they could not vary much for most workers because the technology and work organization of auto manufacturing largely determines the work pace and productivity. Productivity variation could range from almost zero for assembly line workers to perhaps 30 percent for the skilled. Experience, on the other hand, should count little for the unskilled, more for the skilled. Therefore, the research task became one of ascertaining the extent to which supervisors' evaluations of individual employees were based on their social status, human capital characteristics, and experience.

We predicted that payment practices would tilt toward the human capital model (Bae and Form 1986). Management could retain experienced workers by offering them more overtime pay and training them for more skilled jobs. We found that the ratio of the highest to lowest monthly earnings including overtime was very high: 2.84:1, compared to 1.5 to 1 in other countries.

Regression analysis revealed that management had carefully calculated a path that took both social status and human capital factors into account. In determining wage raises, supervisors accorded seniority the most weight followed by skill and marital status. This pattern tilted toward the social status model because skilled workers received only 15 percent more in raises than the unskilled. Variation in seniority pay was much larger than in the West. However, in the regressions on monthly earnings, which took the allocation of overtime work into account, skill contributed the most, followed by seniority and marital status. Here the skilled earned about one-quarter more than the unskilled, a pattern that tilted toward the human capital model. In a tight labor market, management retained the less skilled by rewarding them for their loyalty (seniority) and by recognizing their family obligations (marital status). It enticed the skilled by guaranteeing more overtime work and also recognizing their loyalty (seniority) and family obligations. Management's strategy apparently gave it operational flexibility while demonstrating a sense of social responsibility.

Looking back, my students and I examined labor markets in the United States, India, and Korea, all differently structured. Later, I added France (see chapter 9). None of these markets were entirely free and all of them had to be understood in terms of how the firms and employees were embedded in the institutions of the larger society and its stratification system.

Explaining Economic Ideologies

Many sociologists have been bothered that Americans have not embraced conflicting political ideologies and become highly class conscious. In other words, they do not understand why Americans are not more like Western Europeans. Yet it always seemed to me that Americans are as much aware of their economic interests as the Europeans, that they recognize status differences in society, and that they vote and behave largely in terms of their self-interests. Perhaps, rather than directly inquiring about class consciousness and political ideologies, sociologists might better understand the phenomena by inquiring whether people at different income levels share a wide ranging set of economic beliefs about themselves and others, that is, whether different economic ideologies appear to guide people's political behavior.

I conducted a survey of Illinois adults to examine how economic strata (prosperous, middle income, and the poor) perceive and assess their own economic status and how they judged the fairness of economic inequality nationwide. The three income strata were families in the top 15 percent of the income distribution, the middle 65 percent, and the bottom percent. The survey probed two themes: the extent to which economic status shapes economic ideology and the ability of four theories of stratification to explain them.

Following an earlier research design (Huber and Form 1973), the Illinois survey (Form and Wood 1985) oversampled rich and poor in order to get enough cases at each level for statistical analysis. The respondents were asked to respond to 34 items in five areas of economic ideology: (1) the fairness of their own earnings compared to those of a representative set of other occupations; (2) the appropriateness, fairness, or equity of earnings of four interest groups (corporations, small business, farmers, labor union members), three broad occupational strata (professional, white-collar, and manual workers), and four disprivileged groups (blacks, Hispanics, women, and welfare recipients); (3) the fairness or the justness of the distribution of income and inheritance between rich and poor; (4) the fairness of income tax rates on different levels of income; and (5) the fairness of welfare payments and governmental redistribution programs. All questions on incomes, taxes, welfare payments and the like pertained to *actual current U.S. economic data*. Since the respondents were constantly informed of this, they were not dealing with hypothetical economic conditions, but with reality.

Respondents were classified as rich, middle income, and poor, and also as defined by four theories: Marxist, functional (human capital), elite, and lumpen. For the Marxist theory, respondents were divided into four strata using E.O. Wright's (1979) criteria based on property relations: bourgeoisie (employers and self-employed), managers (with supervisory function), proletariat (employees with no supervisory function), and unemployed. For functional theory, individuals were assigned socioeconomic scores. For elite theory, the elite comprised the top sixth of the income distribution. Finally, for lumpen theory, two income strata, the upper five-sixths and the remaining poor.

When split into three income strata (rich, middle, poor), respondents differed on only half of the economic ideology items. About half the respondents in all strata thought that the pay of their occupations was unjustly low, and this judgment tended to be carried over to about half of the remaining items of economic ideology. Yet the strata agreed that the pay of ten occupations representing the occupational structure (from top executives to minimum wage occupations) was generally just or equitable. Strata consensus was also high that some groups deserved more income than they received: women, small business, farmers, blacks, Hispanics, and middle class, but the rich, more than the middle and poor strata, thought that manual workers, labor union members, and welfare recipients got somewhat more than they deserved. The strata also disagreed on a justifiable upper limit of incomes and justifiable income gap between rich and poor.

Surprisingly, the strata agreed that the just or fair income of the lowest paid full-time worker should be about 40 percent higher than the current minimum wage. There was massive agreement that most income tax rates were unjustly high and they favored the rich. Strata differences appeared in the expected direction on government guarantees for employment, health care, educational subsidy for the poor, and limits on business profits. Yet, the differences in economic ideology did not carry over into the political arena; 75 percent of respondents in all strata identified themselves as middle-of-the-road or conservative.

All thirty-four items comprising economic ideology were regressed on the four strata classifications as defined by Marxist, functional, elite, and lumpen theories. All four were equally weak. Only 30 percent of the regressions of 203 partial regression coefficients were statistically significant and the variance they explained was low, under seven percent for most beliefs. No theory was better than the others in specific content areas of economic ideology.

Overall, race attained statistical significance more often (39 percent) than any other variable, followed closely by education, age, then gender, and income. Least often significant was occupation. Income behaved less consistently in all theories than other strata variables. In sum, no theory was superior in explaining economic ideology. Moreover, combining the theories in various ways failed to produce more robust results. Generally, each theory's most important indicator performed the worst for that theory. Occupational classes, the most important indicator for Marxist theory, ranked last in performance for that theory. The SEI of occupations, the most important for functional theory, also ranked last. Income, fundamental for elite and lumpen theories, also ranked respectively second last and last.

I concluded that the nation may have a mushy stratification system comprised of groups with loose and overlapping economic and social beliefs. A theory to explain it should focus on shifting and amorphous relations among various groups in different contexts. Current stratification theories suffer from a hardening of the categories and need thorough revision.

9

Striking My Own Mark

The medieval silversmith devised a steel stamp to identify his work and struck his mark on everything he produced. The mark I had developed by the mid-seventies was the study of divisions in the working class. Most of my future work would revolve around this theme. In 1977, as our first Illinois sabbatical approached, I wanted to go to France to study the division of the French working class. Joan took three projects in varying stages of completion, rented a French manual typewriter, adjusted to the new locations of several often-used keys, and went to work. As we had visited France several times, my fluency in French was passable. France was an ideal country in which to gather empirical data on a historically solidary and ideologically oriented working class. I could compare it to the fractured and non-ideological (or ideologically pragmatic) American working class. Such comparative studies were rare.

Comparing the French and American Working Classes

I decided to examine three propositions on French and U.S. working-class differences that were widely believed to be true. First, wage differentials among manual workers should be lower in France than in the United States because French labor unions promoted wage equalization. Second, given France's revolutionary tradition, its working class should be more class conscious. Third, French workers should be more politically involved and more radical than the American, given the political stance of their powerful communist and socialist labor unions. These themes extended my four-nation study of blue-collar stratification and later studies of skill cleavages and labor market stratification in the American working class.

I selected Lyon, France's second city, as the research site because I thought it would be more like the rest of the country than Paris. I would limit the study to artisans, first-level foremen and supervisors, skilled and semi-skilled employees, unskilled laborers, and household and service workers. The first task was to obtain accurate wage data, difficult because such data had not been consolidated into a single source and their interpretation was the subject of ideological dispute. Radicals claimed that government data reported higher earnings than workers actually received while employers claimed the opposite. INSEE, the French equivalent of the U.S. Bureau of the Census, gathered earnings data from employers, but not from self-employed artisans and their family workers, government employees, domestics, and illegal immigrants. Everyone agreed that payroll data would be more accurate, but payroll studies were almost nonexistent.

I gathered payroll data from local industries, including glass, plastics, chemicals, and others, comparing them to INSEE data on these industries. Labor union contracts which by law had to be filed in local government agencies turned out to be incomplete and hopelessly out of date. Earnings data of government employees were readily available because salary schedules, prescribed by the national government, varied only by employee seniority and the local cost of living. Wage steps by seniority were also fixed by law. I located several good empirical field studies covering two decades of earnings by artisans (a political force in France), domestics, farm laborers, and immigrant workers. The persons who reported these wages, whether self-employed or employers, doubtless underestimated earnings slightly to avoid higher taxes.

In short, it was possible to largely overcome obstacles to obtaining reliable data. Comparing my payroll studies with those reported by INSEE, I concluded that INSEE earnings data were as reliable as those reported by the U.S. Bureau of the Census (Form 1981). Also, the earnings of government employees by occupational level closely approximated those in the private sector. Importantly, labor unions' episodic drives to lower earnings differentials between the skilled and unskilled turned out to be ineffective. Differentials not only returned quickly to traditional levels but they were also somewhat higher in France than in the United States for twenty major industries. Earnings inequality among the artisan, government employees, and most industrial workers was also higher in France than in the United States.

When I compared France and the United States by gender, race, ethnicity, and industry, I found that French men attained relatively higher levels of education and vocational training than women compared to their U.S. counterparts. The gender earnings gap was higher in France, even with occupation and skill controlled. When I compared the earnings ratio of foreign-born workers in France (largely North Africans) to French native-born with the earnings ratio of American blacks and Hispanics to U.S. whites, the French race-ethnic earnings differentials, controlling for gender and skill, were higher. In short, contrary to the received wisdom, the conclusion was unambiguous: earnings inequality was higher in the French working class than in its U.S. counterpart.

National comparisons of class political solidarity were more hazardous (Form 1981). In the United States, manual workers had increasingly supported the Democratic Party over the decades, thereby increasing the political homogeneity of the working class. Longitudinal data from French social surveys ran in directions contrary to the received wisdom. Political apathy and failure to vote were generally higher in the French than in the American working class. Gender differences in party allegiance were also greater in France, women being more conservative than men. Surprisingly, more French than American workers, especially the skilled, opposed union involvement in politics. Differences in party preferences by skill level were also greater in France because the communist party was a constant source of division. I concluded that with 25 percent of the working class politically withdrawn, 40 percent split into a communist and noncommunist left, and 35 percent preferring center and right parties, a politically unified French working class seems to be as impossible a dream as it is in the United States. The *American Journal of Sociology* asked me to revise and resubmit my article but rejected the revision, presumably because the reviewer reported that I had failed, as he recommended, to make proper use of the theory that Trotsky (1932) developed in *The History of the Russian Revolution.*

The Splintered American Working Class

My next project was to analyze the divisions, cleavages, or strata of the American working class, defined as manual and service workers. I divided them into six major groups: foremen of manual workers (women were excluded from this category), self-employed manual workers, skilled workers, low-skilled workers in the capital intensive heavy industries of the core economy, low-skilled workers in the labor-intensive industries of the periphery, and the marginally employed. The six groups would be compared for income, taking gender and racial divisions into account. Then the groups or strata would be examined for differences in their politics and working-class consciousness.

Despite the liberal orientation of American sociologists, systematic empirical studies of the working class were scarce. From 1895 to 1930, the *American Journal of Sociology* listed only twelve articles on the subject. Subsequent studies revealed general disagreement on its definition and composition. Almost no studies systematically compared the U.S. working class with other working classes. After the 1960s, sociologists began to comment on the economic disparity between the working class and the so-called underclass of poor women, blacks, and immigrants. Despite lack of systematic evidence, sociologists agreed that the working class was being de-skilled and that job dissatisfaction, alienation, and discontent were growing. In the 1970s, researchers became interested in the struggles of workers and managers to control the organization of work. Most of them ignored the earlier research of industrial sociologists who had examined workers' struggles as manifested in their informal organization and shop-floor politics. The 1970 Marxists referred to these activities as "the labor process," a term that gained wide acceptance. Most sociologists apparently concurred with the Marxists that the historical trend was for management to increasingly dominate the labor process by degrading skills and centralizing decision making, ignoring streams of studies of labor union and grass roots movements to resist management control. In short, the literature was rich in theorizing but poor in empirical verification. This was not due so much to lack of data as failure to consult and organize them.

Six Working-Class Strata

The Public Use Samples (PUS) of the U.S. Census made it possible to generate enormous quantities of data that could test various theories. Over time, I conducted eleven studies that were incorporated in *Divided We Stand* (Form 1985). All of them followed a common format. Conflicting theoretical views (Marxist, social structural, and human capital) were first presented, then tested with empirical data. They revealed surprising disparities in earnings, social status, and politics among manual workers. The annual earnings of self-employed manual workers were twice those of employees who worked in periphery firms; the skilled earned 77 percent more than the unskilled; employees in core industries earned 58 percent more than those in the periphery. For family earnings, the disparities were even larger. Detailed regression analysis further confirmed that the six groups or strata differed widely in ascribed social status (like race and gender) and human capital (education and training and other characteristics).

Although no comprehensive study had examined how foremen differed from the workers they supervised, sociologists saw them variously as management lackeys, a separate stratum, an anxious marginal group uncertain of its loyalties, or as a part of the working class. The PUS data showed that foremen, 4 percent of the working class, differed widely in the number of employees they supervised in different industries and occupations. The great majority had previously been manual workers and many moved back and forth between supervisory and nonsupervisory positions. Foremen resembled skilled workers in many ways, slightly better educated and better paid than those they supervised.

I combined several national social surveys to get data on the class consciousness and politics of the foremen. The majority saw themselves as part of the working class and the general public agreed with their self-placement. Politically, foremen were slightly more conservative than skilled workers. In sum, the data revealed that foremen did not differ much from other manual workers and they suffered no sense of marginality or ambiguity about their social status.

Although only four percent of manual workers are self-employed, surveys reveal that at one time or another, 40 percent of blue-collar Americans have aspired to work for themselves. Most sociologists have conceptualized self-employed manual workers as politically conservative members of the lower middle class (petty bourgeoisie). Although their number approximates that of farmers, researchers have virtually ignored them. Yet data were easily accessible in the Census.

The PUS revealed that almost half of the self-employed were craft workers or artisans; the remainder worked in the services and transportation. Compared to employees, more of the self-employed were white, male, older, married, better educated, and had more vocational training. The Internal Revenue Service estimated that they underreported their income by 30 percent. With this correction, they clearly were the most affluent blue-collar workers, even after all characteristics that affected earnings were controlled in regression analysis. Contrary to speculation, proprietors were upwardly mobile and their bankruptcy rates were low. Survey data showed that they were only slightly more conservative than the skilled workers and foremen.

In a previous chapter I reported my findings on the skilled as a special interest group (Form 1976b). There I conclusively demonstrated that their representation in the labor force has not declined historically, that they were not being de-skilled and that they were not falling in economic status relative to the working or middle class. Surveys of annual earnings in various countries revealed that the advantage of skilled over non-skilled ranged from 25 to 400 percent. Compared to the less skilled in the United States, they were better educated, more homogeneous in race and gender, more self-conscious and socially cohesive, and more active in protecting their interests both inside and outside of labor unions. Somewhat more independent and conservative than the less skilled, they nonetheless tended to assume leadership in labor union struggles and (with important exceptions) exerted a restraining influence. In political outlook, they were more politically pragmatic than other manual strata. Despite images of the working class as being homogenous, the three top strata comprised 37 percent of it.

I then divided two of the three lower strata into those who worked in the capital-intensive core and those who worked in the labor-intensive periphery. Differences were startling. Mean annual earnings in the core were 72 percent higher than in the periphery, and they varied greatly by union status, gender, and race. The earnings advantage of the unionized core over the non-unionized periphery was 220 percent. Among the non-unionized, the core earnings advantage was 65 percent.

Sector earnings inequality was much higher for women, especially non-white women. The annual earnings advantage of white unionized men in the core tripled that of women in the non-union periphery, and almost quadrupled that of non-whites. Regression analysis showed that, controlling for all the variables that affect earnings, except for weeks worked and union membership, gender explained earnings more than any other variable. Women's lack of access to complicated machines played an important role in their wage subordination. Finally, core and periphery differences in politics were small but consistent. Workers in the periphery had lower voter turnout, lower identification with the Democratic Party, less splitting of party vote than workers in the core. Both categories had similar class identification.

Finally, the marginally employed are those who worked fewer than twenty-seven hours a week over the year. Ideally, the stratum should be defined as those unsuccessful in finding full-time employment. In that case, they would resemble the permanent poor. But systematic data on this group were difficult to find. Without the restriction, the marginally employed were a heterogeneous lot of high school drop-outs, house-wives not seeking full-time work, the semi-retired, and those who were unsuccessful in finding full-time work. Understandably, their earnings were lower than those in the other strata. Although dominantly employed in the low-skilled periphery, they also appeared in the other working-class strata which suggests that they were politically diverse.

The impact of labor union membership on the strata had not been studied. I obtained tapes of Current Population Reports of annual surveys of 50,000 workers that contained data on union membership. In 1971 and 1981 union members' annual earnings advantages over the unorganized were large in all sectors and occupations. The 65 percent overall advantage (not counting fringe benefits) was large enough to define the unionized as privileged. Unions increased the earnings of workers who already had higher earnings, leaving others more exposed to market forces. The gender, race, and employment advantages of the skilled in the core sector were increased by unionization, after controlling for human capital factors that affect earnings. The union advantage was pervasive at all skill levels, sectors, racial groups, and sexes. However, marriage and head of household status advantaged only men, not women; similarly, men's human capital returns in unionized plants exceeded women's.

Finally, I located a unique national survey of workers' response to technology, technological change, and automation (Mueller 1967). Contrary to popular belief, the survey showed that relatively more women than men operate automatic and semi-automatic machines that restrict their physical mobility while men operate machines that require skill and permit mobility and work autonomy. Contrary to Marxist beliefs, technological change upgraded job skills and increased job satisfaction for both men and women, although more for men. Most men and women liked their machines and accepted technological change as normal.

Having found significant and persistent economic and status cleavages among the six working-class strata and evidence of political differences, the remainder of the monograph intensively explored their political ideology and behavior. In the preceding chapter, I reviewed the findings of an Illinois survey concerning beliefs about the fairness of the economic system for three classes: professional-administrative, clerical, and manual. I also examined the data for extent of disagreements among the working-class strata. They were fewer and smaller than class differences, but strata differed significantly on two-fifths of the economic ideology items. Although the disagreements did not concentrate in specific areas, the lower the stratum, the more its members perceived societal economic injustice. The foremen's beliefs were generally closer to those of the working class than the middle class, confirming earlier findings. In almost two-fifths of the beliefs, the separate working-class strata differed significantly and monotonically, suggesting an increasing sense of grievance against the system among the lower strata. Among the unionized, this sense was greatest among women and African-Americans. To conclude, although considerable fragmentation appeared in the economic ideology of the working class, it was unrelated to political self-labeling as conservative or liberal.

I reasoned that if political consensus occurs anywhere in the working class, it should be highest at the local union level where union officers make a conscious effort to inform members on political issues and mobilize them to vote. A search of the literature from 1960 to 1980 uncovered only sixteen empirical studies of local union politics, but only seven unions (all of them liberal like the United Auto Workers) systematically surveyed members on concrete political issues. The studies revealed high consensus that unions should pursue traditional collective bargaining goals and legislation to expand social security benefits. Fewer than 60 percent supported legislation to improve the economic, social, and civic life of the poor. Neither did the majority support union ties to the Democratic Party, voting for union-backed candidates, or approval of the spending of union dues for political purposes. Opposition to labor's political programs was highest among the skilled, the most politically active members.

Working-class political cleavages were then examined at the national level. I assembled national election survey data for the 1970-80 decade and analyzed them for each of the six working-class strata. Expectedly, the higher the stratum, the higher the voter turnout; union membership increased it somewhat. Stratum effects held after the variables normally associated with voting (income, age, race, home ownership) were held constant. However, stratum effects on identification with the Democratic Party were smaller than for other variables, namely, race, religion, union membership, education, sex, class identification, and income. In six biennial elections, a larger percent in all strata split their party vote than voted for the straight Democratic ticket; the higher the stratum, the greater the ticket splitting. For Democratic voters, when all factors were controlled, stratum effects were negligible, while other effects remained. Yet, the higher the stratum, the more union membership increased Democratic voting. Finally, although the majority in all strata identified with the working class, the higher the stratum, the greater the identification with the upper working and middle classes. Overall, larger turnouts and higher Democratic voting by the lower working-class strata were necessary for Democratic Party victories. Working-class stratification turned out to be greater and more important for politics than earlier investigators had assumed.

While *Divided We Stand* (1985) went considerably beyond other efforts to understand working-class solidarity, I still did not fully understand why organized labor's political efforts were not more substantial. What had gone wrong?. I turned to that problem in my next monograph. Suffice it to say here, that while my findings on working-class stratification were positively reviewed in sociology's main journals, they were not widely cited subsequently because they seemed to run against the prevailing ideology in the discipline.

10

The Illinois Shop

Going to Illinois from Michigan State marked a sea change in institutional environment. The Illinois campus did not compare in beauty to Michigan State's and Urbana-Champaign were two adjacent dreary communities when compared to Lansing, which itself was not exactly sparkling. Although the two cities were about the same size, the university was originally located in Urbana as was the faculty ghetto. Gradually part of the university had spilled over into Champaign. Therefore, the official name of the institution was the University of Illinois at Urbana-Champaign, never the other way around.

Yet, the difference in the intellectual atmosphere of Michigan State and Illinois was striking. The Illinois library was magnificent and Illinois students were a notable cut above Michigan State's. Illinois and its departments were more research oriented, more competitive nationally, and more sophisticated in their approach to scholarship. Even the social sciences faculties, which were not top rate, were more nationally visible than Michigan State's. Despite Illinois' isolation on the prairie, it brought notable cultural events to the campus. The semester system of sixteen weeks compared to Michigan State's eleven-week quarters was an added bonus. Students, especially graduate students, had more time to acquire basic understanding of a course before writing their papers.

A chief concern of the humanities but especially of the social sciences at Illinois was campus domination by the physical sciences and engineering, some of whose faculty seemed to see at least some merit in studying Beowulf and Shakespeare but rather little in studying voting or social stratification. The social sciences had relatively lower status and fewer resources than those available at other outstanding universities. Except for Psychology, other social and behavioral science departments had difficulty retaining their best scholars. Illinois was competitive nationally in attracting good young scholars, but couldn't hold them once they became nationally visible. The year before we arrived, Alejandro Portes had left for Texas; the year before he left, Alvin Gouldner had taken a position at Washington University in St. Louis and Joseph Gusfield departed for the University of California at La Jolla. The department's national ratings had slipped a bit.

Joan and I arrived the same year as Joe Spaeth, an expert in survey research from NORC in Chicago. In our first few years at Illinois, the department hired Kenneth Land in mathematical sociology. Spaeth had done the initial ground work and Land was instrumental in furthering the necessary arrangements for the Social Science Quantitative Laboratory, which played a crucial role in training graduate students and enabling faculty to get their work done. Subsequent hires included Larry Cohen in criminology, Bob Schoen and Linda Waite in demography, Rafe Stolzenberg and Jim Kluegel in methods and stratification, Reeve Vanneman in South Asian studies, and John Mirowsky and Catherine Ross in social psychology. The department regained much of its former lustre. The new crew along with other department members like Harvey Choldin, Norman Denzin, Robert Jones, Clark McPhail, Rita Simon and others published in highly visible journals and, within a few years, the department was outperforming most departments nationwide, as measured by articles appearing in *ASR*, the *American Journal of Sociology*, and *Social Forces*.

Then, repeating past cycles, faculty began to leave. Land and Cohen went to the University of Texas in Austin, Rita Simon who was active in law and criminology left for an administrative position in criminology at American University, Reeve Vanneman went to Maryland, and Linda Waite and Rafe Stolzenberg left for the RAND Corporation. At the end of 1983 Joan Huber left to become dean of the College of Social and Behavioral Sciences at Ohio State and I joined her there in sociology. Some years after that John Mirowsky and Catherine Ross left for Ohio State.

Living in the Institute

At Illinois, I had a joint appointment in Sociology and the Institute of Labor and Industrial Relations (ILIR). The contrasts between the two units were many. The Institute was established soon after World War II when organized labor was a growing powerful force in the nation. ILIR was strictly an interdisciplinary graduate unit, very well funded by the state. Its faculty had a reduced teaching load, eleven-month appointments, and funding for research assistants. ILIR was housed in a new building especially designed for its program. Twenty paces from my office was the ILIR library, stocked with most of the social science books and periodicals that had even a remote connection to labor and industrial relations. Every week the librarian circulated a comprehensive list of articles published in social science journals that bore on industrial relations, very broadly defined. Keeping up with the literature was easy. The Institute employed an editor and sponsored a reprint series of articles published by the faculty, which it distributed widely. It had a large lounge and seminar room, offices for graduate students, lockers for their materials, and a small research laboratory.

Four labor economists and three extension faculty had full-time appointments in the Institute. Economics had four joint appointments as did sociology; psychology had three, business, law, and history had one each. They were released one-quarter to one-half time from teaching in order to do research and were employed through the summer. Each one was given a half- or quarter-time research assistant. About forty of the Institute's students were in the M.A. program, and about fifteen were in the Ph.D. program. Carefully selected, they were required to have two social science minors.

I have never been part of an organization whose morale was as high as ILIR's. Students and colleagues respected one another, talked to one another, helped one another, and often engaged in joint research. They lunched together, visited in each other's homes, and developed strong friendships. The Institute extension faculty in labor and business were well integrated into the Institute's social and intellectual life. ILIR also invited outstanding scholars to present colloquia during the year as well as notable leaders in labor, business, and government. Faculty meetings were rarely contentious. Every year, alumni were invited to a two-day convention in which faculty and invited guests presented papers. Over the years, this custom resulted in a strongly supportive alumni group.

My students, although poorly prepared in sociology, did well in my seminars on industrial sociology and the American working class. Working hard, they performed as well, often better, than did sociology majors. I found great satisfaction in directing student theses and dissertations and participating in the committees directed by labor economists.

Although I had an office in sociology, I found myself spending more of my time at the Institute. Bernard Karsh, a joint appointment in sociology, had joined the ILIR faculty almost at its inception. Trained at the University of Chicago in the peak of its research involvement in labor, Bernie had an intimate knowledge of union affairs. Like many sociologists, he saw labor economists as narrow and provincial in their approach to labor. Gruff and somewhat confrontational in style, Bernie would disparage their outlook. They tolerated his attacks with amusement, but respected his dedication to the Institute and his insights into the labor scene.

Karsh and I had a bantering relationship. While he tended to derogate the economists' outlook, I decided to learn from them. They were a bright, productive, and cooperative lot who respected my contributions. I showed them my manuscripts, worked with their students, and developed close intellectual and social ties. And I encouraged sociology students to take their courses. In my research in the structure of labor markets and in *Divided We Stand*, I tried to weld ideas from both labor economics and sociology in order to understand cleavages in the working class. In short, I learned a great deal from them and perhaps they became more appreciative of sociology. While at the Institute, I was more productive than I ever was or would be.

Mel Rothbaum, director of the Institute, was a warm and supportive colleague who respected interdisciplinary studies. About two years before we left Illinois, he retired as director and I was asked to succeed him. As usual, I refused, but I was happy to learn that my colleagues had confidence in me.

Toward the end of our thirteen-year stay at Illinois, the Institute underwent important structural changes. In the 1970s, with soaring inflation and fading support from the Illinois legislature, the university administration was obliged to look for places to cut spending. The Institute's privileged status made it an attractive candidate. As the power of organized labor was declining statewide, the Institute had become considerably less able to protect its budget. The university pressed the Institute to increase its teaching loads to the levels of other campus units, to eliminate summer salaries for joint appointments, and reduce graduate student assistance from half to quarter-time.

These circumstances more it more difficult to tempt candidates for appointments in the social sciences to accept joint appointments in the Institute. They would have a double load of committee assignments and have to work with two sets of colleagues and students, increasing the costs and reducing the benefits of an ILIR appointment.

By the time that we left Illinois, the number of sociologists on the Institute faculty had been reduced from the four when we had arrived to one: Bernie Karsh. As union membership and the political power of organized labor continued to decline, ILIR students found fewer and fewer jobs in labor relations and more in personnel departments. The College of Business, pushing to increase its academic respectability, reduced the number of its courses in personnel administration. The Department of Psychology was similarly uninterested in attracting faculty to an area that it saw as being more applied than research-oriented. Yet the market demand for personnel experts remained high in the private sector while the supply was limited. Sensing this need, ILIR expanded faculty and courses in personnel administration, now called "Human Resources." In short, over a period of thirty years, the Institute changed its faculty, course structure, its relations to other departments, and reduced its focus on organized labor. Yet, faculty morale remained high and the loyalty and financial support of its alumni organization grew steadily.

The hardest thing about leaving Illinois was leaving the Institute. My colleagues gathered together for a send-off lunch that touched me deeply. They really knew how to say goodbye. We had an informal lunch downtown. Much laughter, with picture taking. A short speech, a Verdi opera as a gift, and a toast from me to them.

Sociology's Politics

Life in sociology contrasted sharply with that in the Institute. When we came to Illinois in 1971, Fritz Fliegel was head. He had been in the Department of Rural Sociology for many years. When Ed Hewlet had stepped down as head of Sociology, the dean pressed Fritz to replace him. Fritz had wanted neither to leave Rural Sociology nor to be head, but accepted the position until "things settled down in Sociology." I warned him that if they wanted me to be the next department head, I would be unavailable.

When Joan and I arrived, Fritz had an associate head, Sidney Kronus, then an associate professor. Fritz, Sid, and Norman Denzin, close friends, regularly got together for a beer at the end of the day. They invited me to join them, but after the first meeting, I resisted further invitations. I didn't feel that I really fit in. Besides, I didn't like beer.

Within two years Fritz decided to step down as head and return to Rural Sociology. As head, he had tried to bring Sociology and Rural

Sociology closer together, as they had been at the University of Wisconsin. When Fritz proposed that Rural appointments should be joint in Sociology, the advisory committee in Sociology agreed to hire and promote Rural candidates only if they met Sociology's criteria. When the first two candidates from Rural failed to meet Sociology's criteria for promotion to associate professor with tenure, Rural Sociology promoted them anyway, which terminated contacts between the two departments.

When Fritz stepped down, he hoped that Sidney Kronus would become head because Sidney had satisfactorily served as associate head. However, several of the faculty felt that it was inappropriate to appoint an associate professor as head and there were other issues as well. I joined others to campaign for long-time department member Bernie Karsh, whom the dean eventually appointed. The disagreement created some hard feelings and Kronus and his wife left the following year.

I accommodated quickly to life in the department. I knew three members from my years at Michigan State. Clark McPhail and Norbert Wylie had been graduate students at Michigan State and I had hired urban sociologist Harvey Choldin, a Chicago Ph.D., when I was chair there. A few of us lunched daily at the Newman Center across the street from Lincoln Hall where sociology was housed, which helped me to become acquainted with other members of the department.

Three political issues dominated department life: the annual election of the Advisory Committee, faculty hiring and promotion, and curriculum revision. The Advisory Committee, which met every two weeks with the head, had on its agenda all issues that came before the department but the bulk of its time was consumed by matters that concerned recruitment, promotion, and tenure. Its recommendations strongly affected department decision making although they were only advisory (not mandatory) to the head. Four of its members were comprised of those tenured faculty members who had received the most votes; the fifth was the untenured faculty member who received the most votes. While we were there, those who were elected to the Advisory Committee represented a variety of opinions but they were persons who possessed organizational common sense and were generally able to compromise and work well with others to reach a viable consensus. Joan and I became members of a group that was determined to improve faculty performance and national visibility. Despite some resistance, the department began to recruit some very able faculty who performed at the top of their fields. Overcoming obstacles, the department improved rapidly and its future appeared bright.

Yet, from the beginning departmental politics were somewhat contentious. Disagreements centered on faculty recruitment, promotion, and the graduate student curriculum, all of which were inextricably intertwined with deep ideological differences over the future of the discipline. One faculty member, a quasi-phenomenologist who was enchanted with European literary fads was also a productive scholar who was reputed to work his students hard. At first his passion seemed to be thick description; he later became something of a deconstructionist. Compulsively anti-quantitative, he crusaded against "positivist" social science, declaring that sociology was not and never could be a science. Many graduate students strongly supported him in resisting additional compulsory quantitative courses.

The quasi-phenomenologist's strongest ally was a longtime associate professor interested in theory. He had done relatively little empirical research and had become increasingly hostile to quantitative analysis. Dissatisfied with the Parsonian theory course taught by a colleague, he wanted that course eliminated from the graduate program and his own substituted. In the ensuing debate at a faculty meeting (later referred to as the Great Theory Fight), the faculty split on what the required theory course should cover, classical or research-oriented theory. A strong supporter of C. Wright Mills's approach to the study of current political issues, the theorist was hostile toward those who, in their teaching and research and relations with graduate students, tried to separate what they thought was true from what they wished were true. Other faculty whose interests lay in classical theory, social movements, symbolic interaction, and qualitative methodology intermittently supported the two allies in some of their causes.

The "positivists" were led by Ken Land, who was supported by a cohesive core of faculty including Ken Southwood, Bob Schoen, Joe Spaeth, Marc Felson, Bill Form, Joan Huber, Harvey Choldin, Larry Cohen, Jim Kluegel, Rafe Stolzenberg, Linda Waite and, later, Catherine Ross and John Mirowsky. This group of faculty proposed to increase the quantitative requirements in the graduate curriculum from two to three courses and expose all students to a core curriculum that covered theory, methods, social organization, and social psychology. The proposal was strongly resisted by some of the other department members, including a number of very vocal graduate students.

The "positivists" generally won the fights because they were more united than the opposition and usually consulted one another on strategy before faculty and advisory group meetings and in departmental elections for the Advisory Committee. Some of them, like Land, Cohen, and Stolzenberg were very outspoken, even somewhat intimidating in debates, not hesitating to call people stupid, dumb, and obstinate, terms which, however accurate, were rarely used in faculty debates. The opposing group, apart from its core (the quasi-phenomenologist and the theorist), was ad hoc, supported by different faculty members depending on the issue. Overall, the "positivists" usually outnumbered other faculty on the advisory committee, thereby increasing the probability that recruitment would focus on empirically oriented faculty who had been well trained in quantitative methods and who pushed for improved quantitative training for the department's own graduate students. However, the anti-positivist camp's continual reintroduction of the same issues in department meetings helped keep the spirit of conflict alive. Yet, on the whole, faculty relations outside of the faculty meetings remained civil, on the surface at least.

The quasi-phenomenologist and the theorist continued their drive to contain the "positivists." In faculty meetings, they would introduce motions that had already been introduced and failed and were certain to be defeated again, but which would entail endless discussion. They would take notes furiously as if they were going to use the material for some weighty purpose, perhaps research or even a lawsuit or two.

The theorist accused me of having sold out, as he put it, of having changed my political views and abandoned the legacy of C. Wright Mills. Carrying his views to a larger arena, he managed to gain permission to speak at an ASA Council meeting where he accused the ASA Publications Committee of sexist, political, and methodological biases in selecting editors who, in turn, were biased in selecting articles for publication because they chose biased reviewers.

One of the theorist's suggestions at that meeting was that the Publications Committee should select a woman as the next editor of *ASR* and in fact a woman, Rita Simon, did become the next editor. When Rita completed the three-year term she had agreed to serve at Illinois, the Publications Committee had failed to mobilize itself in time to select her successor and she did not want to extend her term for yet another year. She recommended me and I reluctantly agreed to serve. At the end of my year, the Publications Committee asked me to serve a full term but I decided I could not do it at the time.

Bernie Karsh enjoyed being the department head and we supported him for a second term, which, he announced, would be his last. At the end of Bernie's second term, the dean appointed Joan as the next head with strong support of the faculty. She had already demonstrated administrative skills when, a few years earlier, the chancellor and the vice chancellor for academic affairs invited her to become the first director of the university's new program in women's studies. Joan continued to improve Sociology's faculty recruitment, shortened and clarified the sociology course descriptions in the university catalog which over time had acquired a patina that betrayed their antiquity, and she successfully coordinated a drive for a core curriculum for the graduate students.

These were difficult times financially for the university because of the high rate of inflation and reduced appropriation from the legislature. Over five years, inflation had eroded our salaries by 25 percent. The legislature not only cut back on its support, it also insisted that the university spend its carefully nurtured reserves. Legislative support of the Chicago Circle campus, as it was then called, increased faster than that for the flagship Urbana-Champaign campus, which threatened some of its programs. Many of us felt at the time (and still feel) that the state of Illinois (which ranks rather low among the 50 states in terms of university support) had a university that was far better than it deserved.

Pressed for resources, the administration was forced to resort to cannibalism, taking resources from weaker units to support the stronger ones. To rationalize the process, all units were reevaluated by a newly appointed university committee on which I was asked to serve. Participation on the committee was most distasteful because we had to ask departments to furnish data that might result in reducing their resources. Just before we left Illinois, Joan chaired the university budget priorities committee, which was charged with advising the administration as to where funds could be reallocated with least damage to university quality.

Years slipped by and life at Illinois was fulfilling. Neither Joan or I contemplated leaving despite invitations from other institutions. In 1983, Ohio State asked Joan to apply for the position of dean of the College Social and Behavioral Science, which then included the Departments of Anthropology, Communication, Economics, Geography, Political Science, Psychology, Sociology, and the School of Journalism. She was not especially interested but was finally persuaded to submit her vita. When invited for an interview, I suggested that she take a look; she could always refuse. Her first visit went well, but she was not keen to leave Illinois. When she was called a second time for another interview, I strongly urged her to take another look. After the second visit, she reported that she finally heard the drums beating. When they called to offer the position, she knew it was time to march. And thus were we persuaded to leave Illinois for Ohio State.

We could not leave that fall because Joan and I were scheduled to teach large sections of Introductory Sociology (about 500 students in each section) and it was hard to find replacements for classes of that size. Our house sold earlier than we anticipated, so we moved into a furnished apartment and moved our belongings to a house we bought in Upper Arlington, near the Ohio State campus.

Just before we left in late December, our colleagues gathered for a going-away dinner. It was a quiet affair. Kluegel, as acting chair, said only a few words as we had asked. Then Joan handed him a $1,000 check. "What's it for?" he asked. "Anything," we said. "Throw a party. Have a good time!"

11

Guild Politics

Offices in ASA

Although many sociologists attend annual meetings, perhaps present papers, and even read the *Footnotes*, the official newsletter, relatively few of them have the opportunity to observe the inner workings of the American Sociological Association (ASA). I attended my first ASA meeting in 1946 while at Kent State. In those days, the meetings were held in Chicago during Christmas break. Attendance was relatively small, little more than that of a typical regional society today. The few special sessions were well attended as was the business meeting. It seemed to me that most of the attenders knew one another because interaction in and out of the meetings was so lively.

The experience was lonely and intimidating. As I had not been trained in a department that had large numbers of graduate students, I knew no one. Consequently, I attended one session after another, not saying anything. I silently observed small groups of happy friends congregated in the halls, engaging in animated conversation. I saw Talcott Parsons in the elevator but didn't dream of introducing myself. A few others seemed as unattached as I, but I was too timid to approach them. What would I say? I ate alone.

In my first years at Michigan State, I attended meetings with colleagues. Although I saw them occasionally, they had their own friends from graduate school days and knew people at other institutions. Not wanting to appear socially dependent, I kept my distance. Sessions where I presented papers comprised the highlight of the convention for me. There I could relax, engage in discussions, and invite people to lunch. After publishing *Industrial Sociology*, I was occasionally invited to be a discussant. Slowly, my circle of friends and acquaintances grew and I no longer felt like an outsider.

In 1960, Charlie Loomis nominated me for membership in the Sociological Research Association (SRA), which had been organized in 1936 by a set of distinguished sociologists who felt that the regular meetings of the ASA were insufficiently dedicated to rigorous research. They wanted serious discussion of important research papers distributed in advance of the SRA meetings, which were held during the annual meeting of the ASA. SRA membership would be limited to the discipline's 100 best researchers. A committee was established to review nominations and those recommended for membership would be voted on at the annual meetings. I was pleased to be elected.

At my first meeting, members gathered for cocktails before dinner at a nearby hotel. I tend to be withdrawn at such affairs, but Charlie introduced me to his friends. With the second martini, I relaxed. We sat down to dinner, enjoying animated conversation. I had studied the long paper that had been circulated before the meeting. After dinner, the author was supposed to summarize it briefly, but he went on for more than half an hour. After the presentation, there were questions and comments from the floor. First to rise was Talcott Parsons, then Robert Merton, Paul Lazarsfeld, Kingsley Davis and a few lesser lights. Glancing about the room, I recognized some very distinguished scholars but I also saw more than a sprinkling whose records were somewhat less than distinguished.

For ten years the ritual at the meetings remained unchanged. Most of the papers presented were of modest quality. Staying alert after cocktails and a big dinner became ever more difficult for many of us. Membership gradually expanded to 150 as members sponsored colleagues and ex-graduate students. Sitting with her sponsor at one meeting was a new Wisconsin Ph.D. who had published a couple of papers in *ASR*. Arthur Stinchcombe, a truly creative sociologist, was inducted at the same meeting.

SRA had lost its original function. The main research game was being played at the ASA meeting's thematic and plenary sessions. SRA had become a mutual admiration society of greats, not quite greats, and their claques. While I enjoyed meeting friends at the annual dinners, I preferred seeing them one on one. I resigned from SRA and wrote to about a dozen members that I saw no point to it. Dudley Duncan resigned as did Peter Blau. Others deferred resigning, indicating that SRA could become the nucleus of an organization to replace the ASA, which even then was seen as becoming overly politicized. Bob Dubin said that he enjoyed the camaraderie too much to resign. Even after resigning, I received occasional letters from SRA congratulating me upon my election to membership. I would inform them of my earlier resignation and the reasons for it. No reply.

In effect, SRA had become a quasi-secret society within the ASA, probably a result of its selecting members through individual sponsorship. An observer told me that once when Bill Whyte was putting his program together as president- elect, he asked Alice Myers if he could have a particular slot for a plenary session. Alice replied that SRA was meeting then. With a straight face but twinkling eyes Bill asked Alice what SRA was. Alice looked embarrassed as there were other Council members present who were unaware both of its existence and its claims for time on the annual program.   In 1964, I was asked to serve on the ASA's MacIver Award Committee to select the most distinguished scholarly contribution in the last year or two. I took the task seriously and spent weeks reviewing books to prepare for the discussions. As the meeting opened, an eminent sociologist with a Harvard degree nominated S. M. Eisenstadt's (1963) *Political System of Empires*. Another Ivy League scholar seconded the motion.

I had problems with Eisenstadt's turgid Parsonian prose, almost 400 pages plus 150 pages of footnotes in very small print. His rambling analyses dealt with conflicting values and cultural orientations, tensions between rulers and subjects, bureaucratic problems of exercising power, growing social heterogeneity, and the demands of outlying regions for autonomy. Many boxes and cells rarely contained more than two cases, which ranged from the ancient Inca empire to nineteenth-century Prussia. His theory failed to consider ecological, technological, and material factors that affected outcomes. My attempt to discuss the book's problems was aborted by a call for a vote, which was taken at once. The committee's work had ended. Other books worthy of nomination were not even considered. I decided it would be fruitless to finish my term on that committee. Yet, from that date on, I served the ASA in one capacity or another for the next twenty-five years.

In 1966 when Charlie Loomis was elected president, he asked me to serve on his Program Committee, usually comprised of five or six members. Charlie decided to hold the meeting in East Lansing rather than in the ASA's headquarters in Washington as was the custom. The only persons to make the trip to East Lansing were Ed Tiryakian and an ASA secretary. Our task was to select session organizers for the annual meeting, the persons who would accept or reject papers to be presented in particular subject areas. The three of us were not as well informed as would have been desirable about competent contributors in some areas of sociology but, doing the best we could, we finished in a few hours. This meeting stands in stark contrast with those I attended later as ASA Secretary which usually lasted at least two full days.

The following year, I was elected to a three-year term on the Publications Committee, a three-person committee charged with supervising the performance of editors, proposing the names of new editors to the Council, reviewing journal budgets, and the like. Convened at the annual meetings, we moved expeditiously through our agenda, except for nominating new editors. In contrast to later practice, neither the editors of ASA journals nor ASA officers participated in our meetings.

At my first meeting, Committee member Alvin Gouldner failed to appear, and arrived late at the second, just as we were finishing our business and about to select the next chair. Al nominated me, the other member seconded the motion and the meeting was adjourned. When I was chair, nothing memorable happened.

In 1972, I was elected to the ASA Council for a three-year term. Council had 12 elected members including the president, the secretary, and the executive officer as an ex-officio member. The Council met during the annual meetings and once or twice during the year in Washington. Most of Council's work deals with ASA administrative matters: budget, final selection of editors, location of future national meetings, nominations, convention resolutions, formation of committees, and so on.

Council meetings tended to be long and tedious. At one Council session (1979) when I was serving as ASA Secretary, President Tad Blalock commented impatiently that we never discussed sociology as a discipline; we should set aside at least one evening during the meeting to discuss intellectual matters, such as the health of the discipline and its future. However, after an entire day of sitting endlessly to deal with ASA affairs followed by cocktails and dinner, few of us had the energy or inclination to discuss sociology. The experiment was abandoned.

Council membership provides an intimate view of the complex operations of the executive office that often involve contentious issues. Typically, the Executive Officer, a professor on leave from a university for three years, is selected by Council to supervise the Administrative Officer, the person to whom the Washington staff (about fifteen persons) reports. The latter has the complex task of keeping track of the budget, supervising the staff who arrange hotel accommodations for annual meetings, publish the convention program, and edit *Footnotes*, the ASA newsletter, and other tasks. When I was on Council, the very competent and energetic Alice Myers had been administrative officer more than two decades.

The Executive Officer, who spends most of the first year in office learning how it is run, is highly dependent on the Administrative Officer, who knows where the bodies are buried, that is, the details of organization's history and operations. The Administrative Officer has considerable latitude in deciding whether to release or withhold information about office operations. Over the years, Administrative Officer Alice Myers had became well acquainted with many influential sociologists from all over the country and she exerted considerable influence on ASA affairs.

As the chief responsibility of the president of the ASA is to plan the annual program in a particular year, the Secretary is in fact its most powerful officer. Elected to a four-year term, the first as an apprentice, the secretary monitors the Executive Office, prepares the budget, chairs the Committee on Executive Office and Budget (EOB), serves on the Publications Committee, makes contacts with prospective editors and nominees for ASA offices, and evaluates the ASA staff, a demanding and time-consuming job. Although the president serves on Council for three years, the duties in the first year (other than being a Council member) involve only the program for the annual meeting. The president's other responsibilities are only for one year: chairing Council meetings and writing letters as needed in the name of the Association. In short, ASA is run by the executive officer, the administrative officer, and the secretary, because presidents in effect serve only one year.

Many of the long discussions in Council meetings arise because Council members do not know how the organization functions and what Council can or can not do. Some new Council members appear at their first meeting with enthusiasm and fresh ideas about new projects that ASA should undertake. They seem surprised to learn that others, who also have new initiatives, are reluctant to accept their ideas. The projects are typically presented with little thought of their costs and the financial well being of the ASA. Despite cautionary signals from the secretary and the executive and administrative officers, many new projects are launched, and many must be later abandoned.

In response to the pressure for new programs, ASA functions have proliferated over time. In turn, budgets have increased as have membership dues and fees. The stream of new programs seems unending:

teaching services, research funding, new journals, new affirmative action programs, the establishment of Congressional fellowships, the entering of court cases, the investigation of violations of academic freedom, the pursuit of funds for new projects, and pushing legislative priorities in Congress. The power of the administrative officer continues to grow as the functions proliferate. The expansion of staff, budgets, and functions reduces the attention given to the association's original purpose: to promote sociological knowledge. One of the main tasks of the secretary is to contain the enthusiasm of Council members for new projects and to remind them of the organization's main functions.

When on Council, I learned that the American Economic Association limits its functions to publishing the *American Economic Review*, the *Journal of Economic Literature,* and arranging the annual meeting. The American Political Science Association (APSA), the same size as ASA, had fewer functions and expenses. APSA avoided election expenses by having its council select its officers. Although most disciplinary associations had fewer functions and smaller budgets than the ASA, many Council members have taken pride in the expanded professional activities that the ASA has pioneered.

Serving on Council should be a requisite for becoming secretary. In 1973, after competing my Council term, I was elected secretary to succeed Milt Yinger. Otto Larson was the outgoing executive officer and Alice Myers, the administrative officer. It was a difficult period because membership was declining, budget deficits were rising, new political movements were pushing their agendas, and dissatisfaction with ASA affairs was mounting. My primary concern was to get budget spending under control. Council and the Publications Committees were perhaps meeting more often than necessary and their expenses were rising. January meetings were sometimes held in Arizona or southern California to escape the Washington weather, which increased travel expenses because ASA staff members had to travel out of town. When I heard that plans were afoot to meet in Puerto Rico, I put my foot down. Later, Jim Short moved that all future ASA meeting be held in Washington, which passed.

Unanticipated deficits arose when the boiler gave out at headquarters, when the Xerox machine wore out, and when rain poured into the basement. These unanticipated expenses played havoc with the budget. I proposed that a building maintenance fund become a separate budget item to cover long-term maintenance contingencies. In addition, an organization's reserves should equal at least one year's operating budget. Our reserve was less than 20 percent; I proposed 50 percent as the goal. In our Washington meetings, we no longer went out to lunch but had sandwiches brought in.

I tried to get an account of expenses from Alice Myers for specific activities and meetings, but never succeeded. She pointed out that the books were not kept that way. When I examined them, I found that it was indeed impossible to figure things out. Nor could we revise our accounting system to do it. Yet, we had to cut services and expenses. The ASA traditionally had given its staff higher cost of living raises than did the federal government, and paid parking expenses as well. We reluctantly decided to reduce the staff's wage advantages over those of government workers. Council meetings were extended one day at the annual meeting to reduce the annual number of meetings. We borrowed money from the Rose Monograph Fund to cover deficits, rather than paying banks higher interest rates for loans. I refused my honorarium and pushed to have them abolished for editors. Slowly, the budget came under control.

The situation at ASA headquarters with a new executive officer was as disturbing as budget problems. Otto Larsen had just returned to the University of Washington after serving two terms in that position. Extremely effective, he got along well with the bright and charming administrative officer, Alice Myers. Over the years she had accumulated a vast store of knowledge about ASA operations. But she sometimes exceeded her authority in dealing with matters that were largely professional. She defined the executive officer as a guest who should not become too involved in the daily affairs of the office. After Hans Mauksch from the University of Missouri was selected to succeed Otto, it quickly became apparent that he and Alice were less than comfortable working together. Since she had announced that she would retire "shortly," Hans wanted to know more about the daily affairs of the office because he wanted more control over them. Moreover, he had his own agenda, which was to increase support for teaching services. Unable openly to confront and contest Alice's authority over the staff, he appeared to be an ineffective administrator. In this uneven contest, Alice had strong support from some past and present ASA officers. Throughout the difficulties, Hans was unfailingly polite, vague in giving orders, timid in the infighting, and generous to a fault in his complaints to me.

In trying to mediate their conflicts, I felt obliged to give the executive officer some support because he was responsible for supervising Alice and the organization. Hans's demand for more detailed knowledge about the organization seemed reasonable since Alice said she intended to retire. But Alice preferred to pass on her knowledge directly to her assistant, who likely would become the next administrative officer. I pressed Alice to set her retirement date, but she was determined to outlast Hans. President Milt Yinger, Secretary-Elect Jim Short and others informed me that Alice thought I was going to fire her, which was not true. They advised me not to press her and reported unfavorable things about Hans's conduct that Alice had not shared with me. The conflict was unresolvable. I made more frequent and exhausting trips between Champaign-Urbana and Washington to monitor the conflict and calm the waters. Hans's term expired on my watch and, while he was willing to stay on for another term, the Committee on the Executive Office and Budget wisely recommended that we seek another executive officer.

As secretary, my task was to get competent people to apply for the position. I asked Otto Larsen whether he would consider returning as executive officer. After a time, he indicated that he would, if the terms were right. Although the Executive Office and Budget Committee (EOB) knew him well, as a candidate, he had to be interviewed along with the others. He reluctantly complied, but was plainly miffed and thought that his record as executive officer made him the obvious choice. But the Committee found his terms excessive and concluded that a new executive officer should deal with Alice's retirement and the reorganization of the office.

When Otto Larsen learned that the EOB Committee had selected Russell Dynes from Ohio State, he was furious with me. In a telephone call that lasted an hour, he dressed me down for asking him to apply and then undercutting him. I despaired because I could not convince him that the Committee thought his salary and other demands were too costly and that they considered him too closely associated with Alice to make a clean sweep of things in the ASA office. Otto could not hold a grudge and we renewed our friendship at the next annual meeting. This conflict was mild compared to the ones I experienced as secretary with Al Lee as president.

In 1975, in the largest electoral turnout in ASA history, Alfred McClung Lee, a write-in nominee, was elected president. Al and his wife Elizabeth were founders of the Society for the Study of Social Problems and they had a strong following among its members as well as among some old timers in ASA, young "progressives," liberals in the Wright Mills tradition, Marxists, and some women in Sociologists for

Women in Society (a direct descendant of the women's caucus). I had known Al for years and our relations had been cordial.

When Al grasped the gavel at the first Council meeting, he announced that he had been elected with the largest majority in ASA history and that his constituents expected him to be an active innovator in ASA affairs. Henceforth, the ASA would take public progressive stands on political issues of the day. He chose as his presidential theme of the annual meeting, "Sociology for Whom?" In political translation, it meant for the underdog. Most sociologists are favorably disposed toward the poor, women, minorities, and the deprived. Although Al's trumpet blast was a bit out of tune, his views were widely shared by Council. But Al was intolerant of those who disagreed with his tactics to achieve them. He stance was rigid, not subject to compromise.

Whenever Al was challenged on Council, he would bellow that he had been elected with the largest majority of any president in ASA history. While the election turnout had been the largest, not unusual in a growing organization, Al's majority had been razor thin. He was unaware of this because the ASA did not publish the number of votes each candidate received. Finally, when Al bragged once too often about his landslide, a knowledgeable ASA official told him that his majority was the thinnest in ASA history. He was not pleased.

Al's imperial nature became manifest in the Program Committee that presidents chaired. His appointees to the committee included a woman who had led demonstrations at her university, a friend at *Sociological Abstracts*, a long-time friend at Texas A & M, and an old-time liberal at an eastern university. I was a committee member by virtue of being secretary, and Jay Demerath and Joe Himes were holdovers from the previous committee. The committee met in Washington to fashion the program, operating in a standard way in the morning. In the afternoon, one of Al's appointees left early to catch a plane, another left soon after, and a third became ill and excused himself. The standard procedure was for a committee member to propose names for appointment as session organizers and briefly describe their qualifications. Then a vote determined the first choice and alternates. The chair typically did not vote except to break a tie.

After two of his appointees left, Al said that they had given him their proxies. I commented that that was hardly appropriate because proxies were for specific items. Absent members could hardly know who would be nominated nor could they profit from discussion of their qualifications. Al ignored my remark. He and his remaining appointee had arrived with their list of nominees. When votes were taken, Al would raise his hand and count it as three votes and his appointee's vote constituted a fourth. Controlling the majority, they always won. There was little sense in my participating in the charade. I became silent until the end of the meeting. Later, when I entered the dining room, Al signaled me to join him at his table. Cordial and pleasant, he acted as if nothing unusual had happened.

The most egregious display of Al Lee's totalitarian liberalism arose in a 1976 Council meeting. Al introduced a resolution to censure Jim Coleman for reporting that his research showed that city-wide student bussing to secure racial balance accelerated white flight from U.S. cities. This finding ran contrary to what some liberals believed and some of them accused Coleman of being racist, politically indiscrete, and methodologically inept. Not all Council members had read Coleman's report but all but one considered him a reputable scholar with liberal values. They refused to censure him whether or not his findings measured up to the most rigid methodological scrutiny.

As Council members continued to speak against Lee's motion, he became more adamant. He replied to each comment at length and then pointed to others to speak, ignoring the order of their requests. As secretary, I sat next to the president at Council meetings, helping Al by keeping track of the order of those asking to be recognized. As I pointed to the next in line to speak, Al roared furiously, "Bill, I am the president of this organization and you are not. At least not yet. Not yet!" Alex Inkeles suggested that Lee relinquish the gavel because he was violating Roberts Rules of Order by actively taking part in the debate and by making decisions as chair. Al would hear none of it. Bill Whyte soberly told Al that he was violating Coleman's academic freedom in several ways. Kai Erikson followed with a strong condemnation of Al's position. Eventually, everyone spoke against Al's motion except his ally on Council who had seconded it.

I finally proposed a substitute motion: that a plenary session at the annual meeting be devoted to school bussing, and that experts on bussing, public policy, and methodology be invited to discuss Coleman's research, and that Coleman be given opportunity to defend himself. The motion carried overwhelmingly. S. M. Miller was chosen to preside; Reynolds Farley, Joyce Ladner, Ray Rist, and David Armor were invited to make presentations and Coleman was invited to respond. The plenary meeting, filled to overflowing, went very well.

In 1988, twelve years later, the Section on Sociology of Education gave Jim Coleman its Distinguished Scholar Award. He closed his acceptance remarks with these words:

> I will accept this award with pleasure. I accept it not only for myself, but for William Form, who back in 1976 encouraged the ASA Council not to censure me, but to hold an open forum. I accept it in the name of Reynolds Farley, who in the same year did not hesitate to change his conclusions about the effects of bussing on white flight when further analysis showed the results to be similar to my own. I accept it in the name of Maureen Hallinan, who opened the pages of *Sociology of Education* to what became a productive conflict. I accept it in the names of Sally Kilgore and Thomas Hoffer, whose reputations were not yet made and who could never have afforded to go it alone. I accept it in the name of all those researchers whose academic freedom was constricted by the norms of the discipline. Perhaps most of all I accept it in the name of all those who have braved these norms and have had their reputations warped, twisted, or destroyed by so doing.

I was relieved when my tumultuous term as secretary ended, thinking that it would end my official involvement in ASA affairs. But in a couple of years, perhaps in 1979, I was asked to run for president against Rose Coser. Bill Whyte was a write-in candidate and he won. Two years later I was again asked to run, this time against Matilda White Riley. She won. Bill Whyte wrote that when he was asked to run, he did not know that I was a candidate and wished me well. After Matilda's victory, she embraced me as soon as she saw me at the annual meeting, saying she was sorry I lost and that she had voted for me. With such noble spirits as friends, my losses were easy to take.

Editing ASR and Publication Politics

In 1986, at age sixty-nine, a year from compulsory retirement, I was asked to be editor of *ASR*. I accepted with some ambivalence because it would delay my research on union politics in America. Yet adding another book to my vita was no big deal so I put my research aside. Past experiences with some editors convinced me that they had not always read the manuscript. I decided to read every paper and write my review before reading other reviews and making decisions.

Craig Jenkins and Bob Kaufman agreed to be the deputy editors. They assigned the reviewers, generally two, as I was always the third. I also relied on them to help me arrive at some decisions. Things worked out fairly well. We ran an efficient shop and processed reviews generally within six weeks, a record.

Over the years, to cut costs, the *ASR*'s physical quality had deteriorated: the paper soon became yellow, the size of the type became smaller,
and the inking of the print became lighter. An annual page allotment
was strictly enforced. Physically, the journal was the worst in the discipline, worse even than the least prestigious regional journal. Although
ASR operated with a large profit, most of it was spent to support other
ASA activities. This reversal of priorities violated my sense of how a
learned society should behave and I decided to do something about it. I
cut a page out of current issues of the *American Journal of Sociology*,
*Social Forces, Sociological Quarterly, Social Problems, Social Science
Quarterly*, and others), joining them with scotch tape to make a scroll
three feet long. Then I cut pages from *ASR* over the past few years to
make another three-foot scroll. I labelled the scroll "The Degradation
of *ASR*."

Circulating the two scrolls to the Publications Committee, I demonstrated that *ASR*'s paper quality had deteriorated, its print size reduced, and the aesthetics of the printing had worsened, all to save
money for other enterprises. The other scroll showed that among all
the journals (even the worst regional one), *ASR* was poorest in physical quality. I pressed for money to improve paper quality, enlarge type
size and blackness, and add more pages. Mike Aiken, then Secretary,
pressed Council for funds to improve *ASR*. It provided some, but not
enough to satisfy me.

Over the years, *ASR* had lost some of its attractiveness as a result of
changes ordered by Council. Book reviews were removed to a new journal, *Contemporary Sociology*, ASA affairs were consigned to the house
organ, *Footnotes*, sophisticated methods articles were shifted to a new
journal, *Sociological Methodology, Sociological Theory* became an
annual and then a semi-annual. *ASR* contained only research articles.
The *American Journal of Sociology* and *Social Forces* and others had
book reviews, more extensive comments, special issues, and were more
fun to read. *Footnotes* rarely published comments on the state of discipline, position papers, or provocative pieces. Its format as a newspaper
made it a natural throwaway. Since its contents were not indexed, members had problems locating specific items.

I tried to introduce a bit of variety in *ASR* by writing editorials and
inviting others. Subject to review, I asked distinguished sociologists to
present position papers on the state of sociology and problems facing
the discipline. I stole a few pages from articles to publish the table of
contents of current issues of all ASA journals to stimulate their being

read. I published the editor's Annual Report in *ASR* where it belonged, not only in *Footnotes*. And I published the names of sociologists who had died during the year, noting the issues of *Footnotes* where the obituaries appeared. I published Errata of previous articles on a separate first page of the issue, where it would be most visible and could be cut out to place with the original article. But the more innovations I introduced, the fewer the pages were available for articles. I partially overcame the deficit by trimming lengthy reviews of the literature and tightening the writing. ASA policy remained rigid on page allotment even though the *American Journal of Sociology*, for example, was devoting more pages to articles than *ASR*. While my innovations made the journal more appealing, subsequent editors did not continue them.

Finally, some good articles had to be rejected simply because of rigid page allotments. To partially overcome the stricture, every year I managed to publish about fifty pages more than *ASR* was allotted. Bill D'Antonio, then the executive officer, was responsible for keeping editors on budget. When he objected to my budget overruns, I asked him to apply my editor's honorarium ($3,000) that I had returned to ASA to cover the deficit.

Returning an honorarium is no simple matter. I had returned them as secretary, then as editor, to the ASA because I thought it unseemly to be paid for service to one's discipline. As a Council member, I had moved several times to eliminate them but always lost. I first asked ASA not to send me the check, but was informed that it couldn't be done. Legally, I had to accept it, pay taxes on it, then I could return it as a gift, deducting it from my income taxes as a charitable contribution.

Bill D'Antonio was reluctant to violate ASA guidelines, but finally let me to have the extra fifty pages. However, the next year he told me that the overruns amounted to more than my honorarium. I offered to pay the balance because I had committed the articles but Bill somehow found funds to cover the cost overruns. I never was able to convince Council that publications should receive the highest priority in the budget of a learned society. Clearly, ASA was becoming less and less an academic society oriented to research.

At the beginning of my term as editor, the elected Publications Committee held meetings with journal editors present. As the number of ASA journals increased, the three elected members of the committee were outnumbered by the seven editors. Although the editors' vote on all issues was advisory and held separately from that of members, the Committee felt outgunned in discussions, made to feel like a minority imposing its will on the majority. It decided to meet separately from the editors and then hold a joint meeting after it had passed on policy issues.

I was not altogether comfortable with the Committee's decision, not because it did not have the right, perhaps even the obligation to meet separately, but because it would come to the joint meeting with policies all threshed out. I proposed that editors also meet separately prior to our joint meeting, so we could discuss the agenda and arrive at the joint meeting well prepared. This worked out very well and expedited our meetings with the Publications Committee.

In my final year as editor, *ASR* was evaluated by Council, a standard practice for all ASA journals. Council member Maureen Hallinan, ASA secretary Terry Sullivan, and Jeylan Mortimer from the Publications Committee made up the subcommittee who carried out the evaluation, inviting a qualitative sociologist at a Midwest university to join them. The subcommittee asked me to provide data on the number of papers submitted to *ASR* that were quantitative or qualitative, the respective rejection rates, referees' sex and race, and other matters.

The gist of their lengthy report to the Publications Committee was that *ASR* articles and their reviewers should represent the sex, race, and ethnic composition of ASA members as well as the substantive and methodological specializations in the discipline. Devices were suggested to make certain that *ASR* articles would be representative. In sum, quotas should be instituted for each area of concern.

I was taken aback by the report. It seemed to be based on two pieces of research that were seriously flawed, first, a 1984 survey of ASA members that showed wide discontent with *ASR*. A "systematic sample" survey of 209 ASA members had elicited a 40 percent response, which Norval Glenn said was "small and probably biased."

The second piece of flawed research, conducted by the qualitative sociologist on the subcommittee, was based on a snowball sample of Marxists and qualitative sociologists to show that *ASR* was biased against qualitative and Marxist research. The letter that accompanied the survey said that its writer was concerned to document the perception of *ASR* as being narrow or specialized; if readers knew of qualitative, theoretical, or other underrepresented researchers who had had submission experiences that seemed to indicate some sort of systematic discrimination, he would like to hear of it. The appendix to the snowball survey included twenty-one letters from ASA members that complained of the unfair treatment they received from *ASR* editors. All of them were unsigned.

The qualitative sociologist had written to Larry Griffen, a Marxist sociologist then at Indiana, who replied that his experience was that I had bent over backward to be fair to Marxist-inspired papers. But Griffin's letter did not appear among the batch reproduced in the Appendix of the subcommittee report. Nor had I been invited to respond to letters that personally attacked me. I prepared a six-page response to the report, then sent it to the Publications Committee before it met at convention in August 1989.

The Publications Committee rejected the subcommittee's recommendations to include randomness in the selection of reviewers, to accept more papers with split reviews, to invite papers from underrepresented areas, to publish special issues, and to add subsections in *ASR* to reflect the breadth of the discipline.

The Publication Committee's actions had to be approved by Council. I wrote letters to Council to ensure it would be fully informed. In the exchange with the opposition on the subcommittee and Council, I extracted a major concession, the admission that there *may be a perception* among some that *ASR* is biased against certain areas and methods of sociology and consequently, authors of such papers may not submit their papers to *ASR*. The solution seemed obvious: those with this perception should be encouraged to submit papers. My review of *ASR* decisions found no difference in rate of rejection of such papers and others.

The conspiracy of the Marxists and some qualitative sociologists to demean *ASR* was so transparent and mean-spirited that I did not understand how the subcommittee could claim to have conducted a disinterested evaluation. In the meeting of the Marxist section at the annual convention, the qualitative sociologist's snowball survey attack on *ASR* was presented. The Fall Newsletter of the Marxist Section also attacked *ASR*, relying heavily on the snowball sample findings.

A former student of mine at Michigan State who then chaired the Marxist section wrote an editorial charging *ASR* and ASA as biased and unfair. I had talked to him at the ASA meeting and given him data that disproved his charges. Among these, was an analysis of three years of papers that had been submitted to *ASR*, coded as qualitative or quantitative and by substantive areas. The number of papers published were proportional to the number submitted; 19 percent of the papers published were qualitative, including papers on interpretive sociology, cultural sociology, discourse analysis, and theory. The rejection rate for these and remaining categories was about the same. I gave him copies of Griffin's and other letters of support and a list of Marxist papers that *ASR* had published. We had increased the referees of Marxist papers by 50 percent. My former student ignored all these data in his editorial. I wrote him again and asked him to publish my response in the newsletter and his response to it, but he did neither.

The controversy in Council and Publications Committee received wide publicity and I received strong support. Andrew Greeley wrote that the Marxists had motivated the "mean-spirited committee report on the *ASR*." Clifford Clogg wrote, that I was a great *ASR* editor. Paul DiMaggio wrote two strong letters supporting me. Larry Griffin wrote, "I have worked with lots of editors since Zelditch and I have never seen anyone do a better job than you." Carla Howry, on the ASA staff wrote that at least a dozen people had come to her at the regional meetings to say much they liked *ASR*.

I then reexamined the reviews of qualitative papers submitted to *ASR*. We had routinely chosen referees who did qualitative research to review papers in their fields. Their reviews turned out to be harsher on average, with two exceptions. Papers with a Marxist orientation reviewed by Marxists had high positive consensus as did qualitative papers dealing with gender issues.

The Publications Committee asked me to continue being editor for another term. Most people are unaware that a three-year term as editor actually involves four years of service. The editor begins receiving manuscripts on 1 July because the first issue appears in the following February. Although the term ends three years later in July, the editor is responsible for processing accepted manuscripts through the December issue, a five-month interval. Having served on the MacIver Award committee, the Publications Committee, Council, twice as editor of *ASR*, and secretary, eighteen years of service to ASA seemed enough.

The issues dealing with the alleged bias of *ASR* have not been settled. They seem to reflect unresolvable cleavages within the discipline on the role of ascriptive characteristics of participants in the publication process and ideological and methodological cleavages. Can consensual and universalistic standards be used to judge the merit of publications in all subareas of the discipline? Will this fissure eventually split the ASA into two societies as it has some of the other disciplines in the social and behavioral sciences?

12

The Ohio State Shop

Introduction

In 1983 when Joan Huber was in her second term as head of the department at Illinois-Urbana, she was invited to apply for a position as dean of the College of Social and Behavioral Sciences at Ohio State University. Approaching Columbus by car for a second interview, I saw the skyline and burst out that I was ready to move whether they offered me an appointment in sociology or not as I had plenty to do. Joan accepted the position and, although I was approaching compulsory retirement age, the Provost offered me a visiting professorship in sociology and the department was eager to have me.

Department Politics

Ohio State was more like Michigan State than the University of Illinois: big campus, unspectacular buildings, large student body, strong land-grant tradition, situated at the state capital, middle- and lower-middle-class students, strong emphasis on athletics. Like most land-grant institutions, Ohio State had a feeling of openness, friendliness, and vitality. The big difference was that Columbus was larger than Lansing, more exciting, and growing. Both Columbus and the university were improving culturally. I knew several department members from my years at Michigan State when we met annually at the meetings of the Ohio Valley [later, North Central] Sociological Association. Knowing what to expect at Ohio State, I immediately felt at home.

The most important difference between Illinois and Ohio State was Ohio State's lower calibre of students. The university had long had an open admissions policy which required that the it accept any graduate of an Ohio high school. Only recently had it begun to require certain high school courses for admission. Ohio State's openness didn't bother me because I had always favored giving students a second chance and knew how to work with them, gaining their confidence, raising their aspirations, and encouraging them to work hard.

Despite hard times in academia, I was struck by Ohio State's opulence compared to that of Illinois. At Illinois, the one long-distance phone that faculty could use was locked in a phone booth, faculty were assigned a Xeroxing quota, two secretaries served the entire department, and faculty did all student advising. Faculty members received $75 for convention expenses if they presented a paper, the money drawn from the small overhead returned to the department from research contracts. While Ohio State pleaded poverty, there were none of these restrictions. Not only did the department have double the secretarial help of Illinois, it funded two student advisors, paid most of the expenses to national and regional meetings, had a research laboratory, and access to additional research funds from college and university. Faculty salaries were considerably higher, especially for full professors.

I had informed Saad Nagi, chair of Sociology, that I expected to be treated like any faculty member and teach a full load of five courses for the year. Before we arrived, Nagi had assigned me two graduate seminars: Social Stratification and Structural Sociology, both of which turned out to be disappointing because the graduate students simply didn't work as hard as they did at Illinois. I didn't repeat the mistake I made in my first year at Illinois when I failed a quarter of the students. But I did wonder whether I wanted to go on teaching graduate seminars. In the spring I taught Introductory Sociology with 400 students. I carefully prepared my lectures, worked the students hard by requiring them to read three books, had them take frequent examinations and write reports. Although they complained, at the end of my last lecture they stood up and applauded. I decided to teach fewer graduate seminars and focus more on undergraduate courses in the areas of work, occupations, and the economy. With enrollments of twenty-five or fewer (smaller classes than at Illinois), classes went very well. However, in my last graduate seminar on the American working class, student performance was still disappointing.

Saad Nagi was improving the department with good appointments, some of whose work was akin to mine, including Mike Wallace, a promising new Indiana Ph.D. who was teaching economic sociology at Yale and eager to return to the Midwest as well as Toby Parcel, doing fine research on labor markets at Iowa, and Bob Kaufman, a young Wisconsin Ph.D. then at Utah who was doing excellent research on race stratification in labor markets.

Mike, Toby, Bob, and I, all engaged in labor market research, began to work together on a research program dealing with technological change. Research funds were readily available from Ohio State and the National Science Foundation. Richard Simpson from North Carolina, noting our stream of publications, dubbed us "The Gang of Four." Kevin Leicht, an Indiana Ph.D., joined the gang for two years as a post-doctoral fellow. Had Kevin and Mike remained at Ohio State, the research program would have prospered. Much to my regret, Mike left for Indiana and Kevin left for Penn State, spelling the end of the gang of four and its research program.

A deep departmental cleavage was apparent from the very first, a split between those who were unhappy with Saad Nagi, the recently appointed chair, and all the others who either supported Saad or were indifferent. This split, which festered for several years, can be better understood by considering the department's recent history. Sociology, one of the oldest departments in the nation, was established in 1898. Raymond Sletto, a measurement expert from the University of Minnesota, headed it for seventeen years until he stepped down in 1967. The Department had earlier been ranked fairly high nationwide but in the early 1960s it began a path of steady decline.

Hoping to revive the department's stature, the dean invited Hans Zetterberg to succeed Sletto. Zetterberg, a wealthy and sophisticated Swedish professor at the University of Uppsala, had a fine scholarly record. His diplomatic skills were less well honed. His first act was to divide the faculty into three groups: core, marginal, and frozen. Then he sent letters to all to inform them of their status. The frozen, told that they would never receive a raise, were advised to leave. Those in the marginal category were told to quickly improve their productivity lest they become frozen. As the majority of faculty were either in the marginal or frozen groups, the department became a cauldron of discontent. Fifteen faculty left within a year. A hurried recruitment effort yielded two or three distinguished appointments and several untried assistant professors.

A vocal opposition soon emerged in response to Zetterberg's imperious and volatile style of administration. In his third year, several department meetings ended in shouts and insults. Without notifying the faculty, Zetterberg suddenly left during the student riots of 1971. At first, the department was unaware that his absence was permanent because he had often gone to Sweden for short visits, leaving Alfred Clarke, the assistant chair, in charge.

To calm troubled waters, the dean hired Edward McDonagh from the University of Georgia to take over as chair in a period made even more difficult by the onset of the 1970 recession, shrinking budgets, and falling course enrollments. After three years, McDonagh was appointed dean of the College of Social and Behavioral Sciences himself and he selected faculty member Russell Dynes as chair in Sociology. When Dynes left three years later to become the executive officer of the ASA, he was succeeded by long-time department member Kent Schwirian.

Schwirian encountered even heavier economic weather. The department budget was cut 30 percent in his first three years in office. Enrollments had declined from their peak level in the late sixties and, with an enrollment-driven budget, the future looked even bleaker. In a drive to remedy this situation, Schwirian, with the energetic support of Simon Dinitz, a distinguished criminologist, developed an expanded criminology program that received support from the provost's office. In part, the program was enacted to thwart the establishment of a separate unit in criminal justice, a strong national trend that was undermining criminology enrollments in sociology departments.

Among the courses introduced in the new curriculum were those essential in criminal justice programs such as forensic science and identification which were taught by experts in the state criminal justice system. The new criminology concentration or major became almost a separate department with applied courses, adjunct professors, a part-time administrator, adviser, secretary, and a support budget. Criminology enrollments and number of majors zoomed, far outstripping those in Sociology.

When Kent Schwirian stepped down from his five-year term as chair in summer of 1982, the department recommended to the dean that Saad Nagi be appointed. An Ohio State Ph.D., Nagi had successfully attracted large research funds whose overhead refunds were directed to the units to which he was attached, the medical school, the Mershon Center for National Defense, and Sociology. His involvement in Department affairs had been modest over the years. Although he had strongly supported Zetterberg, he was not seen as part of a Department clique. Nagi was strongly research oriented and eager to improve the department's national stature that had not improved much since before the Zetterberg years. With rising enrollments and an improving economy, Nagi was promised resources to improve the department.

One of Nagi's first acts was to fund a research laboratory with funds that the criminologists thought had been designated to support the criminology program. At the same time and with the support of the University president, Nagi began to eliminate some applied criminology courses (e.g., finger-printing), to abolish the positions of program supervisor and student advisor, and integrate the criminology major into the sociology major. As if all of this were not enough, there was serious contention on the promotion to full professor of one of the criminology faculty.

I arrived in January 1984 in the midst of the demise of the criminology major. The criminologists and their supporters, perhaps seven or eight who opposed Nagi's unwillingness to support the recommendation for promotion, directed their objections to the highest levels of the administration. In addition, two other faculty members opposed Nagi on personal grounds. Nagi had the support of three women faculty, two men who had strongly supported Zetterberg, and three others to whom he had assigned key department posts. The remainder of the department was indifferent to the struggle and, in effect, went along with Nagi.

I wondered whether I had stepped into a political inferno because I openly supported Nagi's plans to improve the department yet I regularly lunched with his critics, the only group in the department that was socially cohesive. Nagi, who always played his cards close to the chest, shared neither with me nor the others all of his reasons for opposing the promotion. To my dismay, Nagi's critics withdrew from departmental affairs, in part because they had not been appointed to key committees. The remainder of the faculty was silent. In faculty meetings, Nagi's critics sat in stone silence while Nagi made announcements in almost inaudible monologues. Very few persons asked questions or initiated discussions of policies or events. I had never witnessed so low a level of faculty involvement.

Nagi worked hard to improve the department's facilities and standing. He had high scholarly standards and quietly and systematically pursued his vision by hiring junior scholars like Bob Kaufman, Laurie Krivo, Toby Parcel, Ruth Peterson, and Mike Wallace, and senior scholars like demographer Krishnan Namboodiri, political sociologist Richard Hamilton, and social movement analyst, Craig Jenkins. He consulted me and his kitchen cabinet on recruitment and other problems.

Nagi's core opposition were the tenured faculty who had been in the department a decade or more. Apart from their grievance over the fate of the criminology major, they privately objected to Nagi's quiet and non-consultative style of running the department and to his abandoning of valued customs of the old regime. If the department had ever had any solidarity, it was no longer apparent.

Although Nagi's critics were socially cohesive and lunched with one another daily at the faculty club, they were politically passive. I regularly lunched with them and they accepted me even though I supported Nagi's ambitions for the department. I voiced my disapproval of their withdrawal from departmental politics and urged them to work out a compromise with Saad. That would be useless, they said, Nagi would be immovable. In short, I was accepted by both sides of the dispute and tried to bring about their reconciliation.

I decided that promoting the associate professor whose qualifications were disputed was the price to be paid for rebuilding departmental morale. My advice to Nagi supporters was that they show restraint and support the promotion. They reported this to Nagi who came to my office. Without telling me his reasons, he asked me to abandon my efforts. Furious at the pressure to restrain my political rights, I wrote a letter of resignation effective at the end of the quarter and sent it to Saad the next day. I decided not to attend the meeting of full professors that would reconsider the promotion case.

Saad invited me to lunch to dissuade me from retiring, and seemed unable to comprehend why I was so disturbed. He refused to accept my resignation and pressured me to stay on. I wouldn't agree, but he persisted. I told no one in the department of my decision to resign. In any event I was scheduled to retire in two years at the compulsory age of seventy.

About that time, I heard that the ASA Publications Committee was split on nominating the next editor for *ASR*. I had already been editor for a year while at Illinois and was uncertain whether to take another turn at it. I asked whether the post was still available, which soon resulted in a request to be the next editor. Nagi pressed me to accept. It would bring prestige to the department, which would fully support the journal. I could be relieved of all departmental duties.

I decided that the editorship would ease my transition to retirement, accepted the post, and ceased engaging in departmental affairs. Later I learned that Nagi had good reasons for blocking the associate professor's promotion but did not want to embarrass the associate professor or the department by making them public. I devoted full time to the journal and enjoyed the experience. True to his word, Nagi subsidized the journal's operation more than other any institution had in the past. My deputy editors, Craig Jenkins and Robert Kaufman worked hard with me to improve the journal. As I had passed the age of seventy by the end of my tenure as editor, the department invited me to a celebration of my retirement. I never liked such affairs and reneged. On my birthday, someone asked me to step into the seminar room. There was a cake. Everyone joined in singing happy birthday and I was given a Mount Blanc pen. I responded with a one-minute expression of appreciation.

In sum, when Nagi became chair, the department had ranked at about the median of all of the sociology departments listed in the report of the National Conference Board in 1982. In the Board rankings that appeared in 1993, the department was in the top twenty-five, and an issue of *U.S. News & World Report* noted that it was one of the few departments nationwide to rise so dramatically in faculty prestige. Nagi was succeeded by Krishnan Namboodiri who maintained the trajectory with good appointments. He was followed by Barbara Reskin who served two years, then resigned because she did not like administration. She was followed by Betty Menaghan who served as chair almost six years. By the end of her term, faculty productivity had improved greatly. A study done by a department member at the University of Iowa indicated that, considering only the criterion of publication in the discipline's top three journals (*ASR*, the *American Journal of Sociology*, and *Social Forces*), the department ranked in the top three or four.

Institutional Analysis

As the end of my term as *ASR* editor approached in 1989, Maureen Hallinan asked me to contribute a chapter for a book she was editing on *Change in Social Institutions*. The day after my term expired, I moved into the emeriti office and turned to the task. I had always been dissatisfied with how sociologists deal with institutions and this was my opportunity to systematize my thoughts. In two months I wrote the essay (1990) on "Institutional Analysis." Despite a century of thinking about the subject, sociologists had neither arrived at a consensual definition of "institutions" nor agreed on how to operationalize the process of institutional change. Attitudes, values, rules, norms, regulative principles, and large organizations were among the many conceptions of institutions. The use of the term in introductory textbooks revealed a truly chaotic situation.

I proposed an organizational approach to the definition and study of institutions and institutional change. I defined an institution as a number of interacting organizations (complexes) whose boundaries are measured by the extent of their contacts. The regularities that emerge from these interactions are norms, rules, regulations, and laws. Institutional analysis explains how these regularities emerge, function, and change, reversing the traditional approach where they are asserted to exist and then used to explain behavior. My procedure avoided the circularity of the traditional sociological practice where regularities are first posited and then used to explain them.

In an organizational society, organizations compete, bargain, fight, form alliances, or ignore one another. This is what is meant by social processes. Patterns of organizational relationships that emerge from the social processes, I argued, comprise the institutions: economy, polity, education, welfare, family, and others. Since the procedures for identifying all institutions are built upon identifying organizational interlocks, identifying institutions automatically identifies inter-institutional relations. Thus, institutional analysis is at the same time inter-institutional analysis, relating parts (institutions) to the whole (society). As things now stand, most scholars treat institutions separately, conveniently ignoring sociology's main task: to understand society.

To illustrate the utility of the approach, I used the political model of institutional relations used earlier in *Industry, Labor, and Community* (Form and Miller 1961). This model essentially depicts the density of network ties among organizations as they interact to attain their objectives. In ongoing interactions and bargaining among nested organizations, the norms of interactions are derived empirically, not asserted a priori to explain the interactions. I was happy with the piece. Several of my colleagues made it required reading in their courses. Unfortunately, the audience for edited books is small and the chapter's impact was limited. I am currently considering expanding this approach in a monograph.

The New Deal

For the 1985 meetings of the ASA, President Kai Erikson asked me to contribute a paper on his theme, "Working and Not Working." I elected to write a paper on organized labor and the welfare state. Theda Skocpol, who took part in the same panel, was an expert on the New Deal. During the discussion, we disagreed on labor's role in launching New Deal legislation. I decided to immerse myself more deeply in the history of the New Deal, but had put the task aside when I became editor of *ASR*. The paper was finally published five years after its presentation (Form 1990b), just as I was finishing my editorial term.

After finishing the institutional analysis paper, I returned to my study of the New Deal. I discussed my thoughts with my colleague Craig Jenkins who had examined the formation of fiscal policy under the New Deal. We decided to edit a book on empirical sociological research on policy formation during the New Deal. We spent the better part of a year combing the literature, finally selecting a number of papers that hung together nicely. After editing them we made contact with the publishers to assess the cost of royalties to be paid. Then we sent our prospectus to fifteen publishers, indicating that we expected no royalties. All of them turned the project down because paying the royalties was prohibitively high.

We decided to ask all the authors whose articles we had selected to write fresh papers on their topics following a plan and format we had worked out. All but a few, Theda Skocpol and her ex-students quickly agreed. Skocpol negotiated for all of them. They finally decided to join the project if Theda wrote a concluding chapter for the book. Craig and I balked at this because the book could hardly have two concluding chapters. Besides, writing this chapter was the editors' job. Skocpol would not budge even though we offered to submit our final chapter for her inspection prior to publication and would carefully consider her reactions in the final draft. She remained adamant. Without her chapter and those of ex-students who emphasized the state's role in fashioning the New Deal, the book would not be comprehensive. We had to abandon the project.

Labor Politics in America

Yet, all was not lost. The year of intensive reading made me more aware of the role that organized labor played in the Democratic Party's legislative projects. This was the time to write my long-delayed monograph on labor politics. Reviewing the literature since the New Deal, I found that the one comprehensive field study was Greenstone's (1969) *Labor in American Politics,* done in the mid-1960s

Many of Greenstone's provocative findings no longer reflected current reality. The economy, political parties, organized labor, and political processes had changed enormously in the intervening thirty years. Neither was reformulation of Marxist class theory adequate in the face of theoretical developments in labor economics, sociology, and political science. Labor market theory now emphasized segmented markets brought about by the restructuring of the economy and changing patterns of international trade. Political theory had been revised to cope with the resurgence of the Republican Party and its attacks on traditional federalism and the welfare state. These changes called for a revised theory of labor politics that depended less on class and more on the restructuring of the economic, stratification, and political systems. I discerned parallels between economic segmentation and changes in the stratification and political systems that affected labor politics. Exploring the parallels would be the theme of my research.

Greenstone had drawn a parallel between the American Democratic Party and the European social-democratic parties. This parallel failed to hold after the New Deal in the face of the changing class composition of labor and the parties. The Democratic Party had become less dependent on labor as labor's input into manufacturing dwindled. In 1935 less than one-tenth of organized labor was white collar; by 1990, more than four-tenths. As the labor movement declined, its occupational composition began to resemble that of the entire labor force. Moreover, the annual earnings of the unionized sector outpaced those of most sectors labor force sectors. In the 1940s the largest Internationals were in building trades and manufacturing; in 1990, they were in government and services. The changing occupational and industrial composition of labor had changed both its internal and external politics.

Moreover, turbulent economic change had redistributed labor's membership regionally, weakening its political impact. Ebbing party loyalty, the use of mass media in political campaigns, the explosion of Political Action Committees (PACs) in competing interest groups, and the rising strength of gender and racial groups in the Democratic party had reduced labor's party influence. Importantly, the suburbanization of industry and labor union members had weakened labor's influence in urban politics.

Greenstone had portrayed three models of urban labor politics based on labor-party relationships in three metropolitan centers: Detroit, Chicago, and Los Angeles. But the UAW no longer dominated the party in Detroit. The Daley Democratic machine that had so long dominated Chicago had been successfully challenged and changed. Los Angeles's disorganized politics, long dominated by business, had changed in response to changing composition of racial groups and unions in the city.

Greenstone's models no longer held but no alternatives models had appeared.

One of my tasks was to determine how local politics had changed since the 1940s. I found basic changes in the relations among the major participants (business, government, parties, labor, and citizen groups), a more complex pattern of politics, and contrary to neo-Marxist theory, local politics had become more rather than less important. Labor's political machine, the Committee on Political Education (COPE) was built along community lines. Despite massive economic, ecological, stratification, and political changes in American cities, COPE's original operations remained essentially unchanged. This called for a reevaluation of COPE's effectiveness as a vote gathering machine in the city.

I was eager to get into the field again and talk to union officers and the rank and file. The reservoir of first hand observation on which sociologists depend to interpret events dries up over time and must be periodically refilled. I decided on a comparative field study of labor politics in Cleveland, Columbus, and Cincinnati, all metropolitan areas with over a million inhabitants. They were nearby and represented different economic and political patterns. Cleveland, a major manufacturing center was the most consistently Democratic city in the nation; Columbus, a white-collar service center, the most consistently Republican city; Cincinnati, an economically balanced city, was predominantly Republican, occasionally challenged by a revitalized Democratic Party.

Interviews in each city were arranged with the heads of the Republican and Democratic parties, journalists, political science professors, COPE leaders of the AFL-CIO, heads of COPE in the ten largest unions, and presidents of the largest locals of the ten unions. The interviews were exciting but also exhausting. I made many 200-to-300-mile round trips from Columbus to Cleveland and Cincinnati, often for a single interview.

I first reviewed the history of each community's economy, political parties, organized labor, and the role of ethnic-racial groups in politics. In such markedly dissimilar cities, I expected labor to adjust its political operations to local realities but this didn't appear to be the case. In Cleveland, the operations of the Democratic Party were chaotic, those of COPE were uncoordinated, and tensions between the party and COPE remained unresolved. The spectacularly successful record of the Democratic Party in Cleveland was not due to the strength and efficiency of the party or of labor, but to the political traditions of the major ethnic and racial groups. In Cincinnati, a reorganized Democratic Party and a reorganized COPE were struggling to overcome Republican dominance. Innovative and energetic party and labor leaders recognized the enormous difficulties in overcoming the traditional conservatism of their members and the community. Both labor and the party leaders in Columbus ritualistically tried to mobilize the Democratic majority to vote, but with little success. They seemed resigned to Republican dominance in city, state, and national affairs. In short, labor politics in Cleveland banked on tradition; in Cincinnati, on struggling to overcoming tradition; and in Columbus, on adjusting to the conservative status quo.

Since the same ten unions were investigated in the three cities, I examined whether city differences in political climate affected union political behavior. Thus, although the UAW was one of the most liberal unions on the national level, only in Cleveland were its local officers stridently liberal, but in Columbus and Cincinnati they were much more conservative. Even with these variations, within each city, the unions tended to fall into four types. The ex-AFL unions (Carpenters, Electrical Workers, Teamsters, building trades) were consistently the most conservative, while the ex-CIO unions were the most liberal. The Teachers and Government unions, despite their liberal rhetoric, were largely independent, while the Service and Food and Commercial unions were liberal in outlook but low in political involvement. In each city, the more liberal the union officers, the less they represented the political views of the rank and file. Even in Cleveland, the most liberal city, the majority of members of the most liberal union (UAW) thought their union should not engage in politics. In sum, city differences, cleavages within and between the unions, and political segmentation between officers and rank and file were normal conditions.

Critics of labor often point to the enormous electoral help the Democratic Party receives from COPE, but few scholars have examined this claim in the field. COPE routinely recommends political candidates to its members and it involves many volunteers (mostly officers) to turn out the vote. Randall Ripley and Herbert Asher in the Ohio State's Department of Political Science had conducted a statewide survey of the political attitudes and behavior of union and non-union voters. The samples were large enough to draw subsamples for my three cities and compare the responses of union and nonunion members. It was thus possible to examine the extent that COPE influenced the political behavior of union members.

City differences in political attitudes and behavior were evident but small. Likewise, differences between the union and random samples were small but in the expected direction. The most notable finding: almost *half* of union members did not know whether their union engaged in any of eight COPE-sponsored political activities. Of those saying they knew, 61 percent said (contrary to reality) that their union didn't engage in these activities; only 15 percent knew that their union was involved in COPE efforts to turn out the vote. COPE's ability to aggregate the political activities of its diverse unions was small. The survey conclusion was clear: the extent and efficacy of labor's political efforts is not only fractured but highly exaggerated.

Since labor had cast its political fate with the Democratic Party, I tried to gauge its influence on the party's national conventions from 1932 to 1992, particularly in reference to labor planks in the party platform and the selection of presidential candidates. For this stretch of sixty years, I examined consensus within labor and between labor and the party.

Clearly, labor's influence varied from convention to convention, reaching a low point in the 1972 convention. Its influence varied with the conflicts within and between the AFL and the CIO and with the strength and independence of groups in the liberal coalition: party leaders, teachers, women, blacks, and intellectuals. At one time or another, CIO unions were expelled from the AFL, Mineworkers quit the CIO, the CIO expelled Communist unions, the AFL expelled the Teamsters, the UAW quit the AFL-CIO, the AFL-CIO did not back the party's choice (McGovern) in 1972, and the alliances between dissident unions, the NEA, and other groups were unstable. In short, labor rarely spoke with one voice in the conventions and it lost leadership in the party's liberal coalition. With its successes declining, labor's ambivalence about its party alliance had grown.

Party politics may be less important than labor's impact on national elections and Congressional legislation. My interviews with COPE leaders in Washington provided insights into its operations as a coordinating body. From its birth in 1955 to 1990, COPE's organization in Washington was small, decentralized, and underfinanced. The organization did little to educate members on issues and its maximum influence in increasing member voting turnout was 10 percent. Even after the UAW and the Teamsters returned to the AFL-CIO, they both retained their separate political machines. COPE did not coordinate its work with the NEA nor did it conduct reliable assessments of its electoral efforts after elections. Given its resources, COPE did as well as might be expected, which wasn't very much.

Yet, the AFL-CIO's Washington lobby (Legislation Department) of eight professionals and a support staff was remarkably effective. It coordinated the lobbies of sixty International unions and developed ties with 400 labor specialists employed as staff by members of Congress, three-quarter of whom were pro-labor. Apart from influencing legislation, the Legislative Department tried to mobilize with limited success grass-roots support for various bills. Relations with the Democratic Party were strained, resembling ancient family disagreements.

COPE, Americans For Democratic Action (ADA), and the Consumer Federation of America (CFA) allegedly formed a liberal coalition in Washington. I examined how the three ranked the performance of all senators on major issues. ADA's rankings were consistently the lowest, but importantly, the majority of issues the three associations selected were quite different. The common issues they ranked dealt primarily with non-labor issues. The conclusion was that if a "progressive coalition" ever existed in Washington, it has been very loose.

Finally, I examined labor's success from 1947 to 1992 on congressional bills it signaled as important. The bills were coded for their relevance to organized labor and to non-labor issues such as the state of the economy, the general welfare, and class equity. Labor's success in passing specific labor legislation was about the same under Republican and Democratic administrations, but labor did less well on non-labor issues under Republican administrations, especially in the Senate. Over the years COPE targeted more bills for action that dealt with labor than with class equity and the general welfare. Overall, the Internationals in Washington seemed more successful in pursuing their interests than COPE was in pursuing the general interests of labor or those of disprivileged groups in society.

On completing my trilogy of monographs on the working class, I proposed a program for labor as its leading actor. With relatively small increases in resources devoted to organizing and political education rather than vote turnout, organized labor can become more united, more vital, and more successful in improving the lot of the working class and the nation. There are signs that labor can again become a social movement rather than a fragmented pressure group.

My research and writing journey continues. Apparently, they are something I must do. As a change of pace, I first wrote a family biography which was fun. And I turned to fresh fields, the study of social movements from a structural perspective and the sociology of religion. The journey continues.

13

The Changing Journey and Guild

The Journey

Looking back, I did not immediately discern the direction of the journey. Unlike most of my friends who strayed little from their chosen paths, I became bored travelling the same route for more than a few years. In an unpublished paper in which Ronald Burt analyzed sociologists' citation patterns in journal articles using block modeling techniques, I was surprised to find myself placed in the political arena. I had always thought that economy and stratification were my major areas, but on reflection, I concluded that I was constantly trying to integrate social stratification and politics into a single framework. This theme first appeared in my dissertation and persisted in research on work organization, community power, natural disasters, labor unions, political ideologies, and the working class. While the theme was constant, the substantive areas changed.

The same theme also underpinned the work of Wright Mills, my mentor. Hans Gerth first exposed Mills to the German literature on the politics of white-collar workers and Mills in turn directed me to it. The complex relations between Gerth and Mills in translating Weber and dealing with the German literature are fully explored in Oakes and Vidich (1999). Mills pointed me to three translations undertaken by the Works Progress Administration (WPA) during the New Deal: Emil Lederer's (1912) *The Problem of the Modern Employee*; Jacob Marschak's (1926) *The New Middle Class*; and Hans Speier's (1939) *The Salaried Employee in Modern Society*.

Both Gerth and Mills were fascinated by the problem that haunted German Marxists: the role that the emerging "new middle class" of

salaried and white-collar workers would play in bringing about a socialist state. If they sided politically with the old propertied middle
class, together they could block the socialist dream. If they sided with
the proletariat, as they should, socialism would soon be realized. After
all, Gerth and Mills concluded, the new middle class lacked property
and was exploited like the proletariat. With scant evidence, they argued
that the new middle class feared losing social status and so would not
identify with the proletariat. They disparaged clerks, skilled workers,
and artisans as conservative lower-middle-class petty bourgeoisie pawns
who craved respectability.

I did not embrace this view, perhaps because my father was a skilled
worker and my parents wanted their children to become middle-class
professionals. Although I remained sympathetic to the working class,
however defined, I could not pretend that my family of origin, whatever our class, was downtrodden, denied respectability and mobility
opportunities. To me, the matter of intra-class and interclass divisions
was an unsettled question that needed to be empirically examined. Although it was not my original objective in the dissertation, I compared
the income, status aspirations, and political views of Greenbelt's white-
collar and blue-collar workers and was surprised to find much overlap
(Form 1944, ch. 18-20). When Mills (1951) later published *White-Collar*, he focused on political divisions of the middle class, including clerical workers, but ignored how parts of the working class resembled them.
Ignoring interclass resemblances, he never referred to my Greenbelt
findings.

Mills also had me read Gerth's and his translation of Max Weber's
essay "Class, Status, and Party" before they published it in *Politics* (1944)
(see Oakes and Vidich 1999). In Mills' critique of Warner's (1942) *The
Social Life of a Modern Community*, he (1942a) relied on Weber's essay, excoriating Warner for ignoring class and power questions and
emphasizing social status. I studied the Weber essay and used it to an-
chor my dissertation (Form 1944). There I analyzed the life chances
(income, property, indebtedness) of Greenbelt earners, their past and
current occupational status, and their political behavior and ideology.
A summary article appeared in *ASR* (Form 1945), the first Weberian
analysis of the stratification system of an American community.

In *Industrial Sociology* (Miller and Form 1951), my chapters were
the first to use a Weberian approach to analyze the stratification system
of modern industries: an analysis of the power, status and class aspects
of work organization. In the first revision (Miller and Form 1964) I

expanded the chapter on power into three that dealt with power within work organizations, within labor unions, and between labor and management from factory floor to formal contract bargaining. I also expanded the chapters on status and class.

In the late 1970s, sociologists discovered the "new structuralism" in the study of labor markets, unaware that it was a Weberian approach to the labor market. In accounting for earnings, the "new" approach combined workers' ascriptive status (sex, race, ethnicity), the economic and organizational power of market participants (labor unions, enterprise, government), and workers' human capital (education, training, and experience). I had applied this approach in *Industrial Sociology* (1951, 1964) and later refined it in an essay on "Occupational Power" with Joan Huber (1976). In the late 1960s, I used it again to account for the unusual wage structure of an automobile factory in India (Form 1976, ch. 3; Form and Pampel 1978). In the United States, Bibb and I (1977) applied it to the wage structure of American manual workers. Finally, the framework was applied to explain management's wage strategy in a Korean automobile firm (Bae and Form 1986). About the same time that Bibb and Form used their structural framework to explain earnings, Erik Olin Wright (1979) applied a neo-Marxist class scheme to explain income. With the Marxist and the "new" approaches to labor market stratification, research in the area blossomed in the United States.

My research on community, ecology, and society heavily stressed political stratification. In an article in *Social Forces* (Form 1954), I proposed a political theory to explain changes in land use that supplemented traditional ecological theories and provided a framework to analyze the complex political game among four sectors (real estate associations, business organizations, government bodies, and residents) in bringing about land use change. Each sector and different players within them have different interests and resources. Depending on specified conditions, sectors or segments of sectors unite or split in forging alliances to bring about land-use change. Not until the neo-Marxist approach became popular in the 1970s did urban researchers use a political scheme to analyze land-use decisions. Unfortunately, they oversimplified the problem by conceptualizing the process in crude class terms, for example, the collusion of business and government as growth machines to promote central city growth (Molotch 1976; Feagin 1988).

Beginning in the mid-1950s, I began to develop an institutional approach to community decision-making, targeting the respective influence of labor, government, and business. A series of projects led to the first international comparative study of community power (Form and D'Antonio 1959), a systematic examination of the behavior of government, business, and other sectors in El Paso and Ciudad Juarez in resolving issues within and between the two communities. The comparison revealed different structures of inter-institutional interaction in each city in decision-making, an approach that parted from the prevailing emphases on class or individual influentials.

While Mills was interested in the divisions of the middle class, I was interested in what I thought had more payoff for understanding American politics: Why the working class was not more united in pursuing its political objectives. Without planning it, I eventually wrote three monographs on the topic.

Although I was unaware of it, this theme and others like it perhaps originated in my family socialization. My father was a proud skilled worker with a passion for politics. My notions about working-class stratification were anchored on the distinct place that skilled workers had in it and their politics in preserving that place.

In *Blue-Collar Stratification* (Form 1976) I showed that in four countries (the United States, Italy, Argentina, and India) even automobile workers (an allegedly homogeneous occupation) were divided by skill, social status, and politics. Contrary to Marxist theory, the divisions appeared to be larger in the more economically developed countries. The unpopularity of this hypothesis provoked me to explore it further. In *Divided We Stand* (Form 1986), I examined the income, status, and political divisions among American manual workers. Again, skill, sex, and racial divisions were large and structural, resulting in political cleavages that endured for generations. Finally, because advancing working-class interests in the United States required leadership from organized labor, I demonstrated in the third volume, *Segmented Labor, Fractured Politics* (Form 1995), that political differences among the country's major labor unions were historical and growing. Despite this massive evidence of working-class division, most scholars continued to ignore it and to concentrate on the working class-middle class divide.

My interest in stratification broadened over time. Huber and Form (1973) analyzed the way that different stratification ideologies are socially legitimized in a community, how they are translated under varying conditions to explain and justify economic and political inequality. In another empirical study (Form and Wood 1985), I tested the ability of several theories of stratification (pluralism, Marxist, elite, and others) to explain beliefs about economic inequities in society. None of the theories worked well, but sociologists continue to use them as if they are valid. Finally, in an empirical comparative analysis of working classes in the United States and France, I demonstrated that, contrary to common belief, the French working class is more economically and politically divided than the American (Form 1985, ch. 11).

In sum, although I disagreed with Mills in important ways, I shared his aim to integrate the study of stratification and politics in a single framework. My research became increasingly macrolevel and structural. I did not, perhaps could not, follow Mills' broad, largely qualitative, insightful, critical analysis of societal problems. I preferred to study them empirically in concrete organizations: the work plant, management, labor and government, the labor market, the community, and in different institutions in various societies.

The Changing Guild

In my journey of more than fifty years, departmental shops and the sociological guild changed in many ways. A few experiences illustrate how the shop changed. I retired from three state universities: Michigan State, Illinois at Urbana-Champaign, and Ohio State and had spent summers at the Universities of Washington at Seattle, Penn State, and Indiana. In all the shops I witnessed the same drive to improve sociology. Clearly, guild output improved steadily over the years. Doubters should compare articles in *ASR,* the *American Journal of Sociology*, or *Social Forces* in the late 1930s and today. The earlier articles were speculative, value-laden, and empirically barren. The increasing application of quantitative analysis to systematically collected data enormously benefited the discipline by making theory testing possible. The growth in general theory over the years has not been particularly impressive, but growth in sociology's sub-fields has been spectacular. All sub-fields have improved their theory and methods, including demography, organizations, stratification, institutions (e.g., industry, education, family, government, religion, military), criminology, deviance, and law. The accumulation of sociological knowledge has been massive. While in the 1940s, a scholar could grasp what was going on in all of sociology, today that is almost impossible. Yet, recent changes in some fields are disturbing, a matter I discuss later.

Improvement of the discipline has been accompanied by bureaucratic growth of the university which has eroded the serenity of earlier times. When I went to Michigan State in 1947, I don't remember anyone making much fuss about tenure. Charlie Loomis invited me to his office one day and told me that I was now an associate professor with tenure. I didn't even celebrate the occasion. A few years later, Charlie told Al Beegle that he intended to promote him to full professor. Al refused to go along on the grounds that Duane Gibson, a more senior colleague, should be promoted first. At that time, Loomis also proposed to promote me to professor and I also refused. While such a thing is unheard of today, the incident demonstrates the sense of community colleagues then shared. Duane Gibson taught young faculty members his statistical and survey methods skills and we were grateful. A year later, Loomis promoted both Al and me without consulting us.

In neither promotion did we submit a single sheet of paper to the department or the administration. Nor did the faculty submit reports on their teaching or research. Everyone knew what their colleagues were doing in research, teaching, and service in the department and the university. I taught thirty years before being asked to administer a teacher evaluation form.

The current drumbeat about the importance of teaching is mostly what it is: noise. The alleged neglect of teaching in favor of research is overblown. Even in the most research-oriented shops, I am impressed with the time and thought faculty devote to their teaching. With few exceptions, faculty members work hard at teaching because their dignity and self-worth are at stake. It is dispiriting to lecture to students who do not like you and faculty members go to great lengths to avoid this outcome. They need little pressure to do as well as they can.

The ASA's emphasis on teaching is also misplaced. Its teaching journal does not meet the standards of its other journals. The last report I saw showed that the teaching journal accepts 50 percent of submissions in contrast to 15 for the other ASA journals. The ASA office collects course outlines for various subareas of sociology and publishes them. The enormous variety of outlines display little concern for relating subareas to one another or to the discipline's core. No attention is given to students' obligation to learn, only to the instructor's obligation to motivate them. When my cohort went through the higher education system, it was assumed that most students wanted to learn, otherwise, why would they be there?

One of the main reasons given by teaching enthusiasts for including teaching among ASA's missions was to increase ASA membership by involving non-researchers in ASA affairs, apparently on the assumption that keeping abreast of developments in the discipline was insufficient motivation to get them to join or attend annual meetings. Adding the teaching mission to ASA functions failed to increase ASA membership, but provided a status platform for teachers who did no research, a platform once limited to research scholars.

The first time I had to have my teaching evaluated by students occurred twenty years after I received the Ph.D. I submitted my first annual report at Illinois-Urbana around 1975, about thirty years after the Ph.D. The legislature wanted to know not the amount of time that faculty spent on teaching and research but rather the proportion of time spent on each, so that those who worked, say, sixty-hour weeks (thirty hours on research, thirty on teaching) would report the same proportions as those who worked, say, forty-hour weeks with twenty hours on research and twenty on teaching. I was tempted not to submit a report because it was so patently assumed that professors were trying to avoid work, especially teaching. I filled out the questionnaire with crude guesses. With a seventy-hour work week, I felt I was putting in enough time for teaching. The data, with no known reliability or validity, were reproduced in a huge binding. The project calmed the legislators and kept their "research" staff busy indeed. Apparently, it never occurred to legislators that students had to *read something* based on research and the faculty had to provide that something.

Perhaps the threat of lawsuits has resulted in universities demanding more and more reports on teaching effectiveness. At Ohio State, professors are required to observe the teaching of assistant professors every quarter and to write reports to the department chair. It matters little whether the first two reports indicate that the teaching is dazzling. Reports must be submitted quarterly. The department chair also is required to summarize these reports in an annual letter which is given to instructors and placed in their files. In the promotion to associate professor, the file on teaching alone is an inch thick. Over six years, the time spent on evaluating teaching amounts to about 100 hours, most of it a waste of time which could be better spent in intellectual work.

Undertaking departmental or shop chores was once part of a graded system. The most recently hired assistant professor was expected to teach introductory sociology at 8:00 A.M. and at 4:00 P.M., on Saturdays or in the evening. Preparing new courses involved many hours then as it does now. I prepared a new course every other year as a normal part of my duties. The thought of having time off or receiving summer pay for preparing a new course was inconceivable. Newly recruited faculty rou-

tinely took minutes at faculty meetings and were given normal committee assignments as part of their training and socialization.

Today, associate professors, whatever the quality of their teaching
and research productivity, must be reviewed at least once every three
years whether or not they seek to be promoted. If the teaching reports
are consistently negative, little can be done to improve them. Typically,
the research productivity of "stuck" professors does not improve enough
to warrant promotion. Nonetheless, the bureaucracy insists that the evaluations be repeated, not only creating a larger file of unsatisfactory performance, but often resulting in increased bitterness on the part of both
subject and colleagues.

When I arrived at Michigan State, my normal load was four courses
a quarter for three quarters, four different ones in the winter. We did not
complain that the load was oppressive because we had routinely taught
even more. The load was reduced to three a quarter, then two, then five
for the year. As I examined my vita, I was surprised to learn that the
reduction in teaching had little effect on research productivity. I am
unaware of any systematic research on the relation of teaching load to
research productivity.

The current pressure on young assistant professors in research-oriented departments to turn out research can be demoralizing. The unproductive are constantly reminded that their continued employment
is precarious and the marginally productive are constantly anxious over
their ultimate fate. Some faculty are promoted only to become perma-
nently unproductive "stuck" associate professors. Even the most distinguished departments, including Wisconsin, Chicago, and Harvard,
and their like have a quota of these. Others, marginally accepted for
promotion, may become increasingly productive. Again, systematic
research on productivity over the life course is rarely studied.

Departments have slowly changed to help new faculty attain tenure.
The official teaching load of two courses a quarter is rarely enforced
for newly hired assistant professors in research departments. They are
typically given the first quarter off from teaching and sometimes a research assistant and research funds. Their load is gradually increased,
but if they are productive, they may never teach the official full-time
quota. Neophytes are not given normal committee assignments as it
might reduce their productivity. To further ease their burden, they are
allowed to teach courses in their areas of interest. Under optimal conditions of productivity and research funding, they can spend half the year
not teaching. Whether these aids have notably increased productivity

and made tenure more likely has rarely, if ever, been systematically explored.

The neophyte annually submits reports on teaching, research, and service. These are reviewed by a departmental committee and the department chair submits a written report on the neophyte's progress. The third or fourth year review is critical. A poor review is demoralizing and the neophyte begins a job search. A year to the final tenure decision, the candidate submits another detailed report. The materials are sent to external reviewers for evaluation. Then the senior faculty reviews the material and makes a recommendation in writing to the chair, who in turn makes a recommendation in writing to the dean, who in turn makes a recommendation in writing to the provost. The neophyte is sometimes invited to read the evaluations that tenured colleagues and the department chair have sent to the dean. Throughout this process, most committees members do not read the material the candidate submits to evaluate its quality. They count the number of articles published, the prestige of the journal in which they appear, and the number of citations in the Citation Index.

The dean solicits the advice of a promotion and tenure committee; its recommendations and that of the dean are then submitted to the provost's committee for a final decision, a process that entails an enormous amount of faculty time. Whether the procedure has improved the quality of promotions has yet to be tested. Whatever the results, the system seems designed to maximize anxiety in the candidate and hostility among colleagues.

Anxiety may endure for the entire career, expressed in frenetic activity to increase productivity in order to get higher salary increases. Some productive faculty members try to escape departmental activities and find research offices outside the department to minimize their contacts with faculty and students. For twenty years, Robert Merton and Paul Lazarsfeld at Columbia lunched together in their offices daily, talking sociology for at least an hour. Such faculty-faculty learning has probably declined over the years. For intellectual stimulation, faculty may attend departmental brown-bags. Often scheduled during class hours, attendance rarely exceeds half of the faculty.

To be a graduate assistant once was an honor rather than payment for teaching or research assistance. One applied for admission to graduate studies by simply submitting a course transcript and two letters of recommendation. Today, recruitment of graduate students is almost as intensive as that for faculty. Bright students are invited to visit the department for a day or two, all expenses paid. After being interviewed and entertained by several departments, they select the best offer. The stipend I received as a graduate assistant was roughly one-eighth that of an assistant professor; today the ratio is closer to a third.

The rate of expansion of teaching duties used to be slow for graduate assistants. They first attended lectures and helped professors grade papers. Then they were given a quiz section of Introductory Sociology and perhaps in their final year, a section of their own. Today, assistants start as quiz instructors, are soon given a section to teach, then courses at higher levels. This path often is that taken by the least gifted academically. The pick of the crop are offered fellowships with no teaching or research duties. Almost as rewarding is a research assistantship with higher pay throughout the year, including summer.

Departments have become more entrepreneurial, one of their main functions is to generate research funds. The overhead from these funds primarily goes to the university to support research facilities, but the growth of such facilities at the department level are modest at best. Research funds do support students and provide them with more research experiences than in the past. Faculty who bring in research funds tend to receive higher raises whether or not they produce important research. Funded research also pays for released time from teaching as well as graduate student assistance in order to increase number and quality of publications. Thus, funded faculty are doubly rewarded. Students often publish with their mentors, who compete to place them in the highest prestige universities. Sometimes, faculty recruited on the basis of co-authored articles turn out to be unproductive.

There are some drawbacks to the new order. In the 1950s and 1960s graduate students were typically involved in all stages of the research, from designing it, gathering data in the field, coding, writing papers and publishing. A drawback of much current training is the increasing reliance on data banks, often for both the M.A. thesis and Ph.D. dissertation. Throughout their entire graduate experience, students may not have conducted a single interview, engaged in any participant observation, studied an organization, or worked as part of a research team. Most have never studied a foreign language, minored in another social science, or worked in an organization long enough to have a sense of how it functions. A year-long internship in an organization might well be a requirement of graduate training.

The current exposure of students to sociology's subareas is typically limited. When I arrived at Ohio State, master degree students had to pass four examinations in substantive areas; today, none. At the Ph.D. level, students often are examined in only one area. A review of the literature beyond a decade is rarely required. Departments are often divided into shops that have little contact with each other, which lessens student contact with faculty and students in other areas. In the 1950s, large departments had three shops: social organization, demography, and social psychology. Currently, these shops may be divided into subshops organized around special interests of a faculty member who generates large research grants.

Creativity emerges when scholars know two or more subareas of a discipline, another discipline, or a foreign literature. Learning foreign languages used to be standard in Ph.D. programs, and engaging in research abroad was not uncommon. Language requirements were reduced in the 1950s then eliminated in the 1960s in favor of more training in statistics. Even so, only 37 percent of graduate programs require a statistics course and most of these do not require more than one (Huber 1995, p. 209). Today, students who have never been abroad or studied a foreign language write dissertations in comparative sociology or in world systems. It is not uncommon for students to write dissertations on particular industries, organizations, or social movements without ever having entered a factory, lived in a complex organization, or taken part in a social movement. When students use data banks, they are not required to conduct interviews using the original schedule and to code a small sample of interviews to get a feel of how the original data were processed.

The bureaucratizing of research, large research shops, and the use of complex statistical analyses has generally produced better science. Mass-produced automobiles today are much better products than handcrafted ones of earlier times. Yet good sociological research can still be produced on the craft model. To be sure, craft research takes much time and sometimes results in books rather than articles. Comparative historical analysis of revolutions is largely done along craft lines. Intensive case studies of complex organizations provide another illustration. The need for these kinds of studies persists, but it is hard to fund. When well done as books, they have greater impact on the discipline than most articles even in the best journals although when not well done, they sink rapidly from sight. Craft output should not be evaluated by the same criteria used to evaluate articles. In their eagerness to improve their national reputations, departments sometimes under-reward writers who produce well-crafted books.

Problems of the Guild

Many sociologists are concerned with what is happening to the discipline's intellectual core, if there be one. Historically, the discipline exported theory and methods to other disciplines. The exporting first began when social work was expelled from sociology because it was thought to be too applied. We not only lost the opportunity to influence that field (which become heavily psychological), we closed off potential influence on social policy as well as ready research access to the burgeoning welfare sector.

Other social sciences developed institutional audiences for their output. Economists apply their expertise to business and the economy, political scientists to government, psychologists to clinical practice and personnel administration in business and government. Sociologists could have claimed health, education, and welfare in the welfare state as their special niche by examining the effectiveness of programs and policies, but they allowed other social sciences to preempt the area.

Sociologists originated behavioral research in industry and complex organizations and exported their expertise to business schools, which developed their own departments of organizational behavior. Today's major research journal on organizations, *The Administrative Science Quarterly*, has a subscription list of 40,000 while sociology lacks a journal in this area. Sociologists were too distrustful of business to help solve practical problems of human relations and organizational change. Departments in colleges of business initiated research and applications in these areas. Ironically, sociology departments currently experience difficulty recruiting faculty to teach and study organizations, one of the most important areas of the discipline. When sociology does turn out talented students, business schools hire them because they can pay more.

Criminology, once the monopoly of sociology, has largely been taken over by criminal justice departments that willingly tackle applied concerns in that sector. Few sociologists today study or teach penology, an area begging for organizational analysis. Sociology exported its theory and methods to education departments. Although sociologists still study educational institutions, most of the service research to universities, schools, and government agencies is supplied by faculties of colleges of education. Courses in survey research methods were once the monopoly of sociology, but today are more available in departments of political science and business. Yet, survey research data remains the source of most sociological research.

Students in social work, business, criminal justice, education, and political science used to enroll in sociology courses; today, few do so. Evaluation research, desperately needed to evaluate the effectiveness of public policy, is rarely taught in sociology graduate programs. That area is begging for experiments in organization design and the measurement of organizational outputs.

Having refused to develop nonacademic markets for the application of our knowledge, graduate sociology departments largely teach others who will teach sociology. We may arrive at a point where administrators may ask, Who needs sociology? In the past we gained prominence by our ability to innovate theory and methods that other disciplines adopted. Our ability to continue to innovate derives from our unique perspective among the social sciences: studying societies as wholes or macrolevel comparisons of organizations, communities, and institutions. Yet, a macro emphasis in our graduate teaching is becoming scarce.

Whatever the shortcomings of organizational ecology, it innovated by melding insights from two subareas of sociology, ecology-demography and organizations. Sociology of the labor market grew by incorporating insights from economics and organizational sociology. Social movement research was long mired in descriptive case analysis (Form 1997) until sociologists like Mayer Zald and John McCarthy (1987) brought organizational sociology to bear on the area. The study of stratification in Wisconsin's model of status attainment became ritualized until structural and Marxist sociologists brought their theories to bear on occupational placement and mobility. Progress along these lines will continue only if sociology departments encourage more general rather than specialty training.

To what areas of sociology should departments expose graduate students? While there is no easy consensus on the core of the discipline, Huber's (1995) article in the centennial issue of *The American Journal of Sociology* provides a good list: demography, social organization, stratification, and quantitative analysis, all taught in an historical comparative framework.

The Problem of Theory

Whether sociological theory should be part of core requirements depends on what theory is designed to do. Over 70 percent of Ph.D.-granting departments require theory courses (Huber 1995, p. 209) that represent a wide range, including the history of theory, classical theory, contemporary theory, phenomenology, postmodern, and mixtures thereof. The history of sociological theory and classical theory as typically taught look back toward the discipline's origins. With rare exceptions (Turner 1987), the study of classical theory is reverential, not refined to test current research questions.

Neither should the required theory course focus on theories about theories. Many theory courses today tend to be "conceptual jungle-gymning," relating concepts or theories to one another. Conceptual development in some contemporary theories constitute a Babel stripped of empirical referents. Hamilton (1992) selected a example from Bordieu (1996, p. 267, 53) that refers to "logical logic" and "structured structures predisposed to function as structuring structures." The best theory today is probably being taught in the subareas of the discipline as theories of social movement, institutional change, world systems, comparative-historical change, restructuring of stratification systems, and demographic change.

The simplification of theory as presented in some research articles is depressing. First, an issue is selected, as the passage of a piece of welfare legislation, then three theories are offered to explain it: class, state, or pluralism. Regression equations are run, with a single variable representing each theory. The evidence is displayed and a conclusion is drawn: all, none, or a combination of theories explain the outcome. Other researchers consider another legislative outcome applying the same theories and arrive at a different theoretical conclusion. Then, endless arguments ensue whether one theory is superior to another, leading to little accumulation of knowledge. An impediment to disciplinary growth is the practice, often unconscious, of scholars trying to legitimate their political ideology or values. While we all hope that sociology can help bring about the good society, sociology as a discipline should not push an ideological line. At best, it can provide the theory and tools needed to analyze policies, their implementation, and outcomes. Much research begins with the assumption, for example, that modern work is alienating. This is an empirical question that needs to be tested, not assumed. If ideological disputes cannot be settled by empirical research, they are not worthy of attention. Progress in settling ideological disputes can only be made when antagonists agree on what constitutes a fair test and adequate methodology (Form 1980). Otherwise, they are blowing in the wind.

The history of sociology is replete with illustrations of ideological beliefs that stifle research progress (Hamilton 1996). The case of community power research is instructive. This promising research area was abandoned at the point when substantial cumulative progress was being made. The proponents of class and pluralism fought over methodological issues, but were unwilling to compare the power of their theories to explain a representative range of disputes over extended periods. Abandoning the area, whatever passes for community power research today is found in political science departments that teach state and local government.

One of the most dispiriting developments in sociology is the widespread belief that all research is value-laden, and that scholars can never overcome this. While the essential truth of this position can scarcely be denied, how sociologists respond to this dilemma in concrete research is critically important. They should exert every effort to minimize the impact of their values on their research and not accept the position that nothing can be done to overcome the effect of their own values. This was the posture taken by cohorts of sociologists reared in the Great Depression. Although many embraced socialism (Coser, Lipset, Rossi, others), they strove to minimize the impact of their politics on their research, and accepted their findings even when they disconfirmed their values and beliefs. Many Marxists who entered the field in the 1970s did not try to do this and only confirmed what they wanted to find.

While sociology departments should not require students to memorize ancient theories, they should require them to master the empirical literature in given areas over a span of several decades to avoid rediscovering wheels. Older sociologists often find recent articles that rediscover earlier findings, unbeknownst to their authors.

Despite some reservations about current trends in sociology, the field has steadily improved our understanding of societies. I am optimistic that the discipline will survive and grow if it clings to its original charge to understand society writ large.

My sociological journey had been a blessing. It could hardly have occurred differently, given my socialization. My passion for work was home bred, a religious dedication to pursue an illusive unattainable ideal about the truth of work.

References

Abel, Theodore. 1929. *Systematic Sociology in Germany*. New York: Columbia University Press.

Alba, Richard D. 1995. "Assimilation's Quiet Tide." *Public Interest* 119: 3-18.

Armer, Michael and Allen D. Grimshaw (eds.) 1973. *Comparative Social Research*. New York: John Wiley.

Bae, Kyu Han and William Form. 1986. "Payment Strategy in South Korea's Advanced Economic Sector." *American Sociological Review* 51: 120-131.

Baron, James N. and William T. Bielby. 1980. "Bringing the Firm Back In. *American Sociological Revew* 45: 737-765.

Becker, Howard. 1932. *Systematic Sociology of Leopold von Wiese*. New York: Wiley.

Bibb, Robert C. and William Form. 1977. "The Effects of Industrial, Occupational, and Sex Stratification in Blue-Collar Markets." *Social Forces* 55: 974-96.

Bingham, Alfred. 1935. *Insurgent America*. New York: Harper.

Bloch, Heinz. 1965. *Some Social and Economic Consequences of a Departmental Shutdown*. Winterthur, Switzerland: Keller.

Bone, Hugh A. 1941. *Smear Politics*. Washington, DC: American Council on Public Affairs.

Bordieu, Pierre. 1990. *The Logic of Practice*. Trans, Richard Nice. Stanford, CA: Stanford University Press.

Bowers, Raymond Victor. 1938. "Ecological Patterning of Rochester, New York." *American Sociological Review* 4: 180-189.

Braverman, Harry. 1974. *Labor and Monopoly Capital: The Degradation of Work in the Twentieth Century*. New York: Monthly Review Press.

Brookerover, Wilbur et al. 19?? *Youth and the World of Work*. East Lansing, MI: Social Research Service, MSU.

Burgess, Earnest W. 1924. "The Growth of the City." *Publications of the American Sociological Society* 18: 85-97.

Burnham, James. 1941. *The Managerial Revolution*. New York: Day.

Burt, Ronald S, Hajdeja Igic and Charlene Vannuci. 1990. "Sociology Market." Unpblished manuscript. Department of Sociology, Columbia University, New York, NY.

Callcott, George H. 1966. *A History of the University of Maryland*. Baltimore: Maryland Historical Society.

Campbell, Angus, Gerald Gurin, and Ron B. Miller. 1960, *The American Voter*. New York: Wiley.

Carhart, George S. and Paul A. McGee (eds.) 1928. *Magic Casements*. New York: Macmillan.

Chinoy, Eli. 1955. *Automobile Workers and the American Dream*. Garden City, NY: Doubleday.

Clark, Burton (ed.). 1987. *The American Academic Profession*. Berkeley: University of California Press.

Cox, Oliver C. 1948. *Caste, Class, and Race.* New York: Monthly Review Press.
D'Antonio, William V. and William Form. 1965. *Influentials in Two Border Cities.* Notre Dame, IN: University of Notre Dame.
D'Antonio, W. V., W. Form, C. P. Loomis, and E. C. Erickson. 1961. "Institutional and Occupational Representations in Eleven Community Influence Systems." *American Sociological Review* 26: 440-6.
Davidson, Percy E. and H. Dewey Anderson. 1937. *Occupational Mobility in an American Community.* Palo Alto, CA: Stanford University Press.
Devereux, George. 1939. "Maladjustment and Social Neurosis." *American Sociological Review* 4: 844-851.
Dewey, John. 1920. *Reconstruction in Philosophy.* New York: Henry Holt.
Dodson, Linden S. 1939. *Social Relations and Institutions in an Established Urban Community.* Washington, D.C. Farm Security Administration, Report No. xvii.
Dodson, Linden S, Douglas Ensminger, and Robert N. Woodworth. 1940. "Rural Community Organization in Washington and Frederick Counties, Maryland. College Park, MD: Agricultural Experiment Station Bulletin 437.
Dressel, Paul L. 1987. *College to University: The Hannah Years at Michigan State University.* East Lansing: Michigan State University Press.
Duncan, Otis Dudley and Beverly Duncan. 1955. "Residential Distribution and Stratification." *American Journal of Sociology* 60: 493-505.
Durkheim, Emile. 1933 (1902). *The Division of Labor in Society.* Tr. by George G. Simpson. New York: Free Press.
Eisenstadt, S. N. 1963. *The Political System of Empires.* New York: Free Press.
Faris, Ellsworth. 1937. *The Nature of Human Nature.* New York: McGraw-Hill.
Feagan, Joe R. and Robert Parker. 1989. *Building American Cities: The Urban Real Estate Game.* Englewood Cliffs, NJ: Prentice-Hall.
Firey, Walter. 1945. "Sentiment and Symbolism as Ecological Variables." *American Sociological Review* 10:140-48.
Form, William. 1941? "Adult Education in Action." County Extension Bulletin, no. ?. College Park, MD.
____. 1944. *The Sociology of a White-Collar Suburb: Greenbelt, Maryland.* Ph.D. dissertation, College Park: University of Maryland.
____. 1945. "Status Stratification in a Planned Community." *American Sociological Review* 10: 362-375.
____. 1946. "Toward an Occupational Social Psychology." *Journal of Social Psychology* 17: 85-99.
____. 1954. "The Place of Social Structure in the Determination of Land Use." *Social Forces* 32: 317-323.
____. 1963. "Sulla sociologia della ricerca sociale." *Rassegna Italiana di Sociologia* iv: 463-81.
____. 1965. "C. Wright Mills and Conflict Sociology." Paper presented at the Annual Meeting of the Michigan Sociological Association.
____. 1971. "The Sociology of Social Research," pp. 3-42 in *The Organization, Management, and Tactics of Social Research*, edited by Richard O'Toole, Cambridge, MA: Schenkman.
____. 1973a. "The Internal Stratification of the Working Class: System Involvements of Auto Workers in Four Countries." *American Sociological Review* 38:697-711.
____. 1973b. "Autoworkers and Their Machines." *Social Forces* 52:1-15.
____. 1973c. "Field Problems of Comparative Research: The Politics of Distrust." pp. 83-117 in *Comparative Social Research*, edited by Michal Armer and Allen D. Grimshaw. New York: Wiley.
____. 1974. "The Political Crisis of Argentine Workers or American Professors? Re-

ply to Petras and Rhodes." *American Sociological Review* 39: 759-61.

_____. 1975. "Comment on Spenner." *American Sociological Review* 40: 532-6.

_____. 1976a. *Blue-Collar Stratification: Auto Workers in Four Countries*. Princeton, NJ: Princeton University Press.

_____. 1976b. "Conflict Within the Working Class: The Skilled as a Special Interest Groups." pp. 51-73 in *The Uses of Controversy in Sociology*, edited by Lewis A. Coser and Otto Larsen. New York: Free Press.

_____. 1976c. "Reply to Spenner." *American Sociological Review* 41: 165-8.

_____. 1977a. "An Accidental Journey." *American Sociologist* 27:31-54.

_____. 1977b. "Can Social Movements Explain Societal Change?" Unpublished manuscript.

_____. 1987. 'On the Degradation of Skills." *Annual Review of Sociology* 12:29-47.

_____. 1980. "Resolving Ideological Issues in the Division of Labor." pp. 151-55 in *Sociological Theory and Research*, edited by Hubert M. Blalock. New York: Free Press.

_____. 1981. "Workingclass Divisions and Political Consensus in France and the United States." 4: 263-296 in *Comparative Social Research*, edited by Richard F. Thamasson. Greenwich, CT: JAI Press.

_____. 1986. *Divided We Stand: Essays on the American Working Class*. Urbana: University of Illinois Press.

_____. 1990a. "Institutional Analysis: An Organizational Approach." Pp. 259-73 in *Change in Social Institutions*, edited by M. T. Hallinan, D. Klein, and J. Glass. New York: Plenum.

_____. 1990b. "Organized Labor and the Welfare State." Pp. 319-42 in *Work in American Society*, edited by Kai Erikson and Peter S. Vallas. New Haven, CT: Yale University Press.

_____. 1995a. "Mills at Maryland," *American Sociologist*. 26:41-68.

_____. 1995b. *Segmented Labor, Fractured Politics: Labor Politics in American Life*. New York: Plenum.

_____. 1997a. "An Accidental Journey." *American Sociologist* 27: 31-54.

_____. 1997b. "Can Social Movement Theory Explain Societal Change: The Welfare State as Exemplar." Unpublished manuscript.

_____. 1999. *On the Shoulders of Immigrants: A Family A Family Portrait*. Columbus, OH: North Star Press.

_____. 2000. "Italian Protestants: Religion, Ethnicity, and Assimilation." *Journal for the Scientific Study of Religion* 39:

Form, William and Kyu-Han Bae. 1988. "Convergence Theory and the Korean Connection." *Social Forces* 66: 618-44.

Form, William and Albert Blum (eds.) 1965. *Industrial Relations and Social Change in Latin America*. Gainsville: University of Florida Press.

Form, William and H. Kirk Dansereau. 1957. "Union Member Orientations and Patterns of Social Integration." *Industrial and Labor Relations Review* 11: 3-12.

Form, William and William V. D'Antonio. 1959. "Integration and Cleavage among Influentials in Two Border Cities." *American Sociological Review* 24:801-14.

Form, William and James A. Geschwender. 1962. "Social References Basis of Job Satisfaction: The Case of Manual Workers." *American Sociological Review* 27: 228-237.

Form, William and Joan Huber. 1976. "Occupational Power." Pp. 751-806 in *Handbook of Work, Organizations, and Society*. Edited by Robert Dubin. Chicago, IL: Rand-McNally.

Form, William and Charles P. Loomis. 1956. "The Persistence and Emergence of Social and Cultural Systems in Disasters." *American Sociological Review* 21:180-185.

Form, William and Delbert C. Miller. 1949. "Occupational Career Patterns as a Socio-logical Instrument." *American Journal of Sociology* 54: 317-329.

_____. 1960. *Industry, Labor, and Community.* New York: Harpers. Form, William and Signund Nosow. 1958. *Community in Disaster.* New York. Harper.

Form, William and Fred C. Pampel. 1978. "Social Stratification and the Development of Labor Markets in India.: *Social Forces* 57: 119-136.

Form, William, Joel Smith, Gregory P. Stone, and James Cowhig. 1954. "The Com-patibility of Alternative Approaches to the Delimitation of Urban Sub-Areas." *American Sociological Review* 19:434-40.

Form, William and Gregory P. Stone. 1955. *The Social Significance of Clothing in Occupational Life.* Agricultural Experiment Station, Technical Bulletin 246. East Lansing, Michigan.

——. 1957. "Urbanism, Status Anonymity, and Status Symbolism." *American Jour-nal of Sociology* LXII: 504-514.

Form, William and Claudine Wood. 1985. "The Consistency of Stratal Ideologies of Economic Justice." *Research in Social Stratification and Mobility* 4:239-69.

Friedmann, Georges. 1955. *Industrial Society; the Emergence of the Human Prob-lems of Automation.* Edited by Harold L. Sheppard. Gencloe, IL: Free Press.

Galpin, C. J. 1915. "The Social Anatomy of an Agricultural Community." Madison: Wisconsin Agricultural Experiment Station Research Bulletin 34.

Gans, Herbert. 1979. "Symbolic Ethnicity: The Future of Ethnic Groups and Culture in America." *Ethnic and Racial Studies* 2: 1-20.

Gardner, Burleigh B. 1945.*Human Relations in Industry.* Chicago, IL: Richard D. Irwin.

Geiger, Roger L. 1993. *Research and Relevant Knowledge: American Universities Since World War II.* New York: Oxford University Press.

Gerth, H. H. and C. Wright Mills. 1944. Translation of M. Weber's "Class Status, and Party." *Politics* 1: 271-78.

Glazer, Nathan and Daniel P. Moynihan. 1970. *Beyond the Melting Pot.* Cambridge, MA: MIT Press.

Gosnell, Harold. 1935, *Negro Politicians.* Chicago, IL: University of Chicago Press.

Hamilton, Richard F. 1996. *The Social Miscontruction of Reality.* New Haven, CT: Yale University Press.

Hannah, John A. 1980. *A Memoir.* East Lansing, Michigan State University Press.

Hawley, Amos H. 1944. "Ecology and Human Ecology." *Social Forces.* 22: 399-405.

Henderson, L. J. 1935. *Pareto's General Sociology.* Cambridge, MA; Harvard Univer-sity Press.

Hinkle, Roscoe C. 1994. *Developments in American Sociological Theory: 1915-1950.* Albany: State University of New York Press.

Hirschman, D. L. 1983. "America's Melting Pot Reconsidered." *Annual Review of Sociology* 9:392-432.

Hobhouse, L. T., G. C. Wheeler, and M. Ginsberg 1930. *Material Culture and Social Institutions of the Simpler Peoples.* London: Chapman & Hall.Holt,

Holt, John B. 1936. *Under the Swastika.* Chapel Hill, NC: University of North Carolina Press.

_____. 1936. *German Agricultural Policy 1918-1934.* Chapel Hill, NC: University of North Carolina Press.

_____. 1940. "Holiness Religion. *American Sociological Review* 5:740-747.

Homans, George C. and Charles P. Curtis. 1934. *An Introduction to Pareto: His Soci-ology.* New York: Knopf.

Horowitz, D. L. 1977. "Culture Movements and Ethnic Change." *Annals* 433:6-18.

Huber, Joan. 1995. "Institutional Perspectives on Sociology." *American Journal of Sociology* 101: 194-216.

Huber, Joan and William Form. 1973. *Income and Ideology.* New York: Free Press.

Hunter, Floyd. 1953. *Community Power Structure.* Chapel Hill: University of North Carolina Press.

Inkeles, Alex. 1960. "Industrial Man: The Relation of Status to Experience, Perception, and Values." *American Journal of Sociology* 66:1-31.

Johnson, Barry V. 1995. *Piterim A. Sorokin: An Intellectual Bigraphy.* Lawrence: University of Kansas Press.

Jones, Alfred Winslow. 1937. *Life, Liberty, and Property.* New York: Lippincott.

Kerr, Clark and J. T. Dunlap, F. H. Harbison, and C. A. Myers. 1960. *Industrialism and Industrial Man.* Cambridge, MA: Harvard University Press. Hobhouse, L. T., G. G. Wheeler, and M.

Lederer, Emil. 1912. *The Problem of the Modern Salaried Employee.* Tr. WPA project, 1937?, No. 165-6999-6027. NY.

Lederer, Emil and Jacob Marschak. 1926. *The New Middle Class.* Tr. WPA project, 1937. No. 165-97-6999-6027. NY.

Lenski, Gerhard. 1966. *Power and Privilege.* New York: McGraw-Hill.

Lichtenberger, James. P. 1925. *Development of Social Theory.* New York: Century.

Loomis, Charles P. 1967. "In Praise of Conflict and its Resolution." *American Sociological Review* 32: 875-890.

Lundberg, George A. *Social Research.* New York: Longmans, Green.

Lynd, Robert S. and Helen M. Lynd. 1937. *Middletown in Transition.* New York: Harcourt, Brace.

Mannheim, Karl. 1936. *Ideology and Utopia.* New York: Harcourt Brace.

____. 1940. *Man and Society in an Age of Reconstruction,* tr. E. Shils. New York: Harcourt, Brace.

Marglin, Steven. 1974. "What Do Bosses Do?" *Review of Radical Economics* 6-33-60.

Mayo, Elton. 1939. *The Social Problems of an Industrial Civilization.* Boston, MA: Graduate School of Business Administration, Harvard University.

Mead, George Herbert. 1934. *Mind, Self, and Society.* Chicago, IL: University of Chicago Press.

Merton, Robert K. 1938. "Social Structure and Anomie." *American Sociological Review* 3: 672-682.

____. 1995. "Opportunity Structure." *Advances in Criminological Theory* 6: 3-78. New Brunswick NJ: Transaction.

Michael, Jerome and Mortimer J. Adler. 1932. *Crime, Law, and Social Science.* New York: Harcourt, Brace.

Michels, Roberto. 1930. *Italien von Heute.* Zurich u Leipzig: Orellfussli Verlag.

Miller, Delbert C. and William Form. 1951. *Industrial Sociology.* New York: Harper.

____. 1964. *Industrial Sociology,* 2nd ed. New York: Harper.

Mills, C. Wright. 1939. "Language, Logic, and Culture." *American Sociological Review* 4: 670-680.

____. 1940a. "Methodological Consequences of the Sociology of Knowledge." *American Journal of Sociology* 46: 316-330.

____. 1940b. "Situated Actions and Vocabulary of Motives." *American Sociological Review* 6: 904-913.

____. 1942a. Review of W. Lloyd Warner and Paul S. Lunt, *The Social System of the Modern Community. American Sociological Review* 7: 263-271.

____. 1942b. "Review of Logan Wilson, *The Academic Man." American Sociological Review* 7: 444-446.

____. 1943a. "A Sociological Account of Pragmatism." Ph.D. dissertation. Madison: University of Wisconsin.

_____. 1943b. "The Professional Ideology of Social Pathologists." *American Journal of Sociology* 49: 165-180.

_____. 1944. "The Powerless People: The Role of the Intellectual in Society." *Politics* 1: Number 3.

_____. 1945. "The American Business Elite," *Journal of Economic History* 4: 20-44.

_____. 1951. *White Collar: The American Middle Class*. New York: Oxford University Press.

_____. 1956. *The Power Elite*. New York: Oxford.

_____. 1966. *Sociology and Pragmatism*, edited and Introduction by Irving Louis Horowitz. New York: Oxford University Press.

Mills, C. Wright and H. H. Gerth. 1942. "A Marx for the Managers." Review of James Burnham, *The Managerial Revolution. Ethics* 32: 200-215.

Molotch, Harvey. 1976. "The City as a Growth Machine." *American Journal of Sociology* 82:309-32.

Moore, Wilbert E. 1946. *Industrial Relations and the Social Order*. New York: Macmillan.

Mueller, Eva, et al. 1967. *Technological Advance in an Expanding Economy*. Ann Arbor, MI: Braun-Brumfield.

Myers, Charles A. and George P. Shultz. 1951. *The Dynamics of a Labor Market*. New York: Prentice-Hall.

Nosow, Sigmund. 1956. "Labor Distribution and the Normative System." *Social Forces* 35:25-52.

Oakes, Guy and Arthur Vidich (1999). *Collaboration, Reputation, and Ethics in American Academic Life: Hans Gerth and C. Wright Mills*. Urbana: University of Illinois Press.

Odegard, Peter H. and E. Allen Helms. 1928. *American Politics*. New York: Harper.

Odum, Howard W. 1936. *Southern Regions of the United States*. Chapel Hill: University of North Carolina Press.

Odum, Howard W. and Harry E. Moore. 1938. *American Regionalism*. New York: Holt.

Pareto, Vilfredo. 1923. *Trattato di Sociologia Generale.* Firenze:

Parsons, Talcott. 1937. *The Structure of Social Action*. New York: McGraw-Hill.

Pease, John, William Form and Joan Rytina. 1970. "Income and Stratification Ideology." *American Sociologist* 5:127-137.

Petras, James F. and Robert I. Rhodes. 1974. "Comment on 'Internal Stratification of the Working Class.'" *American Sociological Review* 38:757-59.

Pigors, Paul. 1935. *Leadership or Domination?* Boston, MA: Houghton-Mifflin.

Reynolds, Lloyd G. 1951. *The Structure of Labor Markets*. New York; Harper Brothers.

Riesman, David. 1953. *The Lonely Crowd*. Garden City, NY: Doubleday.

Roethlisberger, F. J. and William J. Dickson. 1939. *Management and the Worker*. Cambridge, MA: Harvard University Press.

Sanderson, Dwight and Robert A. Polson. 1939. *Rural Community Organization*. New York: Wiley.

Sewell, William. H. 1988 "The Changing Institutional Structure of Sociology and My Career," pp. 119-141 in *Sociological Lives*, edited by Maltilda W. Riley. Newbury Park, CA: Sage.

_____.1988. Private Communication.

_____.1989. "Some Reflections on the Golden Age of Interdisciplinary Social Psychology." *,Social Psychology Quarterly*. 52:88-97.

Smith, Joel. 1954. "A Method for the Classification of Areas Based on the Basis of Demographically Homogeneous Populations." *American Sociological Review* 19:201-07.

Smith, Joel, William Form and Gregory Stone. 1954. "Local Intimacy in a Middle-Sized City." *American Journal of Sociology* LX: 276-84.

Sorokin, Pitirim. 1927. *Social Mobility*. New York: Harper.

____. 1937-41. *Social and Cultural Dynamics*. New York: American Book.

Sower, Christopher, et al. 1957. *Community Involvement*, Glencoe, IL: Free Press.

Speier, Hans. 1939. *The Salaried Employee in German Society*. Tr. WPA project No. 465-970391. NY.

Spenner, Kenneth I. 1995. "The Internal Stratification of the Working Class: A Re-analysis.: *American Sociological Review* 40: 513-31.

____. 1976. "Reply to Form." *American Sociological Review*. 41:160-165.

Steiger, Thomas L. and William Form. 1991. "The Labor Process in Construction: Control Without Bureaucratic and Technological Means." *Work and Occupations*. 18:251-270.

Stone, Gregory P. and William Form. 1953. "Instabilities in Status: The Problem of HIerarchy in the Community Study of Status Arrangements." *American Sociological Review* 18:149-62.

Taussig, F. W. and Carl S. Joslyn. 1932. *American Business Leaders*. New York: Macmillan.

Toennies, Ferdinand. 1887, 1940. *Fundamental Concepts in Sociology*. Tr. and supp. Charles P. Loomis, New York: American Book.

Trotsky, Leon. 1932. *The History of the Russian Revolution*. vol. 1. Trans. Max Eastman. New York: Simon and Schuster.

Turner, Jonathon H. 1991. *The Structure of Sociological Theory*. Belmont, CA: Wadsworth.

U. S. Bureau of the Census. 1880, 1890, 1900, 1910, 1920, 1930, 1940. *Population: General Characteristics*. Washington, DC: U. S. Government Printing Office.

Veblen, Thorstein. 1938. *Absentee Ownership*. New York: Viking

____. 1933. *The Engineers and the Price System*. New York: Viking.

____. 1943. *The Instinct of Workmanship*. New York: Viking.

Warner, W. Lloyd and Paul S. Lunt. 1941. *The Social Life of a Modern Community*. New Haven, CT: Yale University Press.

Weber, Max. 1944. "Class, Status, Party," *Politics* 1: 271-278, tr. H. H. Gerth and C. Wright Mills.

____. 1946. *From Max Weber: Essays in Sociology*, ed. and tr. H. H. Gerth and C. Wright Mills. New York: Oxford University Press.

Wilson, Logan. 1940. "Psychiatrists and the Messianic Complex." *Social Forces* 18: 521-525.

____. 1942. *The Academic Man*. New York: Oxford University Press.

Windelband, W. 1938 (1893). *A History of Philosophy*. Tr. James H. Tufts. New York: MacMillan.

Wright, Erik Olin. 1979. *Class Structure and Income Determination*. New York: Academic Press.

Yinger, Milton J. 1985. "Ethnicity." *Annual Review of Sociology* 11:151-=80.

Zald, Meyer and John McCarthy (eds.). 1987. *Social Movements in An Organizational Society*. New Brunswick, NJ: Transaction.

Index

235